NUTTS CORNER
IN WAR AND PEACE

1941–1963

GUY WARNER and ERNIE CROMIE

COLOURPOINT

Published 2024 by Colourpoint Books
an imprint of Colourpoint Creative Ltd
Colourpoint House, Jubilee Business Park
21 Jubilee Road, Newtownards, BT23 4YH
Tel: 028 9182 6339
Fax: 028 9182 1900
E-mail: sales@colourpoint.co.uk
Web: www.colourpoint.co.uk

First Edition
First Impression

Text © Guy Warner and Ernie Cromie, 2024
Illustrations © Various, as acknowledged in captions

All rights reserved. No part of this publication may be reproduced, stored in a retrieval system or transmitted in any form or by any means, electronic, mechanical, photocopying, scanning, recording or otherwise, without the prior written permission of the copyright owners and publisher of this book.

The authors have asserted their right under the Copyright, Designs and Patents Act, 1988, to be identified as authors of this work.

A catalogue record for this book is available from the British Library.

Designed by April Sky Design, Newtownards
Tel: 028 9182 7195
Web: www.aprilsky.co.uk

Printed by GPS Colour Graphics Ltd, Belfast

ISBN 978-1-78073-395-1

Front cover: (top) Liberator AM910 taking off from Nutts Corner. *(Roger Freeman Collection americanairmuseum.com)*
(lower) Postcard of the civil airport buildings including cars belonging to the staff park by the control tower. A Viking can just be made out in the background. *(Mike Charlton Airportpostcards.com)*
Rear cover: (top left) King George VI meets some of 120 Squadron's ground crew. *(Ernie Cromie Collection)*
(top right) A very striking image of the Cambrian Airways Dakota, G-ALXL. *(Guy Warner Collection)*
(lower left) A Hellcat of 891 NAS, after an incident while landing. *(Gill and Gerald Worner Collection)*
(lower centre) An aerial view of the terminal area at Nutts Corner in 1961. *(Author's Collection)*
(lower right) A press advertisement for BEA's Ulster Flyer first class service. *(Guy Warner Collection)*

About the author: Guy Warner is a retired schoolteacher and former civil servant, who grew up in Newtownabbey, attending Abbots Cross Primary School and Belfast High School before going to Leicester University and later Stranmillis College. He now lives in Greenisland, Co Antrim with his wife Lynda. They have two daughters and four grandchildren. He is the author of more than 30 books and booklets on aviation, naval and military history, as well as several hundred articles for magazines in the UK, Ireland, France, Italy, Portugal, Canada and the USA. He also acted as a consultant to museums and universities, reviews books for several publications, gives talks to local history societies, etc and makes contributions to TV and radio programmes, discussing aspects of aviation history.

Contents

Foreword by Michael Strain 5

Ernie Cromie, An Appreciation 7

Introduction 9

Nutts Corner Part 1
RAF NUTTS CORNER

Chapter 1	The Early Days 1940–41	15
Chapter 2	Coastal Command 1941–42	18
Chapter 3	Gliders 1942	47
Chapter 4	Army Co-operation 1943	54
Chapter 5	Operational Training and Heavy Conversion 1943–44	56
Chapter 6	Transatlantic Ferry 1943–44	61
Chapter 7	The Coronados of Sandy Bay 1944	76
Chapter 8	B-17G Flying Fortress 42-97862 1944	84
Chapter 9	Accommodation, Food and Welfare 1944	86
Chapter 10	Weather Forecasting and Area Flying Control 1944–45	88
Chapter 11	Heavy Conversion 1944–45	92
Chapter 12	Fleet Air Arm 1945–46	96
Postscript	A New Life 1946	100
Appendix	Nutts Corner – A Military Timeline	102

Nutts Corner Part 2
THE CIVIL AIRPORT FOR NORTHERN IRELAND

Chapter 13	Introduction	107
Chapter 14	Nutts Corner in the 1940s	111
Chapter 15	Nutts Corner in the 1950s	131

Chapter 16	Northern Ireland's Worst Air Disaster	136
Chapter 17	Transatlantic Travel	140
Chapter 18	Nutts Corner in the 1960s	161
Chapter 19	End of an Era	174
Chapter 20	Not Quite the End	182
Appendix	Passenger and cargo figures 1944–1963	184

Bibliography	185
Acknowledgements	187
Index	188

Foreword
by Michael Strain

"Training, it's in our DNA", This is what I tell guests when presenting at Transport Training Board for Northern Ireland (TTB). Well, that is ever since I was introduced to Guy Warner and listening to him talk about the incredible history of the grounds our training centre sits on today, here in Nutts Corner.

My first slide, as a nod of respect, always contains an aerial photograph of the airfield and a collection of Air Crew whose footsteps we walk in, to this very day.

Today, those noises of take-offs and landings have been long replaced with that of apprentices learning their trade as automotive technicians, the crunching of gears as learners take their first step to become HGV drivers or the quiet of an Electric Vehicle workshop silently introducing leaners to future technologies.

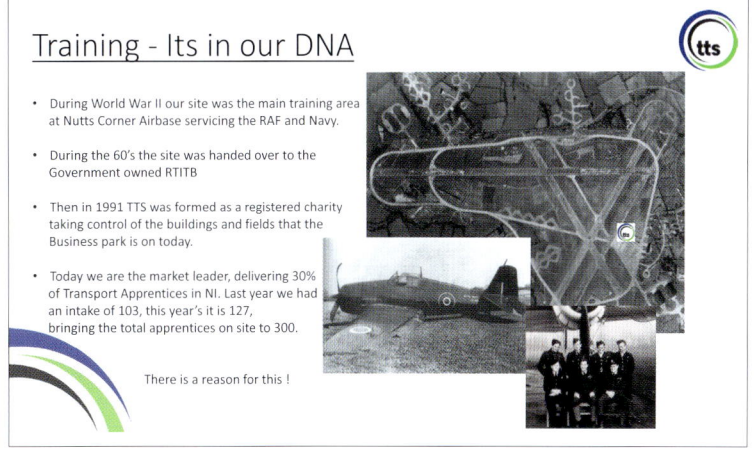

As a charity we deliver this training with passion and commitment to the transport industry and take immense pride in the fact that we do this in an area synonymous with providing a critical training hub and strategic outpost during the Second World War, followed thereafter by taking a seminal role in the development of civil air transport in Northern Ireland.

TTB's partnership with Ernie Cromie and Guy Warner started with our then Chairman in 2019 Mr Ted Hesketh inviting them both to explore ways of commemorating the history of this location, and one of these is this very book you read today. Ernie, sadly passed away in 2021 leaving Guy to see the project through to the end, now with the added pressure of doing it in memory of his dear friend.

TTB are proud to support this worthy project, acting as facilitators for Guy by inviting donations to be made, the subsequent holding of these funds and the location of its launch event.

Guy kindly asked that I write this preface for the book, and as timing would have it, his request was on the 6th June which was the 80th Anniversary of D-Day. Quite fitting, I think, as the reason for this book is similar to the reason for these celebrations, that we do not forget!

The book details the significance Nutts Corner played during the Second World War in a multiplicity of roles with the RAF, USAAF and RN. It guides us through its construction, its effect on the local community, it details aircraft types, their roles and records the tragic loss of lives during operations, whose names are herein recorded and their memory honoured. It then goes on to describe the trail-blazing activities post-war as our aerial gateway, expanding the reach of our businesses, encouraging tourism and providing job opportunities. The tragic loss of 27 lives on 5th January 1953 is not forgotten nor are the seven who perished on 23rd October 1957.

Above all, however, Nutts Corner was a happy place at which to work, with a unique atmosphere, which I believe continues to this day.

Michael Strain
Chief Executive Officer
Transport Training Board for NI

Grateful thanks are due to the Esmé Mitchell Trust, Northern Ireland War Memorial, Belfast International Airport, Antrim and Newtownabbey Borough Council, the Arts Council of Northern Ireland, the Transport Training Board and Mr Joe Brown for their generous sponsorship.

Esmé Mitchell Trust

Mr Joe Brown

Ernie Cromie,
An Appreciation

Ernie and I worked together on many projects: books, talks and exhibitions, over the course of 20 years. In all that time, we never had a cross word. He was one of my best friends and we were of support to each other in times of ill-health. More than once Ernie would have said to me, 'You know, I have so much archive material, I have forgotten exactly what I have.'

When I spoke to him last, when he was in hospital, he asked me to promise that I would finish this book. With the generous co-operation of the Northern Ireland War Memorial, I have gone through his lever-arch files and photograph albums relating to Nutts Corner and have come across this little gem, which is reproduced below as a tribute to Ernie's life-long dedication to all aspects of the history of aviation in Northern Ireland but, in particular, those items which speak of our Ulster character. Ernie annotated a cutting from the *Ballymena Guardian*[1] as follows, 'This poem was composed by Tommy O'Hara from Ballymena. He and his father helped build the airfield.'

> I remember well Nutts Corner in the year of '41,
> For the erection of an aerodrome the work had just begun,
> The workers came from far and near, from Belfast and Broughshane,
> From Crumlin and from Derry, they worked with just one aim.
>
> The farmers of the district where this aerodrome was made,
> Worked as a team with labourers and shovel, pick and spade,
> I remember well the horse carts that came from miles around
> And also mules and donkey carts, or conveyance to be found.
>
> The job was for to scraw the ground and cart the sods away,
> There were hundreds of them at this work of carting loads of clay,
> But this was only the beginning of a very heavy task,
> And we were exposed to winter with its rain and snowy blast.
>
> There were also trees and hedges to be uprooted from the ground,
> And also large farm buildings that had to be pulled down,
> Then at last we all got to the task of the runways being laid,
> And we had to stick hard to our task with shovels, picks and spades.

---

1 *Ballymena Guardian* 19th February 1976

The job was then to sink the roads, about six feet of clay,
And that was north, south, east and west, six miles of run-a-way,
And then this all had to be packed with rocks of stone and spall,
And treaded o'r the level with tarmac overall.

And then there were the hangars built to house the aeroplanes,
And aprons for them to rest, or turn and fly again,
And this completed the aerodrome, and it was all, no doubt, worthwhile,
For it was considered the best in the British Isles.

So to conclude and finish, I am going to write no more,
But pay tribute to the builders, Graham Brothers of Dromore,
And also their gallant workers, who worked with just one aim,
To build the aerodrome that got Nutts Corner for its name.

I am sure that Ernie would agree that we should dedicate this book to our families, whose love and support, tea and biscuits have been so valuable and so greatly appreciated.

Guy Warner
Carrickfergus 2024

Introduction

Nutts Corner airfield was conceived and built during the Second World War. It was not, as some commentators would have it, previously a civil airport; rather, it was one of 22 new airfields that were constructed in Northern Ireland during the war, for military use. Before being acquired for construction it consisted of farmers' fields in the townlands of Dundesert and Aughnamullan in the parish of Killead,[1] four miles to the east of Lough Neagh in Co Antrim and a couple of miles to the south east of Aldergrove airfield, which itself had been in existence since 1918. With the addition of Langford Lodge, from 1942, no less than three substantial airfields would be concentrated in this relatively small geographical area (see the maps overleaf).

The road sign preserves an ancient name. *(Author's Collection)*

Many place names in Ireland start with the letters 'dun' and relate to the existence of a fort, or in Irish, *dún*, which is one of a number of terms used for the most common type of fort or defended habitation site in Ireland: the ring-fort. The second part of the townland's name is similarly derived from Irish, *díseart*, and from Latin *desertum* 'deserted place', being a hermitage or monastic retreat. It is known that a substantial ancient earthen ringfort or *ráth*, probably dating from the Early Christian Period, stood on this land, enclosing a space within of between two and three Irish acres; and within the walls of this were, until about 1800, the remains of a church and graveyard from a later period and *díseart* in the townland name here clearly refers to a monastic hermitage which was connected with this early church. These were apparently destroyed by local farmer, Robert McCune, at about that date. According to the farmer, as recorded by the Ordnance Surveyor, James Boyle, in 1838, 'In the interior of the ruined church were an immense number of human bones, skeletons, ashes and several iron pikes [of a pattern dating from the mid-17th century] and pieces of glass and brass including a small glass seal with the initials ER.' In the burial ground, Boyle added, the farmer found more pikes, a gold brooch, baptismal fonts, silver coin, an iron bow and steel arrowhead and a 6-lb cannonball. In contrast, Aughnamullan or *Achadh na Muileann* translates as Field of the Mill and, indeed, the Surveyor noted two mills, owned by George Cunningham, one for corn and the other

---

1 Regarding the parish name, Killead, the first element of the place-name is Irish *cill* 'church' but the meaning of the final element is obscure (perhaps a lesser-known personal or saint's name). The hamlet of Killead, which contains the modern Church of Ireland church, is in the townland of Seacash (*Suí Cais* 'Cas's seat or stronghold'). However, the medieval parish church of Killead (of which no trace remains) was close to the village named Killead Corner, roughly two miles to the north-east in the townland of Killealy (*Cill Aileach* 'church of the stone or rock') in the *tuogh of Killelagh* which consists of the northern two thirds of the parish of Killead, along with the parish of Grange of Muckamore.

This map of 1837 from *A Topographical Dictionary of Ireland* by Samuel Lewis, clearly shows Killead in the barony of Lower Massereene, to the east of Lough Neagh.

for flax, but both in a poor state of repair. The Ordnance Survey 6-inch map of 1832 displays 'Gredin Mill' (Corn Mill) on the western boundary of the townland, by the time of the 4th edition map (1905), the mill is marked as being 'unused' (The remains of this mill are still there). Sadly, the full story of the events that took place on the site have not been thus far uncovered.

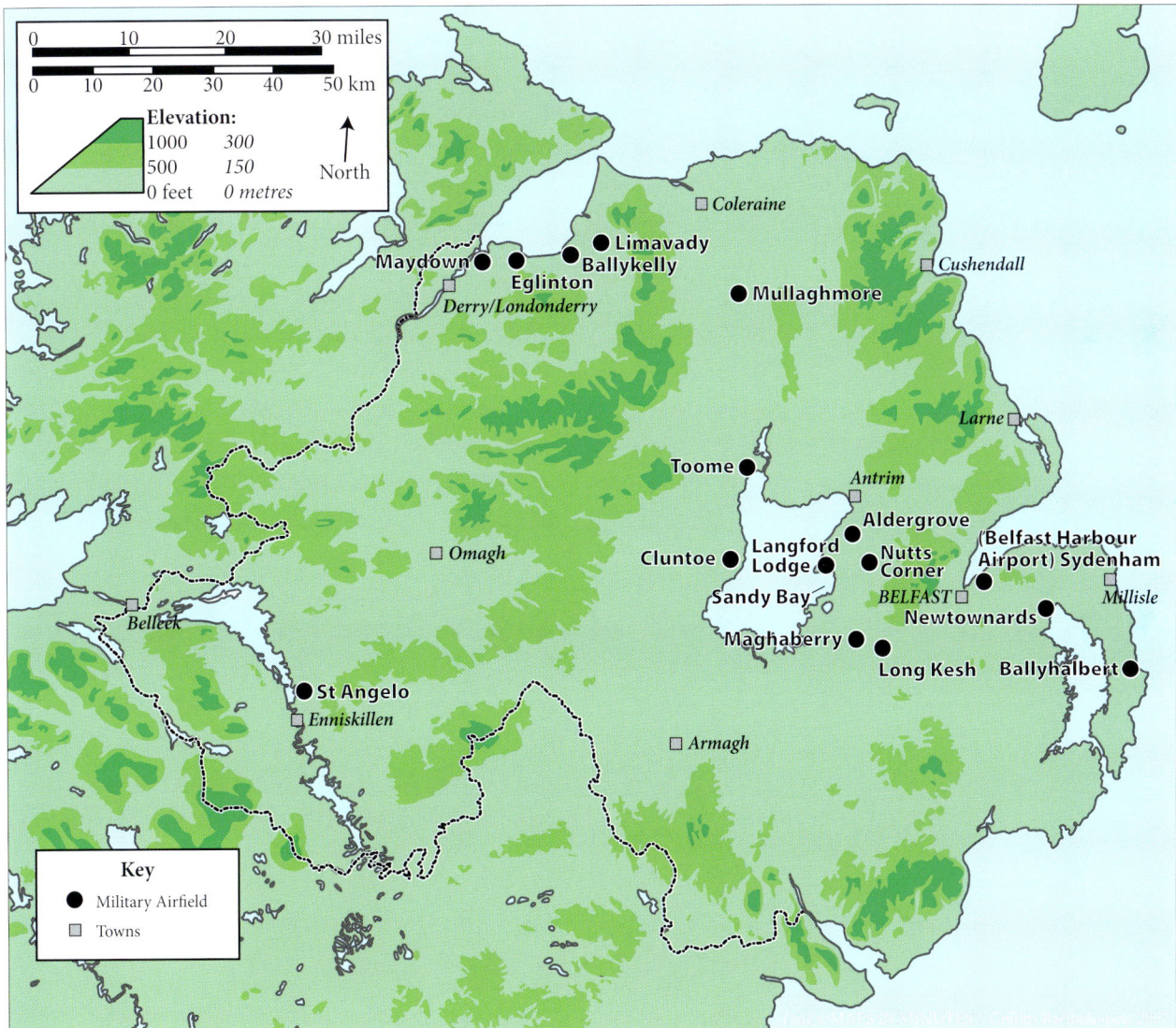

Nutts Corner Part 1
RAF Nutts Corner

Chapter 1
The Early Days
1940–41

It was in June 1940 that construction was first approved, on the basis of a survey carried out on behalf of the Air Ministry Airfields Board. At this stage of the war, it was envisaged that Nutts Corner would be developed as a satellite airfield for RAF Aldergrove, within No 15 Group, Coastal Command, headquartered in Liverpool, with accommodation for one

This aerial photograph, taken on 9th December 1940 is the earliest known of Nutts Corner under construction.
(Ernie Cromie Collection)

General Reconnaissance (GR) squadron only. Two phases of construction were envisaged, anticipated completion dates for which were April 1942, for the main work and September 1943 for supplementary works. A contract was awarded to the civil engineers, Graham of Dromore, Co Down, a company with roots going back to the 18th Century. It is apparent from an aerial photograph dated 9th December 1940 that work on the actual airfield had not begun much earlier.

However, plans were changing almost daily so, when the airfield was officially opened in May 1941, construction work was far from complete and the first aircraft to arrive on operations, on 8th May, constituted a small detachment of three Boulton Paul Defiant single-engine, two crew, turret-equipped night fighters of No 264 Squadron from their base at RAF West Malling in Kent.

Significantly, this was a response to the catastrophic air raids on Belfast and other urban centres in Northern Ireland that had occurred during the nights of 7-8th, 15-16th April and 4-6th May 1941 but, although no one could have known it at the time, Belfast and Northern Ireland had seen the last of aerial bombing. At 01.25 hours in the morning after their arrival, Flight Lieutenant Thomas and his air gunner Sergeant Shepherd took off in Defiant N3444 on a defensive patrol, returning 35 minutes later with nothing to report. He was followed into the air at 02.30 and 02.45 respectively by the other two aircraft, N3453 and N1801, the pilot of the second of which was a young man from Belfast, Flying Officer Desmond Hughes, with his air gunner, Sergeant Gash, but they too did not encounter any Luftwaffe aircraft and so it continued for the following ten days. The third crew were Sergeants Lauder and Chapman. As a result, Fighter Command recalled the Nutts Corner detachment from what had been the first night fighter deployment to Northern Ireland. Nevertheless, for Desmond Hughes, who would achieve many successes against the Luftwaffe later in the war and, later still, 'Air' rank, it had been a welcome opportunity to operate over his homeland.[1]

Remarkably, though, a 'night incident' did occur on the day following the Defiants' return to West Malling. It involved Lockheed

The air gunner of a No 264 Squadron Boulton Paul Defiant about to enter the gun turret. *(Guy Warner Collection)*

---

1 Later Air Vice Marshal FD Hughes CB, CBE, DSO, DFC + 2 bars, AFC, ADC (1919–1992).

Hudson Mk 1, N7296, of No 233 Squadron based at Aldergrove, which was being flown by the Squadron's Commanding Officer, Wing Commander EC Kidd, AFC, AFM. During the course of non-operational, night flying practice he landed at Nutts Corner, however, the aircraft crashed when the undercarriage collapsed, then catching fire and being destroyed. Fortunately, all the crew managed to get out in time.[2]

A formation of six Lockheed Hudsons of No 233 Squadron in echelon. *(Guy Warner Collection)*

---

2 According to the Court of Inquiry, the brakes had acted more severely than expected, due to the pilot's unfamiliarity with a new Lockheed modification which had not been notified. Despite having the dubious honour of Nutts Corner's first air crash, it seemingly did not affect Wing Commander Kidd at all. Seven days later on 28th May, he manoeuvred his Hudson in order that his rear gunner could shoot down a Heinkel He 111, after exhausting his front guns on another He 111 moments earlier.

Chapter 2
Coastal Command
1941–42

By 1941, alarmingly, the United Kingdom and its allies were losing merchant ships to U-boats and marauding Luftwaffe maritime aircraft in the Battle of the Atlantic at a much faster rate than it was possible for them to be replaced.

Despite the efforts of the Royal Navy and RAF Coastal Command, the number of operational U-boats at sea was increasing as their rate of construction exceeded losses. Between the outbreak of war and May 1941, despite numerous sightings, Coastal Command's record was two U-boat 'kills' shared with the Royal Navy and one exclusive 'damaged' by a 502 (Ulster) Squadron Armstrong Whitworth Whitley operating from RAF Limavady. Better times were in prospect however as the Command was about to receive a new very long range (VLR) aircraft type which, in time, equipped with the new Air-to-Surface Vessel

Sunrise over a convoy. Photographed from flightdeck of the escort carrier, USS *Bogue* (CVE-9), in mid-Atlantic. *(US NHHC NH 80-G-86005)*

(ASV) Mark 2 radar and more efficient 250-lb depth charges then being developed would prove to be the most effective in its inventory and help overcome the U-boat threat. This was the four-engine, American Consolidated B-24 Liberator.

The cockpit of an early model Liberator. In 120 Squadron a great deal of 'learning on the job' had to be carried out by aircrew and ground crew alike. Even for a pilot fully qualified on the type it could be a brute to fly. *(Chaz Bower Collection)*

The Liberator was well-armed, including these twin .50 calibre (12.7 mm) Browning machine-guns, mounted one either side in the waist positions. *(Chaz Bowyer Collection)*

The first squadron chosen to receive the type was No 120, a First World War squadron[1] which began to re-form at Nutts Corner in June for the specific purpose of closing the mid-Atlantic 'gap' in air cover which U-boat commanders were exploiting so successfully. The availability of suitable airfields at this time was very limited and Nutts Corner was not ideal in some respects for, as has been noted, the first phase of construction was far from complete and this inevitably caused problems. For instance, only a 5000-feet length of the main runway had been completed, barely enough to enable a fully-laden Liberator to become safely airborne and there were no hangars or enough purpose-designed hard-standings large enough to facilitate maintenance and proper dispersal of the aircraft. By the time construction of the first two T-type hangars was completed in the early summer of 1942, 120 Squadron was just about to be transferred to its new base at RAF Ballykelly. In any event, it hardly mattered as a Liberator's wingspan was too wide for the aircraft to be taken in nose or tail first!

Being a wartime airfield, living and communal facilities for personnel, such as mess halls

---

1 Formed as a day bomber unit on 1st January 1918 but used in a communications role with the single-engine Airco DH.9, and the twin-engine DH.10 Amiens, until disbanding on 21st October 1919. One of its young pilots was Lieutenant James Fitzmaurice (later Colonel 1898-1965), who became the CO of the Irish Air Corps in 1926 and on 12th April 1928 was one of the crew of Junkers W.33, *Bremen*, along with Captain Hermann Köhl (1888-1938) and Freiherr von Hünefeld (1892-1929), on the first non-stop east to west crossing of the North Atlantic by an aeroplane.

and indoor recreational facilities, were in the form of metal or wooden huts or basic brick structures grouped into numerous dispersed sites, the most distant of which were up to a mile from the airfield and on which construction was also far from completed. Even the Officers' Mess was not opened until 12th September 1941.

Nominally, 120 Squadron's initial establishment was nine Liberators but it took time for that to be realised. Although the Anglo-French Purchasing Commission had issued a letter of intent in 1940 to purchase 165 of the first version of the aircraft and had subsequently negotiated and paid for the initial release of 20 for Coastal Command, their delivery was protracted with the result that it was August 1941 before the first, serial number AM928/A, of what became a batch of 11 operationally equipped Mark 1 B-24s was received by 120 Squadron, with the last, AM929/H, not being delivered until one year later. Meanwhile, during the second week of June, four unmodified examples of the type were delivered to Nutts Corner on loan from the British modification plant at Scottish Aviation, Prestwick,

When this photograph was taken, on 26th July 1941, 120 Squadron had only four Liberators on strength, on loan for training and familiarization purposes. All of which appear here, with one of the aircraft being two-thirds of the way along the runway to the left. Note also the dummy hedgerows – an attempt to camouflage the airfield. *(Ernie Cromie Collection)*

to facilitate familiarisation and training. They were AM911, AM913/Z, AM914 and AM922. At the end of July 1941, they were the only Liberators in use in the whole of RAF Coastal Command.[2]

For its time, the Liberator was a sophisticated and technically advanced aircraft which the Americans had found demanded prolonged pilot training programmes. These, however, were not available to the pilots of 120 Squadron so a great deal of 'learning on the job' had to be carried out by aircrew and ground crew alike. Even for a pilot fully qualified on the type it could be a brute to fly and it was eventually cleared to operate at such comparatively great weights that take-off could become marginal. To begin with, instruction was given to the pilots by Colonel McReynolds USAAC and Homer G Berry from Consolidated Aircraft, who was, 'masquerading as a RCAF Squadron Leader.' Lend-lease to the Allies had started in March 1941 but with the USA a non-belligerent, the men of 120 Squadron were warned to be very circumspect about their instructors' background.

Liberator AM910 taking off from Nutts Corner. *(Roger Freeman Collection americanairmuseum.com)*

The most senior officer at Nutts Corner at this time was the Station Commander, Group Captain NAP Pritchett. On 5th June, he was joined by Wing Commander WN Cumming, DFC, who took command of 120 Squadron on posting from No 204 Squadron, which was operating Short Sunderland flying-boats from Reykjavík in Iceland. Over the course of the summer, he was followed by numerous officers on transfer from at least eight maritime squadrons, of various nationalities, backgrounds and experience. Ulstermen were well represented; within a matter of weeks for instance, they included Flying Officer Brian Bannister DFC and Flight Lieutenant Jack Harrison (who was destined to take command of the Squadron in July 1942), both of whom had been educated at Campbell College, Belfast. They were joined, early in August by another Old Campbellian, Flight Lieutenant Terence

---

2 AM911, AM914 and AM922 were not given Squadron code letters, as they were used for training only.

Flight Lieutenant TM Bulloch with his crew at RAF Nutts Corner in October 1941. They are (L to R starting with the back row) Sergeant McColl, flight engineer, Sergeant Hollis, gunner, Sergeant Turner, radar operator, Sergeant Miller, gunner, Pilot Officer Mitchell, navigator, Terry Bulloch, Pilot Officer Dear, 2nd pilot. MF Dear (by then a Flying Officer) was killed on 21st August 1942, when the Liberator III, LV340, of which he was the captain, crashed near Carnlough on the East Antrim coast. *(Ernie Cromie Collection)*

'Terry' Bulloch, DFC[3] whose contribution to the work of Coastal Command would become widely celebrated and an inspiration to many.

Earlier in 1941, during his supposedly 'rest' period, he had helped deliver Boeing B-17 Flying Fortress, Consolidated Liberator and Lockheed Hudson aircraft from the USA to the UK on behalf of Ferry Command so was well experienced on American types.[4] Flying Officer Eric Esler[5] was another Ulsterman who, like Jack Harrison[6], had come from 502 (Ulster) Squadron and there were local men too amongst the NCOs and other ranks, including Wireless Operator/Air Gunner (WOp/AG) Malcolm Ritchie from Bangor as well as Corporals Alec Gibson from nearby Dundrod and David Anderson from Belfast. Throughout the summer, they were

Pilot Officer Eric Esler is pictured (fourth from left) with the crew of his Liberator. During his time in Coastal Command, he attacked 15 U-boats, damaging several. *(Peter Clegg Collection)*

Alec Gibson attained the rank of Flight Sergeant and was awarded a Mention in Dispatches in 1944. *(Gibson Family Collection)*

---

3 Later Squadron Leader TM Bulloch DSO & bar, DFC & bar (1916-2014).
4 Including Lockheed Hudson III AE523 on 28/29th August 1941, from Montreal to Prestwick, via Gander and Nutts Corner.
5 Squadron Leader SE Esler DFC, AE was born in 1918 and became a test pilot after the war, he was killed in the crash of Avro 707 VX784 on 30th September 1949.
6 Later Wing Commander, DFC (1913–1973).

joined by more personnel and the memories of some of them make interesting reading. One such was Sergeant Pilot Harry Wilson who recalled:

'When I was posted to Nutts Corner, I travelled on the boat to Ireland with Sergeant Corkran, an Aussie, and eventually arrived at Crumlin Station. We waited around at Crumlin until we found a RAF lorry which was going to Aldergrove. The lorry gave us a lift to Aldergrove and from there we finally made it to Nutts Corner. The Nissen huts were dispersed and none of them even had electric light then. There were no ablution facilities and we had to draw water from a well in order to wash and shave. We were taken, once a week, to Aldergrove for a bath. I could only compare it with Flying Training School in Rhodesia where I was a member of the second course and – well – there was just no comparison! However, as time went by, things improved and there was a small farm nearby, we were able to buy eggs, milk, butter and bread and we used to settle down to scrambled egg on toast, cooked over a stove in the hut.'

A local inhabitant, Joe Brown remembers:

'This could well refer to my father Andy Brown's farm on now 6 Boltnaconnell Road where there was almost a small business grew up and friendships established with the military. An interesting outcome of a report to the Ministry that Andy Brown was selling fresh milk was that, following a visit from officials, the dairy etc was investigated and instead of a reprimand the small operation was officially registered, and to Andy's amazement a grant that was associated with the selling of fresh milk was paid.'

Another newcomer was WOp/AG Eddie Cheek:

'In June 1941, I was posted to 120 (General Reconnaissance) Squadron at Nutts Corner, in Northern Ireland; of course, nobody had heard of the place. After crossing the North Channel on the Stranraer/Larne ferry, I eventually arrived at Nutts Corner. After reporting to the Orderly Room, I found I was to fly on Liberator aircraft, whatever they were. I asked for directions to the Mess and was more than surprised to be told that it was one mile up the road, with another walk of half a mile to the accommodation site. My first impressions of Nutts Corner

(L to R starting with the back row) Sergeant Ken Owen, flight engineer, Sergeant Eddie Cheek, WOp/AG, Sergeants Ian and Archie Graham, WOp/AGs (and cousins), Flight Sergeant John Spiller, 2nd pilot, Flying Officer Peter Cundy, captain, Pilot Officer George Fabel, navigator. At just 18, Eddie Cheek was the youngest member of the Squadron. *(Eddie Cheek Collection)*

were, though it was not the end of the world, if the Good Lord decided to give the world an enema, here was the place. Living conditions could hardly be described as comfortable on this vast dispersed station. We were housed in those semi-circular monstrosities called Nissen huts, with just one eighth of an inch of corrugated metal separating us from the far from benign Irish elements. We used to say that if one could see Lough Neagh then the rain was approaching, if one couldn't then it was raining. Whether this form of accommodation was dictated by financial stringency or the urgency of war, or was a deliberate attempt by their 'Airships' to toughen us up I do not know but if it was the latter, I have to say that the most hardened criminals enjoyed far better accommodation as guests of His Majesty. Small coal-burning stoves with long, narrow chimneys protruding through the roof heated the room. One would sit in the room, in front of the fire, boiling in front and freezing behind. Our reveries were often disturbed by what was considered a harmless prank. A 'friend' would climb on to the roof and drop the filling of a Very cartridge down the chimney. The effect was both frightening and fantastic: the cartridge burned fiercely, building up sufficient pressure for the small inserts on top of the stove to be hurled up to the ceiling and the room would be suffused with an intense light, the colour of which depended upon the cartridge selected. Although one's heart soon returned to its normal place, it took some minutes before normal sight returned, by which time one's 'friend' had made a leisurely escape.'

A photocall for No 120 Squadron's aircrew at Nutts Corner in 1941. *(Eddie Cheek Collection)*

Flying Officer Rae Walton was an experienced pilot joining the squadron:

'In June 1941, three crews, namely those of Brian Bannister, Peter Cundy and myself, had completed a full tour of operations with No 53 Squadron and were posted to Nutts Corner to form with about six other crews, the reconstituted 120 Squadron, flying Liberators. These were new to the RAF and we spent some months learning to fly them and also learning the anti-submarine and convoy protection work which up to then was being done by Sunderland and Catalina flying-boats. Following re-formation, we visited and gleaned knowledge from Sunderland, Catalina and Hudson squadrons doing Atlantic protection work. We formed a small navigation school at Nutts Corner and spent long hours there, largely teaching ourselves by taking advantage of those who had special training skills. We lived in wooden huts dispersed about a mile from the runways, on gently rising ground to the east. The runways were quite long for those days but the aircraft was always fully loaded and required every inch for take-off. One officer on attachment to the Squadron remarked that the 1600-yard runway available was marginal with a fully-loaded Liberator and aircraft were often pulled off the ground at 125 mph with 50 yards to spare. To service a 110-foot wingspan aircraft in a 90-foot hangar meant that it had to be lifted on trolleys and dragged in sideways. He also commented that the aerodrome at Nutts Corner was built on what was partially a bog and as the runways were of tarmac they give trouble. If an aircraft leaves the runway it gets bogged down at once. The dispersal parks had concrete taxi tracks and these had been covered with tar and stone chippings for camouflage. The stones came loose and damage to propellers resulted. The hard-standings were excellently arranged, being a series of circles round which an aircraft could easily be taxied and were far superior to a narrow track terminating in a concrete square on which it would be impossible to turn a big aircraft.'

No 59 Squadron was called upon to provide three crews for the new 120 Squadron – among the volunteers was Flight Lieutenant David Evans:

'We all arrived at Nutts Corner early in June 1941 and within days we decided that whoever called this new and only partly finished airfield Nutts Corner knew what they were about. Living conditions were initially liable to be fairly primitive, especially for those who, like ourselves, had been living in relatively luxurious accommodation, superbly designed and built, as was that at RAF Thorney Island in the hey-day of the mid-1930s expansion of the Royal Air Force. Leave and other facilities or amenities were more accessible in the South of England – enemy bombing notwithstanding. The new wartime airfields were hutted and dispersed to various sites in order to reduce potential enemy bomb damage, even though in the case of Nutts Corner they were beyond the radius of action of contemporary enemy bombers. Thus, we had to walk about a mile along a country road from where we slept, to the 'domestic site' where we ate, relaxed or bathed. The airfield offices and aircraft operating areas – including already I think, at least one hangar – were a mile further on still. There were also dispersal points off the perimeter track where aircraft were parked. As RAF transport was in short supply, even bicycles were apparently unobtainable and as we had not been allowed to ship our own cars across the Irish Sea, Shank's Pony was the normal and tedious method of getting from A to B. It all wasted time and energy – we were relatively young and impatient, no doubt, that not enough was being done – but I'm sure that the Station Commander – Group Captain Pritchett – and 120's CO – Wing Commander Cumming who I think had a DFC and used to fly for Imperial Airways – tried their best to alleviate our discomforts.'

He was very impressed with the Liberator:

'Compared to the Blenheim, the accommodation was spacious and luxurious. The instruments, switches and levers were well-designed and positioned, the controls positive and infinitely adjustable. There were soft seats, close carpeting, individual ashtrays and, above all, a reliable Sperry 'George'. The Liberator gave an instant impression of size and power.'

Liberator I, AM923, with its ASV radar aerials clearly visible to the rear of the fuselage and under the wings. The radar operator could select either the forwards (wing-mounted) or sideways facing (on the fuselage) aerials, but not both at the same time. The latter would usually be used first to locate a contact to port or starboard, switching to the former and turning for the run-in to target, as illustrated in Diagram 1. This aircraft survived the war, finally being struck off charge at Prestwick in 1947. *(Ernie Cromie Collection)*

After five and a half hours dual instruction from Colonel McReynolds and Squadron Leader Berry, Evans went 'solo' on 2nd July – with five other pilots on board. He and some of the other pilots also spent a week with the Hudsons of No 224 Squadron at RAF Limavady, 'to learn more about submarine hunting and convoy escort.'

For the WAAFs (Women's Auxiliary Air Force) stationed at Nutts Corner, matters were even worse. Mrs Jean Davis remembers:

'We were billeted in the local Orange Hall in Dundrod, which meant about 50 of us in this large cavern, lit by candles most of the time. We had to break the ice at the village pump to wash and our idea of bliss was to hitchhike into Belfast

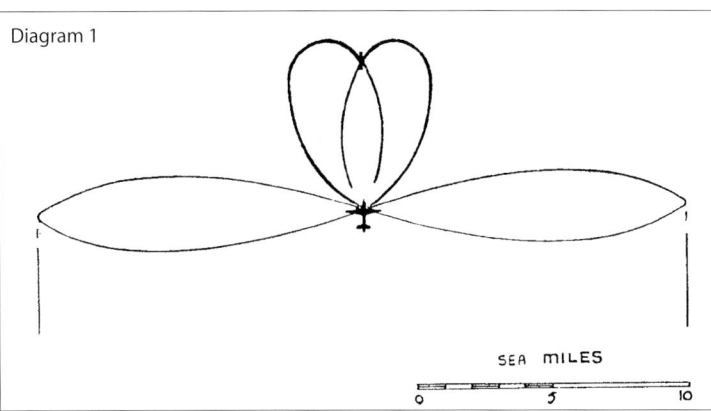

Diagram 1

and have a 'chance bath' at the Grand Central Hotel for one shilling and sixpence. After which we treated ourselves to tea there because luxury was being able to put the milk in last if we wanted to instead of 'cha' ladled out of buckets – one with and one without sugar, in the Mess. The catering arrangements were pretty basic – my abiding memory is of the charming habit of those who delivered the food to the cooks, dumping first the paraffin and then the sack of potatoes on the door mat so that everything in retrospect seemed to have been flavoured with paraffin. I also seem to remember a stern lecture from our WAAF Admin Officer in reply to complaints which, in effect, informed us that there was, after all, 'A War On'. We were there during the early snowy winter nights and we used to pool all our bedclothes and 'biscuits' and make a sort of communal bed for two or three – which was frowned on by authority as being immoral but as we were only determined on not dying of the cold during the nights and being huddled together gave us a united front against the rats that danced over us in the night, for once we took little notice of our superiors.'

By July, a pattern of life was emerging at Nutts Corner, with the aircraft now being flown to/from Prestwick on both training and maintenance flights. The station suffered its first fatality on 22nd July, although it wasn't the result of an aircraft accident; Aircraftman AJ Watkins, a fitter, was killed following a tractor accident on the perimeter track. A native of Birmingham, his body was taken there for burial. On 27th July, as the training programme continued, AM911 and AM922 flew down to RAF St Angelo in Co Fermanagh, where both runways were observed to be in an unfinished state, whilst just over a week later on 6th August, Wing Commander Cumming flew to Prestwick to test-fly the first completely fitted operational Liberator, AM928/A, in which he returned to Nutts Corner the following day. The aircraft was equipped with a ventral four 20 mm cannon pack as well as two tail guns and one in each beam position, together with a full array of ASV radar aerials on the rear fuselage and mainplanes. According to Terry Bulloch this made the aircraft, 'look like a Christmas Tree.'

The first ever night flying practice took place at Nutts Corner on 6th August, by Flight Lieutenant Harrison and Flying Officer THA Llewellyn, making sure to remain well clear of the nearby Divis Mountain which became the scene of a number of crashes.

The 20 mm four-cannon pack of this Liberator 1, AM916, can be seen underneath the front fuselage. *(JD Oughton)*

On 23rd August 1941, Wing Commander Cumming was replaced as the squadron commander by Wing Commander Vincent McBratney,[7] a native of Cork who had moved to Northern Ireland and was now resident in Magherafelt. Already experienced in Coastal Command, McBratney had recently formed and briefly commanded No 413 Squadron at RAF Stranraer, operating Consolidated Catalina flying-boats.

Two additional, fully equipped Liberators, AM924 and AM925, arrived from Prestwick on 23rd August 1941. *(Peter Clegg Collection)*

Two additional fully equipped aircraft, AM924/D and AM925/X, arrived from Prestwick on 23rd August while, on 28th August, 'boffins' arrived to add Sperry bomb sights to all three operational machines, the next few days being spent testing them.

Ironically, there was little operational need for this equipment as most attacks were carried out at very low level. 3rd September saw the Squadron suffer its first aircraft unserviceability when AM914, returning from a local training sortie, burst a tyre on landing, suffering only minor damage. For the remainder of September, local flying and navigational exercises continued as the Squadron worked up towards becoming fully operational. What could have been its first 'kill' came on 18th September when Pilot Officer Wightman and crew in AM910/M sighted an enemy submarine; unfortunately, the aircraft was not on an operational flight and there were no depth charges on board! The sighting was immediately reported to HQ 15 Group who ordered strike action to be initiated but, after circling the area for some time, Wightman had to return to base, undoubtedly feeling resentful about a great opportunity missed.

For nearly a year, 120 was the only VLR squadron that was operational in Coastal Command. The first such sortie was on 20th September, when Flight Lieutenant Harrison carried out an uneventful anti-submarine patrol, finally landing back at RAF Limavady. On the same day, a second patrol was carried out by Flight Lieutenant Bulloch in AM928/A although this sortie too was uneventful. 'The Bull' was destined for greater things. Carrying a full war load, the Mark 1 could remain on station 1100 miles from base for three hours, far beyond the capabilities of

Squadron Leader Terry Bulloch (left) with Flying Officer MS Layton DSO, from Montreal, who was Bulloch's navigator when he sank U6111. *(Ernie Cromie Collection)*

---

7 Later Group Captain, AFC (1913–1996).

Sunderlands and Catalinas. As a result, patrols of up to 17 hours duration were possible, on which Terry Bulloch commented, 'there wasn't much heating but we'd cook meals on solid fuel stoves and we had an Elsan chemical toilet, so we survived OK.'

Fully modified aircraft continued to arrive from Prestwick so that by 21st September there were five on operational strength, AM910/M, AM924/D, AM925/X, AM926/F and AM928/A. The anti-submarine patrols were now taking the aircraft as far out into the North Atlantic as 22° west and lasting for several hours.

Overall, aircraft serviceability was quite good, however, this quickly changed when, after getting airborne in company with AM910/M, the undercarriage of AM925/X, Flying Officer Bannister, failed to retract. After a few anxious minutes considering what to do, Bannister flew to Lough Neagh where the depth charges were jettisoned, following which it returned to overhead Nutts Corner to circle for four hours to burn off fuel before being gently put down on the tarmac there – much to the relief of the crew. Later, when AM910/M, Flying Officer Wightman, was recalled, it was discovered that its bomb doors had been damaged by faulty depth charge release gear. AM924/D also sustained damage to its bomb doors due to the operation of the emergency bomb release and although not serious, all these minor servicing issues meant the aircraft were non-operational for a few days which in turn meant important patrols could not be flown. Towards the end of September there were further tests with the Sperry bomb sight, this time under the guidance of Wing Commander CL Dann[8] of the Technical Branch; the sights probably being tested on the Lough Neagh bombing ranges. As 120 Squadron was now more or less fully operational in anti-submarine techniques, it began the practice of periodically detaching one or two aircraft to operate from other strategically placed stations, AM913/Z departing on just such an assignment to Prestwick and thence to the Inner Hebridean island of Tiree on 28th September.

October was to see an upturn in 120's fortunes when, on 4th, AM910/M and AM924/D were on anti-submarine sweeps with Convoy OG 75. Shortly after midday, AM924/D, piloted by Flying Officer T Llewellyn, met the convoy and began the usual pattern search for U-boats reported by the Senior Naval Officer (SNO) to be in the area. Whilst engaged in this search a Focke Wulf Condor, four-engine, long-range, patrol aircraft was sighted one mile to starboard.

Immediately the big Liberator was banked over in hot pursuit. Dropping to a height

A port side view of a 120 Squadron Liberator flying over the sea on 25th November 1941. *(Ernie Cromie Collection)*

---

8 Later Air Commodore CBE (1909–1965).

The Focke-Wulf Fw 200 Condor was originally developed pre-war, as a long-range airliner and subsequently used as a maritime patrol aircraft. Winston Churchill called the Fw 200 the 'Scourge of the Atlantic' due to its contribution to the Allied shipping losses, not only by sinking merchant ships but also pin-pointing the position of convoys for attack by U-boat. *(Guy Warner Collection)*

of 600 feet, it began to overhaul the Condor. Closer and closer Llewellyn crept until at a range of some 800 yards the Liberator began to vibrate as the front cannons pounded 184 shells towards the enemy. Caught by surprise, the lumbering Condor swung to starboard in a desperate bid to avoid further attacks, quickly finding the safety of the low cloud base. Llewellyn turned his Liberator on an intercepting course, every eye scanning the sky for the enemy aircraft. Suddenly, there it was again, 'Six o'clock high, six o'clock high', the intercom crackled. Instantaneously the tail gunner opened fire on the Condor, 200 feet above, but he could only get in a short burst as his line of fire was suddenly interrupted by AM924/D's tail-fin. This time, the big Condor broke away and dived to starboard, allowing the Liberator's beam gunners to get in a burst from 600 yards; down it continued, to 300 feet. The Liberator's gunners, having got the scent of victory, fired continuous short bursts from 600-800 yards when, suddenly, their aircraft's starboard inner engine began to race and had to be shut down. The chase was over and although AM924/D had received two hits it returned to base without crew casualties. This particular action was the Squadron's first brush with the enemy and although bitterly disappointed at having had to withdraw from the action the whole Squadron was proud of AM924/D's performance.

In the middle of October there was some changing of aircraft, with AM911 and AM913/Z, both non-operational types, being flown to Prestwick, the latter leaving Nutts Corner on the 10th whilst in the opposite direction that day came AM921/B followed by AM923/W two days later. The Squadron was now slowly building up to its supposed initial complement of nine fully operational aircraft and by mid-October the following were on strength – AM910/M, '921/B, '923/W, '924/D, '925/X, '926/F and '928/A. On 22nd October Flight Lieutenant Bulloch was airborne in AM926/F on escort duty to Convoy SL 89 with which he rendezvoused at 08.15 hours. After almost five hours monotonous patrolling, at 13.11 hours, a signal was received from the Senior Naval Officer (SNO) that a Condor was in the vicinity. Immediately, the crew's concentration was again at a peak; then, at position 51°31'N, 10°22'W whilst flying at 700 feet, a Condor was spotted off the port bow, about a mile away and flying at around 1000 feet. Bulloch opened the throttles and climbed for a head-on attack; at about 500 yards the Condor was given two short bursts from the underbelly cannons, the first burst going wide but after the second burst, tracers were seen to smash into the Condor. Approaching the Liberator head-on, the German replied also with his front cannon, registering a strike on a propeller although this wasn't noticed until the aircraft had returned to base. Such was the courage and determination of Bulloch that a third burst was fired from his cannons as the Condor passed some 200 feet overhead.

The Liberator, now in a precarious nose-up position, was immediately put into a dive to prevent the onset of a stall, allowing the tail gunner to get in a two-second burst, exchanging fire with the Condor's rear gunner who managed to get a strike on one of AM926/F's engine cowlings before his aircraft was swallowed up by the low cloud. Ten minutes later, the Condor was spotted again, close to the convoy and again at 1000 feet. Once again Bulloch manoeuvred for a head-on attack, managing to fire a burst from his cannons from about 500 yards but this time the Condor didn't want to get involved and climbed steeply into cloud. It would appear it had done its work though for, just over an hour later at 14.45 hours, a U-boat was sighted by AM926/F's crew three miles away on the port bow. Without hesitation, Terry pushed the nose down, at the same time shouting out orders for the impending depth charge attack. Commencing his run-in, he saw the submarine crash-diving but, making allowances, dropped three depth charges across the path of the 'boat just ahead of the wake termination. The third depth charge was estimated to be a hit, the underwater explosion causing considerable disturbance to the surface just at the end of the U-boat's track. Although AM926/F remained in the area for some time afterwards, nothing more was seen. Thus ended the Squadron's first tussle with a U-boat, which has defied identification but might have been U-203 which reported slight damage after being attacked on that date by an unidentified aircraft.

The first Liberators had arrived with the Squadron painted in standard Bomber Command camouflage, black undersurfaces and dark earth/dark green upper surfaces. Coastal Command's Operational Research Section, under Professor Patrick Blackett, had been considering the best colour scheme to adopt to make patrol aircraft less likely to be spotted by a U-boat's lookout. So, in the winter of 1941 the Liberators

The Mk VII depth charge [or wasserbombe as it was known to the U-boat crews, and 'ash can' as referred to by the US Navy] was a 450 lb (200 kg) bomb fitted with a hydrostatic device to detonate it at a pre-set depth, therefore allowing a submarine to be attacked by aircraft or naval vessels when submerged. Diagram 2 shows the normal method of attacking a U-boat, with a stick of eight depth charges released at 100 foot intervals. *(Guy Warner Collection)*

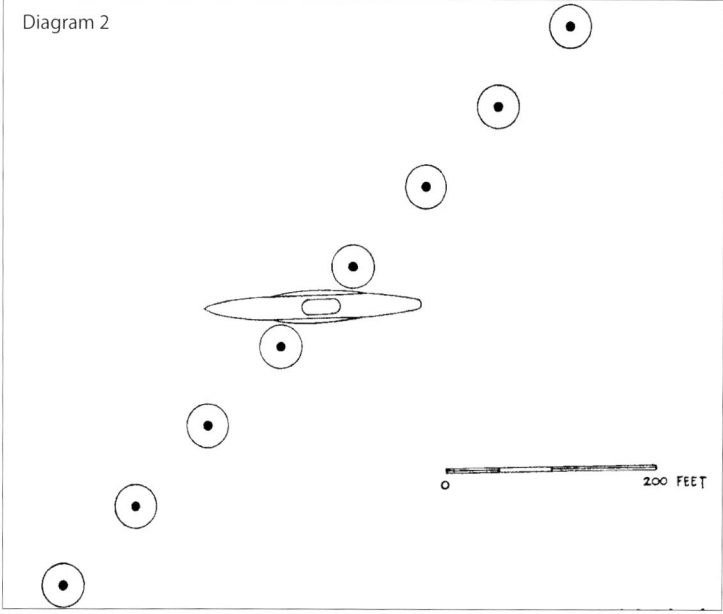

A U-boat crew's view of a 120 Squadron Liberator, in this case AM910. *(Roger Freeman Collection americanairmuseum.com)*

A Lockheed Hudson of No 206 Squadron, as flown by Terry Bulloch. The Squadron was based at RAF Aldergrove between August 1941 and June 1942. *(Ernie Cromie Collection)*

were re-painted with white undersurfaces and dark sea grey/slate grey upper surfaces. In the words of the renowned author, Dr Alfred Price, 'It was tacit recognition of the advantages of a colour scheme gulls and other sea birds had adopted some millions of years earlier.'

A typical cold, wet and windy November brought with it the Squadron's first serious accident when, on the 6th, AM910/M, captained by Squadron Leader RTF Gates returning to Nutts Corner at 23.00 from an anti-submarine patrol, landed heavily, collapsing the undercarriage and coming to rest on the runway, fortunately without serious injuries to the crew. Next day, No 1 Section of No 11 Repair and Salvage Unit, Mallusk, arrived to remove the aircraft from the runway, ostensibly to be repaired elsewhere. According to records however, in April 1942 it was re-categorised a write-off, to be reduced to spares and produce.

On 22nd November a pleasant honour befell Terry Bulloch when he travelled to Buckingham Palace to receive, from King George VI, the DFC he had earned a full year earlier, when he was with No 206 Squadron flying Hudsons over the North Sea.

Two days later, it was Nutts Corner's turn to host a member of the Royal Family when Air Commodore the Duke of Kent arrived to inspect the station, which was immaculately turned out. On the day after that, three new Liberators, AL513/K, AL553/O and AL560/Y were delivered from Prestwick, the first of a small number of the Mark 2 versions which 120 Squadron would have on strength until October 1942. They were received with mixed feelings. To many pilots, the Mark 2 was an improvement on the Mark 1, being the first variant to be equipped with power-operated gun turrets, one in the dorsal position immediately aft of the wings and one in the tail, while the fuselage forward of the cockpit was extended by two and a half feet to provide more crew space. Unfortunately, this resulted in a significant increase in weight and decrease in range to which Terry Bulloch for one took an immediate aversion, preferring the much longer range capability of the Mark 1 to enable him to seek out U-boats as far and wide as possible. Moreover, the onboard catering facilities were somewhat basic as former crew member, Bernard Harvey, later recalled:

'All you had to cook with was an electric kettle. I used to put two tins of soup in there, heat them up and, when they were done, take them out, take out the labels which were floating around in the water, put the eggs in there and have another boil-up until the eggs were hard-boiled, take the eggs out and make the tea with the water that was left. It was all that you could do.'

So far, 120 Squadron had been fortunate not to experience any aircrew fatalities but this changed during the evening of 10th December when disaster struck. Following a short detachment at RAF Dyce, Aberdeen with 18 Group, in the early afternoon AL513/Z and later AM926/F departed for Nutts Corner. AL513/Z arrived but AM926/F became overdue and was subsequently reported as missing. Growing concern among members of the Squadron turned to sadness when it was learned later in the evening that the aircraft had crashed at around 18.30 hours in the Ochil Hills near Alva just north of Alloa, killing all five crew members, the loss of whom would make the first Christmas at Nutts Corner a rather sad occasion.[9]

12th December introduced an additional aspect to the nature of operations carried out by 120 Squadron. Liberator AM924/D was tasked with a shipping strike in the Bay of Biscay and on the following day Terry Bulloch and crew were similarly tasked, in AM928/A, armed unusually, with 500-lb bombs. It was nearly their undoing. Just after 09.00 hours, near Biarritz, they attacked, at low level, two German naval ships steaming line ahead about a quarter of a mile apart. In a beam attack on one vessel, beginning with cannon fire which raked the ship's superstructure, they dropped a bomb from almost funnel height, timed to detonate after 11 seconds but it fell just short. This provoked intense return fire which damaged the tail of AM928/A and seriously wounded the rear gunner, Sergeant Hollis, who lost an eye in consequence. To ensure he was hospitalised as soon as possible, Terry turned around and headed for the UK, landing at RAF St Eval in Cornwall.

Later in the month the Squadron received the Admiralty's formal congratulations for its work in protecting Convoy HG 76, following the sinking of its escort carrier, HMS *Audacity* on 21st December.

Two Squadron members, Flying Officer Walton and Pilot Officer Layton had a memorable, if not enjoyable, week before the year drew to a close. They were dispatched to the Naval Base, Londonderry to proceed on board HMS *Northern Spray* and HMS *Northern Pride*, a pair of 900-ton escort trawlers, for 'observation duties.' The trip to Iceland and back was eventful, losing the convoy in mid-Atlantic in hurricane force

One of the pair of escort trawlers used to give two young officers of 120 Squadron some 'sea-time.' *(www.deepseatrawlers.co.uk)*

---
9 Flying Officer James Rae, Sergeant Roland Magson, Sergeant David Clark, Sergeant Robert Dear, Sergeant Douglas Bartell.

winds which caused the trawlers to roll 50-degree each side of vertical, reaching the coast of Iceland in thick fog, searching for Reykjavik with binoculars and finally running a test of vertical-launch, anti-aircraft rockets which, 'fizzled miserably over the side into the sea when launched.' Rae Walton summed up his feelings as follows:

> 'I was never more glad to reach The Minches [off the west coast of Scotland] on our way back to Londonderry. When we were opposite Oban, the Skipper produced a signal from the Admiralty, sending us immediately back to Iceland. The ship turned north and I was devastated. However, after the moans had died down, it turned out that the Skipper had played a hoax on me!'

1942

In January 1942, Coastal Command began to receive another American type, the Boeing B-17 Fortress. Although it was rated 'long range' rather than 'very long range', nevertheless it proved eventually to be a worthy addition to the inventory. Fortunately for Coastal, following trials with No 90 Squadron, Bomber Command, the B-17 had been considered unsuitable as a bomber, especially for night operations. Again, Nutts Corner was chosen for its introduction to anti-submarine duties and the unit nominated initially to be equipped with the type was No 220 Squadron, Coastal Command, which had been operating Lockheed Hudsons from RAF Wick in Caithness. Declared non-operational at the beginning of January 1942, to afford time for conversion, its personnel began to move with their remaining Hudsons to Nutts Corner where they were joined by men on transfer from No 90 Squadron. Simultaneously, command of the Squadron passed from Wing Commander CFC Wright to Wing Commander RTF Gates who had previously been with 120 Squadron as a Squadron Leader.

Sadly, 220 Squadron's time at Nutts Corner started inauspiciously. On 4th January, Hudson AM670 was en route from Wick with six men on board when it became lost in a snowstorm and crash-landed on the lower slopes of Agnew's Hill, Co Antrim. Two crew were injured but fortunately everyone survived and the pilot, Flight Sergeant George Gamble, was later awarded the British Empire Medal for the 'initiative, endurance and gallantry' he had displayed during this incident. On 1st February another of the Squadron's Hudsons, AM615, was involved in an exercise to test the defences of RAF Aldergrove when in the course of a very low-level attack against troops close to Nutts Corner, it hit a hedge, went out of control and crashed, killing the six men on board.[10] The tragedy was witnessed by a member of 120 Squadron whose memory of arriving at Nutts Corner was referred to earlier – Sergeant Eddie Cheek, Wireless Operator/Air Gunner.

> 'During the defence exercise I was in the 120 Squadron crew room. I should first explain that there had been attempts to camouflage this new airfield. One of the

---

10 Flight Sergeant George Ireland, Flight Sergeant Colin Morley, Sergeant Falkner Young, Sergeant Ronald Walker, Sergeant Wallace Watts, Sergeant Kenneth Horton.

features was that some stretches of the original hedges had been left to grow within the airfield perimeter; of course, they presented no hazard to the normal operation of aircraft. As we were watching this aerial activity I saw a Hudson aircraft start an extremely low run over the airfield, from east to west. The aircraft struck a section of hedge, immediately going up into a very steep climb and from a height of a few hundred feet it either stalled or was uncontrollable and dived into the ground. At that time, our aircraft dispersals were located on the northern side of the airfield, that is, on the northern side of the Belfast/Crumlin Road, the airfield proper being to the south side of the road. We made our way to the crash site, arriving sometime after the crash rescue services; there were no survivors. I estimate that the point of impact was fairly close to the Belfast/Crumlin road, to the north, some 500 yards west of the westernmost aircraft dispersal. As I recall, our reaction to the horror was barely detectable, secure in the emotional insulation of the young.'

That day was an especially tragic one inasmuch as two additional Hudsons were written off in circumstances related to the same exercise, both of them at and close to Aldergrove where they were on the strength of 206 Squadron.

In one case, which was almost a mirror image of the Nutts Corner tragedy, four crew of AM604 were killed[11] but there were no fatalities in the other case[12], fortunately. On becoming aware of the other two crashes, Eddie felt moved to further comment, 'At the time I thought, what a bloody silly way to run a war.'

As with the B-24, delivery of new B-17s was slow to get under way. In fact, it was mid-February before the type made an appearance, when four aircraft were flown to Nutts Corner from RAF Polebrook in Northamptonshire, to which crews of 220 Squadron had travelled at the end of January to begin type conversion training. However, the aircraft were not new, they were B-17C hand-me-downs, AN527, AN530, AN531 and AN537. A fifth, AN520, did not arrive until April, again from Polebrook. These early B-17C variants (Mark 1 to the RAF) had no tail armament and a smaller tail-fin with no dorsal extension, making them instantly distinguishable from later versions which 220 Squadron did not begin to operate until July 1942.

Lockheed Hudsons of 206 Sqn Aldergrove, which suffered two crashes on 1st February 1942. *(Ernie Cromie Collection)*

Meanwhile, training continued at Nutts Corner, to facilitate which AN531 and AN537 were adapted to carry depth charges and were maintained at a very high level of serviceability.

---

11 Pilot Officer Hugh Fraser, Sergeant Archibald Campbell, Sergeant Philip Fry, Sergeant Geoffrey Kettle.
12 This crash involved Hudson AM613 which was also taking part in a Station Defence Exercise. Taking off from Aldergrove, there was a partial failure of one engine. The resulting swing caused the undercarriage to collapse and the aircraft was destroyed in the ensuing fire.

Boeing Fortress Mk I, AM529, at RAF Heathfield, near Prestwick, shortly after its arrival from the USA in 1941. *(Guy Warner Collection)*

Training activity intensified throughout March and April, with navigation flights both in Fortresses and Hudsons being flown almost daily as part of a full programme also involving ground instruction, fighter affiliation, air-to-air and air-to-ground firing and bombing, taking advantage of the nearby Lough Neagh ranges. When circumstances permitted, Fortresses AN531/O and AN537/L took part in anti-submarine searches and convoy escort. By the end of April, satisfied that the required state of efficiency had been accomplished, Wing Commander Gates declared the Squadron fit for operations, notwithstanding that only 'O' and 'L' were fully equipped for operational work. As time would tell, the Mark 1 Fortress sorties were largely uneventful, with one notable, but embarrassing exception.

Fortress I, AN537, NR-L, of No 220 Squadron over a convoy, early in 1942. *(A Price Collection)*

On 18th May, the crew of AN537, thinking they had spotted a submerging U-boat, delivered an accurate attack but it was on what proved to be a school of porpoises, with some hits. The incident resulted in the following sarcastic signal from Group HQ in Liverpool, 'Congratulations to crew of 'L' 220 for successful attack on enemy in which 50 were destroyed.' Just over a month later, on 20th June 220 Squadron was transferred from Nutts Corner to Ballykelly, flying from which base it redeemed itself emphatically, destroying two U-boats within four days of each other in February 1943, flying Mark 2 Fortresses.

Since January 1942, 120 Squadron's Liberators had been continuing to operate from Nutts Corner although they were increasingly making use of the new airfield at Ballykelly, Co Londonderry, which was really only becoming fully operational in that month and to which the Squadron was destined to be transferred, in July 1942. Meanwhile, the anti-shipping strikes in the Bay of Biscay that had been a novel feature of operations in December 1941 continued into 1942. The official Coastal Command narrative of the time reported on a particularly interesting and prolonged example. On 11th January, Liberator AM924/D 'Donald Duck' took off from Nutts Corner at 04.10 hours, under the control of Flying Officer Peter Cundy[13].

At 15.20 hours, west of Cape Finisterre, they spotted a Heinkel He115 seaplane torpedo bomber/minelayer approaching the Liberator from below and behind and immediately turned to attack it, firing from beam and rear guns. Although fragments were seen falling from the Heinkel, which was emitting what was taken to be smoke from the starboard engine, it disappeared into a rain squall. Twenty-five minutes later, the crew sighted a large merchant ship about five miles away and a surfaced U-boat close by, both hardly under way. The ship was the MSS *Elsa Essberger* (a blockade runner, carrying among other cargo, some 4000 tons of rubber) in company with U-373, the captains of each vessel being aboard the U-boat 'in conference'. Losing height rapidly and passing the ship on the vessel's port side, Peter Cundy decided to make for the U-boat first, opening fire with the underbelly cannons at 800 yards range while closing to drop five depth charges set to explode at 50 feet depth. That was probably the saving of the U-boat from destruction as it was still on the surface when the depth charges entered the water, although after it submerged a large patch of oil was seen in the foaming water where the U-boat's stern had been observed sticking above the surface before disappearing. Next, Peter climbed the Liberator and attacked the ship, beam-on, using his cannons which raked the hull and superstructure whereupon the He115 suddenly reappeared. Turning attention again to the enemy aircraft, AM924/D exchanged fire with it and chased it off before resuming his attack on the ship, only to be interrupted for a second time by the Heinkel's reappearance. Both aircraft again exchanged fire which resulted in smoke streaming from the starboard engine of the Heinkel which, as before, dived towards sea level and disappeared. By now, it was 16.15 hours and, short of ammunition and fuel, Cundy decided it was time to leave the scene, landing at St Eval in Cornwall at 19.40 hours.

Flying Officer Peter Cundy at the controls of a Liberator. *(Eddie Cheek Collection)*

A Heinkel He115, three-seat seaplane, a type which was used as a torpedo bomber and also for reconnaissance and minelaying. *(Guy Warner Collection)*

---

13 The rest of the crew were as follows: 2nd Pilot Flight Sergeant Spiller, Flying Officer Fabel (Navigator), Sergeant Owen (Flight Engineer) and Sergeants Graham, Cheek and McKie (WOp/AG).

The attack on the Elsa Essberger as photographed from Liberator AM924. *(Eddie Cheek Collection)*

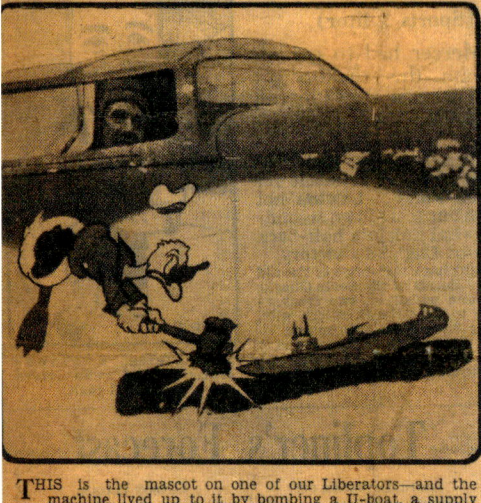

The attack was reported 'fairly concisely' in *Flight* magazine but made a bigger splash in a newspaper, with the headline 'Donald Duck Took Them All On'. Eddie Cheek annotated this cutting, 'Flight Sergeant John Spiller is in the cockpit. In those days each crew operated its own aircraft; ours bore the letter D and a superb painting of Donald Duck.' *(Eddie Cheek Collection)*

It was later established that *Elsa Essberger* had sustained significant damage. She entered the Spanish port of Ferrol on the following day, remaining there for a little under two months and transferring some of her cargo to smaller ships, before leaving and entering Bordeaux in early March, where, by October, she was being loaded with machine tools intended for Japan. Just as she was getting ready to sail, on 7th November, she was heavily damaged in an air raid on Bordeaux by Bomber and Coastal Command, so much so that she was declared a total loss. U-373 had been damaged and entered the La Rochelle U-boat base at La Pallice on 13th January, remaining until 24th February, apparently under repair. For this action, Flying Officers Cundy and Fabel were each awarded the DFC on 24th January.

The following month, on 18th February 1942, a dreadful tragedy unfolded at Nutts Corner, involving Liberator AM925/X and nine crew.[14] Fully loaded for an anti-submarine patrol, at 04.50 hours the aircraft lifted off the eastern end of the main runway (now at its full length of 6000 feet) but, failing to gain enough height, almost immediately struck a radio mast, losing the tail unit, impacting the ground and careering across some fields before coming to rest to the south of the A52, Belfast Road opposite the airfield communal site, exploding and bursting into flames. The consequences were horrific due to the inflammatory nature of 3000 gallons of high octane fuel, ordnance, ammunition and sea markers containing

---

14 Flying Officer BS Bannister DFC (Captain, injured); Sergeant WJ Wilson (2nd Pilot, injured); Pilot Officer WM 'Pop' Densham (Observer, fatally injured); Flying Officer H Wakefield DFC (Supernumerary Navigator, injured); Sergeant P Welford (Navigator, killed) and Wireless Operator/Air Gunners Pilot Officer PG Fuller, killed, Sergeant AA Middleton, killed, Sergeant H Mines, injured and Sergeant JF Waite, injured.

powdered aluminium. Rushing to the scene, medical personnel found Sergeants Waite and Mines on their feet but severely shocked. Efforts were made immediately to get them to Sick Quarters but it would appear that Waite, although injured about the head, back and leg, rushed into the blazing wreckage and succeeded in extricating Pilot Officer Densham who was then found lying close to Flying Officer Bannister, both of whom had suffered severe injuries.

While Station Medical Officer, Flying Officer Claydon, and his assistant, Aircraftman Gilbert, were administering immediate aid to them, more depth charges exploded, causing Claydon and Gilbert to shield both injured men with their own bodies. Having done all they could for Bannister and Densham, Claydon and Gilbert then attended to Sergeant Wilson who was also severely shocked, lying by the roadside. Flying Officer Wakefield, meanwhile, although suffering from burns and shock, had somehow made his own way to Sick Quarters. It wasn't until first light that the bodies of the remaining three crew members were found amongst the wreckage.

Flying Officer Brian Bannister is on the extreme right of the middle row. This photograph was taken in 1940 when he was on a training course at No 2 School of Army Co-operation, Andover. *(Ernie Cromie Collection)*

Remarkably, in the course of time, those men who had survived the crash recovered from their injuries, except Densham who died from his injuries two days later. Age 32, he had been nicknamed 'Pop' and had previously flown with Brian Bannister when both men were members of 53 Squadron but this had been his first mission with 120 Squadron. A few months later, Sergeant Waite's courage was recognised by the award of the George Medal. With tragic irony, not long after Bannister's recovery, he was one of 13 passengers and crew on board Hudson N7253, of No 24 Squadron, which was flying from Sydenham to London when it came to grief during a thunderstorm over the Welsh Mountains, killing all on board, on 17th July 1942.

Operations continued however, in all weathers and with no reduction in intensity, ranging from the Bay of Biscay area to Iceland and beyond. In April, for instance, 120 Squadron's aircraft carried out 31 sorties amounting to 385 flying hours. On 26th April, a record was set for Nutts Corner when six sorties were carried out, involving Liberators of 120 Squadron as well as a Hudson and a Fortress of 220 Squadron.

The navigator of Liberator AM925, Sergeant Page Welford, lost his life in the crash at Nutts Corner on 18th February 1942. *(Mrs Susan Haughton Collection)*

Close to home could be hazardous too. On 4th May, Liberator II,

AL558/V, was on local night flying exercise when it impacted Divis Mountain, which was part of the high ground fringing North Belfast, five miles from Nutts Corner. One of the crew, Sergeant J Gooder, was killed and three others were injured. A report on the accident recommended that a beacon be placed on Divis.

There were occasions when the Liberators were tasked with long range reconnaissance missions off the coast of Northern Norway in indirect support of the Russian convoys. In their own way, these were every bit as dangerous and harrowing as anti-submarine and anti-shipping sorties, possibly more so as Flying Officer Rae Walton and his crew[15] were to discover. On 22nd May Walton flew AM924/T to RAF Stornoway in order to carry out a radar sweep off the North Cape of Norway on the following day. They returned to Stornoway without incident but, two days later, in carrying out a similar sweep they sighted and attacked a U-boat with cannon fire but without evident effect. Three days later, on 28th May, carrying out yet another operation, they were attacked by three Messerschmitt 109s which caused two engines to fail. Having seen off the 109s, they had just turned for home when the third engine gave up and they were forced to ditch within very distant sight of the Norwegian coast. Tragically, two of the WOp/AGs, Flight Sergeant Allgood and Sergeant Smith, did not survive the action but the remaining men managed to get into their dinghy and start to paddle for the coast. On the following day they were still paddling when a storm blew up, during which Flight Sergeant Culnane died of cold and exhaustion. On the day after that, 30th May, the survivors reached an offshore island where they were captured by two German soldiers. When one soldier left to fetch support, Walton and his colleagues overcame the other one, left him tied up, then managed to find a boat and reach the mainland. Fortunately, before leaving on the actual sortie they had made up two emergency packs of food which they had brought from the aircraft. With the aid of the food, by marching at night and living off the land they succeeded in surviving a gruelling trek to neutral Sweden which they reached on 30th June, utterly exhausted. There they were found, fed and, after a few days, taken to Falun where they were interned for seven weeks before being repatriated. During the trek, Sergeant Pickering who had been wounded in the arm by a piece of shrapnel during the engagement with the 109s, had to undergo surgery by razor blade to have it removed. Later, medals were awarded to all four survivors, the MC to Walton and Corkran, the MM to Sergeant Booker and the DFM to Sergeant Pickering.

By May 1942, it was patently clear that, despite the best efforts of 120 and 220 Squadrons, Coastal Command was still woefully short of a sufficient number of long range and very long range aircraft required to help overcome the U-boat threat, especially Liberators. One of the many problems that confronted Coastal Command for most of the war was the indifference, some might say downright opposition to its very existence that was displayed by some implacable advocates of the strategic bombing policy of Bomber Command. The first sign of a softening of that attitude was manifested at Nutts Corner early in the

---

15 Flying Officer Rae Walton, Pilot Officer TJ Corkran, Flight Sergeants J Culnane and EA Allgood and Sergeants JD Pickering, BF Smith and EJ Booker.

month when five new Liberators, AL520/N, AL542/O, AL551, AL552/H and AL553/Q, arrived from RAF Lyneham.[16] They were Mark 2 versions constituting a detachment of No 160 Squadron which it had been decided would be made available to operate as part of 120 Squadron. This was significant because 160 Squadron was a Bomber Command unit that was actually in the process of moving to the Middle East initially, for night bombing raids on enemy ports and bases. The aircraft were air tested and fitted out for Coastal Command operations as much as possible in the time available while the crews, under their Commanding Officer, Wing Commander DIP McNair, began a series of lectures and ground instruction on relevant procedures. Operations began on 10th May when McNair and his crew carried out an anti-submarine patrol in AL552/H but nothing was sighted. AL542/O was similarly tasked on 11th May when convoy escort was the order of the day and for the next fortnight. On 25th May, flying training was temporarily suspended and maximum effort was called for, AL555/U being employed to escort a naval force which was not actually met because of bad weather. On the same day, AL551, with ground personnel, was detached to Stornoway to operate with the small 120 Squadron detachment of Mark 1 Liberators there. It became unserviceable but spares were flown up in a Hudson and AL551 returned the following day. 31st May turned out to be a distressing one. When AL520/N was on convoy escort duty, the aircraft fell foul of a particular hazard to which Coastal crews were not infrequently exposed; it was mistakenly fired on and hit by naval gunfire from one of the ships, which seriously injured one of the air gunners, Sergeant Thomas O'Shea from Co Tipperary. Although the damaged aircraft was flown to Tiree as quickly as possible, Sergeant O'Shea died from his wounds the following day and was subsequently buried in St Joseph's Churchyard, Glenavy. One of the detachment's last operations, which was carried out on 7th June by Wing Commander McNair in AL555/U flying from Nutts Corner to RAF Predannack in Cornwall to operate from there, was a shipping strike off the Spanish coast but, due to fog, his quarry was not found. Shortly afterwards, he and his colleagues left Nutts Corner with their aircraft to re-join the main part of 160 Squadron in the Middle East.

They were replaced, on 11th June, by another batch of aircraft, of a type not normally seen at a Coastal Command station, on detachment from No 44 (Rhodesia) Squadron, Bomber Command, RAF Waddington. This Squadron had already made history as the first to introduce the Avro Lancaster to operations on Christmas Eve, 1941. The detachment consisted of around 60 officers and men together with seven Lancasters Mk I: L7568, R5489, R5494, R5603, R5624, R5665 and R5858. Their stay was only marginally longer than that of 160 Squadron, until 19th July, but in a number of ways it was more eventful and it too began with some very hurried training in general reconnaissance, anti-U-boat tactics and convoy escort duties. To help, an experienced Observer with a Wireless Operator/Air Gunner from 220 Squadron flew on each Lancaster sortie until the detachment returned to Waddington.

---

16 AL551's Squadron code letter was not listed in the ORB.

Three Avro Lancaster B.1s of No 44 (Rhodesia) Squadron in 1942. From bottom to top: W4162 `KM-Y', flown by Pilot Officer Tom Hackney and his crew, W4125 `KM-W', captained by Sergeant Colin Watt RAAF, and W4187 `KM-S', flown by Flying Officer Jim Stephens DFC, DFM. *(memorialflightclub.com)*

On 12th June, Flying Officer PA Ball DFM and crew flew Lancaster R5603 for seven and three quarter hours on an uneventful navigation and fuel endurance exercise. On the following day, Flight Lieutenant TPE Barlow DFC and his crew flew the same aircraft on a convoy escort patrol which lasted just over 11 hours. They met the convoy and on the instructions of the SNO carried out a fruitless search for a U-boat. Any sense of complacency that might have been engendered was dispelled on 14th June, not long after Pilot Officer DF Nicholson and crew left Nutts Corner at 09.05 hours in R5858 'G'. The Lancaster was new, with only 18 hours flying time on the clock and was tasked with escorting Convoy ONS 102, outward bound to West Africa. Nothing had been heard from the aircraft until, at 16.42, 15 Group HQ reported hearing an SOS from 'G' after two engines had failed. This was followed at 22.30 hours by a message reporting that all the crew had been rescued from the sea by one of the RN destroyer escorts. It later transpired that 'G' had experienced a fuel feed problem resulting in both port engines failing and an enforced but successful ditching. It was a problem that had much earlier been experienced during raids over Europe. Some weeks later the Squadron received a rude postcard from the crew, including two members of 220 Squadron, by then safely delivered to Freetown in Sierra Leone.

It is tempting to think that 44 was a lucky Squadron and, given more time would have made an even greater impact in Coastal Command, which seemed to be confirmed on the following day, 15th June. Three Lancasters were tasked to escort Convoy HG 84, L7568 captained by Flight Lieutenant Barlow which took off at 08.25, R5489, captained by Flying Officer Ball which took off at 11.55 and R5494 which left at 12.00, captained by Warrant Officer E Dainty DFM. Unfortunately, half an hour after take-off, R5494's radio failed and Dainty aborted the sortie. Meanwhile, when approaching the estimated position of the convoy, at 12.41 hours, Barlow spotted a submarine on the surface three miles ahead. He immediately dived to attack only to see the U-boat submerging. Nevertheless, he dropped six depth charges very close to the U-boat which the bomb-aimer reported he could just see outlined beneath the surface as they passed directly over it. An oil stain was then seen so Barlow decided to hang around. Forty minutes later, the conning tower of a U-boat broke the surface but after a few seconds submerged again. Barlow then dropped a bomb from 800 feet before returning to Nutts Corner where he arrived at 17.45. In his Combat Report, Barlow noted that a formidable German Junkers Ju88 had been spotted in the vicinity the convoy, 'but he disappeared into cloud we were unable to find him.' The 44 Squadron historian later noted, 'Quite what he expected to do when he did catch him is a little difficult to imagine.'

An aerial attack on a U-boat, note the gunfire and depth charge splashes. *(Guy Warner Collection)*

A few hours later, Ball also spotted a U-boat about five miles from the convoy and carried out an attack with six depth charges dropped from 50 feet, 15 seconds after the U-boat had submerged but he then had to leave immediately because of a low fuel state, touching down at Nutts Corner at 22.15 hours. These attacks were the first to be made by Lancasters against U-boats actually at sea. Some further convoy patrols were carried out uneventfully before the Lancasters ended their detachment on 19th July.

In June 1942, King George VI and Queen Elizabeth made an official three-day visit to Northern Ireland to carry out a strenuous programme of engagements, arriving at Belfast Harbour on 24th in the light cruiser HMS *Phoebe*, with air cover provided by six Supermarine Spitfire Vbs from No 504 (County of Nottingham) Squadron, stationed at RAF Ballyhalbert.

RAF Ballyhalbert's Spitfires kept a close watch on the King and Queen. *(Ernie Cromie Collection)*

The Squadron would maintain a series of protective patrols during the entire course of the visit. In Belfast, they were greeted by numerous dignitaries including the Governor, Earl Granville and his wife, Prime Minister JM Andrews, and the Air Officer Commanding, RAFNI, Air Vice Marshal JB Cole-Hamilton CBE,[17] before inspecting the shipyards and the Short & Harland aircraft factory and then proceeding to

---

17 As a young officer in the RNAS, Cole-Hamilton (1894–1945) had been one of the airship pilots patrolling the North Channel from Luce Bay to Bentra.

RAF Maghaberry was used primarily as a base for aircraft ferry squadrons and also as a transit point for casualty evacuation, due to the proximity of the US Army's 79th Station Hospital at Moira. After the war many hundreds of aircraft were broken up for disposal, including some 200 Stirlings at Maghaberry alone, many of which can be seen here. *(Ernie Cromie Collection)*

Parliament Buildings, Stormont for lunch. Afterwards, it was back to Belfast Harbour to visit and have tea with Royal Navy units before travelling to Hillsborough to spend the night as guests of Earl Granville and his wife at Government House, where mobile anti-aircraft defences had been temporarily installed for the duration of the visit. On the second day, before returning to Hillsborough to spend a second night, the Royal Party visited units of the US Army at various locations in County Down, including Ballykinler and Rostrevor[18]. The final day of the visit, 26th June, was equally intensive, commencing with an inspection of elements of the 72nd Infantry Brigade and 59th Infantry Division of Home Forces of the Army near Moira followed by a visit to RAF Maghaberry.

From there, the King and Queen were conveyed the 14 miles to Nutts Corner, where they were greeted by the Air Officer Commanding No 15 Group, Air Vice Marshal D Colyer CB, DFC and Group Captain Pritchett, before inspecting personnel and aircraft of three RAF squadrons, the resident Liberators and Lancasters of 120 and 44 Squadrons, respectively, and three Fortresses of 220 Squadron which were flown back from Ballykelly to be part of the impressive line-up.

18 In May 1942, the First Armored Division USA arrived in County Down and made Castlewellan Castle its headquarters, under the command of Major General Orlando Ward. Quite remarkably, US troops were stationed in Rostrevor House, built by the widow of Major General Ross whose army captured Washington in 1814, burning the White House and Capitol.

Far left: King George VI inspects the Fortress Is of 220 Squadron, flown in from RAF Ballykelly. *(Ernie Cromie Collection)*

Left: The King meets some of 120 Squadron's ground crew, the tall officer to the left is Wing Commander McBratney. *(Ernie Cromie Collection)*

Far left: Squadron Leader Jack Harrison and his crew are presented to the King. *(Ernie Cromie Collection)*

Left: Group Captain Pritchett is on the far right as the King leaves the Officers' Mess. *(Ernie Cromie Collection)*

Far left: The crew and ground crew of a Lancaster of No 44 Squadron meets the King. *(Ernie Cromie Collection)*

Left: Queen Elizabeth visits RAF Nutts Corner on 26th June 1942. *(RCB Ashworth Collection)*

Personnel line the road and cheer the King and Queen as they leave Nutts Corner. *(Ernie Cromie Collection)*

Half a dozen 120 Squadron Liberator IIIs at RAF Aldergrove in 1943. *(Ernie Cromie Collection)*

Also present for inspection was a detachment of cadets from the Belfast Wing of the Air Training Corps. After lunching in the Officers' Mess, the King and Queen went their separate ways to attend different functions before meeting up again for tea in Ballymena. Their tour ended in the port of Larne where they inspected elements of the Royal Navy and US Navy before departing on board the Hunt Class destroyer HMS *Bicester*.

Early in July, Wing Commander SJ 'Jack' Harrison DFC assumed command of 120 Squadron, which later in the same month, moved to RAF Ballykelly on the north coast. Shortly before the move, the Squadron began to receive its first Liberator IIIs.

Royal Air Force Northern Ireland

The departure of Coastal Command aircraft from Nutts Corner was marked, in July 1942, by the transfer of the airfield to Royal Air Force Northern Ireland (RAFNI). Significantly, this organisation was created in 1940 with responsibility for general administration, and out of consideration for the various issues unique to Northern Ireland of which the prospect of a German invasion of the country, directly or indirectly, was very topical. Although in the nature of a Command, it was part of the overall structure of the RAF and did not assume the functions of other Commands such as Coastal, Fighter, Army Co-operation, Bomber and so on. Effectively, Nutts Corner went into Care and Maintenance which did not, as we shall see, render it unavailable for use or an unimportant military asset.

Chapter 3
Gliders
1942

Although the successful use of airborne troops during the Second World War was pioneered by the Germans, lessons were soon learned by the British Army, resulting, inter alia, in the formation of the 11th Special Air Service Battalion in 1940, the Glider Pilot Regiment in February 1942 and the Parachute Regiment in August 1942, as well as the establishment of an Airborne Forces Depot and Battle School in Derbyshire in April 1942.[1] Meanwhile, in January 1942, to oversee the means of delivering airborne forces to battle, No 38 Wing was formed within the RAF at Netheravon in Wiltshire, to which Nos 296 (Glider) and 297 (Parachute) Squadrons were relocated from RAF Ringway, Manchester, becoming the Wing's first Order of Battle. At Netheravon, the squadrons worked up to operational standard and, as part of their training it was decided that, from the beginning of July, a regular Glider Ferry Service would operate, subject to weather, to and from Northern Ireland with the aim of providing troops and aircrew with long distance training in single or formation towing, sea crossings, ditching drill and long distance navigation as well as facilitating the development and testing of equipment required. The route initially envisaged, flying at a maximum height of 2000 feet or below cloud base as necessary, was Netheravon – Shobdon – Wrexham – Carlisle – Dumfries – Portpatrick – Newtownards – Long Kesh and return. The following combinations of aircraft were authorised (a) tug towing one General Aircraft Hotspur (b) tug towing two Hotspurs (c) tug towing three Hotspurs or (d) tug towing one Airspeed Horsa; tugs would be one of the following types – Armstrong Whitworth Whitley, Vickers Wellington, Short Stirling, Handley Page Halifax, Avro Manchester or Lancaster. Passengers or freight could be carried; however, for the first month of the service only a single Hotspur training glider was to be towed and it was stipulated that two pilots would be carried in each glider.[2]

---

1 On 31st August 1941 the decision was made to form the 1st Parachute Brigade under Brigadier Richard Gale. This was to be located at Hardwick Camp near Chesterfield in Derbyshire. Hardwick Hall became the new nucleus for parachute training and physical selection for airborne forces.

2 No 296 Squadron was formed out of the Glider Exercise Unit at Ringway on the 25th January 1942, consisting at that time of a mixture of Hawker Hector and Hawker Hart aircraft. Several days later the Squadron moved to Netheravon, where they trained with GAL Hotspur gliders carrying troops of the 1st Airlanding Brigade. A conversion to Whitley aircraft began in June 1942, and during the following month the Squadron was divided into 296A and 296B Squadrons. The former reverted to 296 Squadron on the 12th August and was moved to RAF Hurn, whilst 296B was renamed the Glider Pilot Exercise Unit. On the 10th November, the Squadron performed its first operational sortie with a leaflet dropping mission over France.

A pair of General Aircraft GAL.48 Hotspur gliders, which were mostly used for training. *(Guy Warner Collection)*

Armstrong Whitworth Whitley tow aircraft, shown here at RAF Sleap in Shropshire. *(The Glider Pilot Regiment Society)*

In the event, although a same-day return, a trial flight was carried out on 18th July when Squadron Leader AB Wilkinson of 296 Squadron, piloting an Armstrong Whitworth Whitley, towed a General Aircraft GAL.48 Hotspur[3], of 296B Squadron, flown by Wing Commander TB Cooper DFC.[4] The service did not actually commence until 1st August, with the glider being flown by Flight Lieutenant Taylor.

Moreover, a further change of plan resulted in the Northern Ireland terminus being switched from RAF Long Kesh to Nutts Corner. Taylor was followed by Sergeant EA Smith on 5th and Sergeant C Wild on 9th. The overall total of return flights was seriously limited by adverse weather conditions. In August, only nine were successfully accomplished and only three in September. Records are a bit obscure but it appears that only three or four took place in October. Because of deteriorating weather, shorter daylight hours and increasing demands upon squadron aircraft required for other purposes the decision to suspend the Glider Ferry Service at the end of October was taken by the Air Officer Commanding-in-Chief, Army Co-operation Command, Air Marshal Sir Arthur 'Ugly' Barratt KCB, CMG, MC.

Although the operation was comparatively short-lived and the flights few, they were not uneventful, as two in particular will demonstrate. The first, fortunately, did not end tragically but in its own way was remarkable. It occurred on 11th August and involved a Hotspur II, BT536, towed by a Whitley flown by Pilot Officer Hyde. In the glider on this occasion were an Australian, Sergeant MCC Wallis, one of the two pilots who normally made up the crew and 28-year old Lieutenant Mervyn Dennison from Belfast, with six fellow riflemen

---

3 The Hotspur was conceived as an assault glider, requiring a compact design with room for no more than eight, including the two pilots, a change in tactical philosophy soon favoured larger numbers of troops being sent into battle in gliders. Due to this, the Hotspur was mainly relegated to training where it excelled and it became the basic trainer for the glider schools that were formed. Although relatively heavy with a high sink rate, the Hotspur exhibited good flying characteristics and could even be flown aerobatically, allowing novice pilots to quickly gain proficiency.

4 Later Group Captain (1908–1949). Tom Cooper had been awarded the DFC while commanding No 502 (Ulster) Squadron in 1941. On 5th March 1949, he lost his life while test flying Gloster Meteor F.4, RA 382, from Boscombe Down.

of the 1st Battalion Royal Ulster Rifles, part of the 1st Air Landing Brigade, who were taking a fortuitous opportunity to travel home to spend some leave. As the Whitley/Hotspur combination approached the Antrim coast, fog was encountered, at which point Mervyn Dennison takes up the story:

'Fog grew thicker as we reached the Belfast area and soon became solid. The tow pilot called, 'Cast off, cast off'. In flying a glider, it is essential to keep the tow rope as taut as possible and there should be no 'angle of dangle' because with no visibility the glider could be chucked forward then the rope would intermittently go slack until its nose would be pulled out.

I watched the very rudimentary instruments over the shoulders of our pilots and the altimeter fall lower and lower from about 2000 feet down to 800 feet and go lower in the fog. We cleared the fog at about 300 feet, the pilots did one circuit of a field (with stone walls) about the size of two tennis courts and approached it to land. Half a dozen cows and a horse ran about madly. Hotspurs had very thin struts and landing wheels used for take-off. They landed on a large ski-thing under the belly. The pilots did a splendid job of it but we soon tilted and a wing-tip hit the ground. We skidded along over a rough old field, sustained some holes in the belly of the fuselage and ended up with the nose banging into a stone wall. We soldiers kicked open the jammed door and got out. A Corporal Eddie Dempster from Donaghadee said to me 'This is a right oul cod of an airport, it is well named Nutts Corner!' The only casualties were the two pilots who had some facial cuts from the broken Perspex in the nose of the glider.

After about 10 minutes, an RAF corporal arrived, out of breath, and invited us all to come with him. He led us to a semi-underground bunker, with telephone, bunks and cooking facilities. He explained to me that they were on a form of duty to run a decoy runway (with lights). The bunker was about 400 yards from where we pranged. He got through to Nutts Corner, of which I am quite certain; I got on the line, asked for a truck and got to the Duty Officer with my request for him to phone 1 RUR near Netheravon and report our safe arrival and sad circumstances. Not far, say 100 yards from the bunker was a modest farmhouse among tall trees. The dear lady provided a lovely cup of tea and soda scones! The truck arrived and took us, with the pilots, to Nutts Corner. The pilots made a report, so did I and we left them there. The RAF truck drove us to the RUR Depot and we went off on our leave. We all got warrants and eventually returned to England by sea at the end of our leave. Soon afterwards, I transferred to the Parachute Regiment which seemed to provide a much safer form of transport!'

In further correspondence, Mervyn told the author that he regarded the Commanding Officer of 1 RUR as having 'worked a smart trick' in supporting the Glider Ferry Service inasmuch as it had the incidental benefit of providing a quick means of transport for his soldiers going to Northern Ireland on leave. He also mentioned another, perhaps questionable, but understandable benefit. One of his fellow officers arranged for a Belfast butcher to be their agent for purchasing turkeys for No 38 Wing for Christmas and with the authorisation of the then temporary Station Commander, Squadron Leader F Kennedy OBE, he secured the use of a hut at Nutts Corner in which to store them. Allegedly though, so much thieving was occurring from it that it became necessary to put an armed guard on the hut!

On 23rd August, Whitley BD417 of 296 Squadron, flown by Pilot Officer Thomas Tennyson, left Netheravon for Nutts Corner in the forenoon towing Hotspur BT666, piloted by Sergeant Petley, with a number of troops on board. Nearing the Calf of Man, the tow broke but Petley successfully ditched the glider which remained afloat long enough for a RN destroyer to rescue him and his passengers who were eventually landed at Gourock. Meanwhile, Tennyson, who had circled the downed glider for an hour and a half until the destroyer arrived, made for RAF Ronaldsway to take on fuel. Unable to source the necessary 100 octane petrol required, he took off again and at 16.20 hours managed to reach RAF Andreas, which was also on the Isle of Man, where fuel was available. Prior to leaving Andreas, however, he was prevailed upon, against his better judgement, by the Station Commander, Wing Commander EV Knowles DFC[5], to hand over the aircraft to him, as he wanted to take a civilian girlfriend, Thelma Kersley, for a short flight, accompanied by a Major Geoffrey Killigrew Wait MC, the officer responsible for the defence of the Station and Pilot Officer AB Paton, the Duty Pilot of the day. Having deferred to rank and experience and handed over responsibility, Tennyson reported to Flight Control, leaving on board at the back of the Whitley, Corporals Butler, Salt and Williams and Leading Aircraftman Alfred Henderson. At 17.38 hours, Knowles took off but almost immediately the Whitley stalled, crashed and split in half, whereupon the front half burst into flames, killing Knowles, Wait, Paton and Kersley. The four men in the rear portion of fuselage survived the initial impact but LAC Henderson had severe head injuries and died later in hospital in Onchan. Subsequently, his body was taken for burial to Polmont, near Falkirk; the others were buried in the local churchyard at Andreas. It was a tragedy which, even today, is the subject of unresolved questions.[6]

On 18th September 1942, observers of the Nutts Corner scene could have been forgiven for thinking 120 Squadron was moving back from Ballykelly. As anyone familiar with squadron codes painted on aircraft would immediately have realised however, the single aircraft that unexpectedly arrived on that date was not from 120 but from No 224 Squadron, the second of the Coastal Command squadrons to be equipped with Liberators.

---

5 Before the war 'Teddy Knowles' had been one of the early members of the Meteorological Flight at Aldergrove.
6 Killed: Wing Commander EV Knowles DFC, BA, Mus.B, ARCM, ACTL, Flying Officer AB Paton, Major GK Wait MC, Mrs T Kersley, died of injuries: Leading Aircraftman A Henderson, uninjured: Corporal TP Butler, Aircraftman F Williams, Aircraftman CA Salt. A summary of the accident report is as follows: Aircraft took off, climbed, stalled and crashed. Court of Inquiry: Due to pilot E of J [error of judgement] in using full flap during take-off causing the nose to rise beyond control of the elevators. Error probably caused by effects of drink. The AOC wrote: No evidence to show that flaps were down on take-off. May have misused trimming controls and lowered flaps before striking ground. Pilot had too much to drink and is entirely responsible. CI(A) [Chief Investigator (Accidents)] concurs.

A Liberator III of No 224 Squadron, receives the attention of the ground crew at RAF Beaulieu in December 1942. *(Andy Thomas Collection)*

Five more arrived on the following day, carrying the Squadron Commander, Wing Commander WH Kearney, numerous officers, airmen and equipment. Although 224 Squadron was actually based at RAF Beaulieu in Hampshire, to which they had moved only a week earlier from Tiree, they were in the process of working up to operational standard on the Liberators and, not only did Nutts Corner afford quick access to the Lough Neagh Bombing and Gunnery Ranges and ground training facilities at No 1 Armament Practice Camp at Aldergrove, Beaulieu lacked the facilities to enable night flying practice to be carried out there, having only opened for use in August in an uncompleted state of construction. On 24th September, two crews completed their training at Nutts Corner and returned to Beaulieu to be replaced by two new crews. Two days later, four crews and aircraft returned to Beaulieu, leaving two still at Nutts Corner until they also departed on 27th September.

US Parachute Infantry

During the latter half of the month, Nutts Corner played a unique role during the course of extensive military manoeuvres which were carried out in Northern Ireland and lasted from 21–28th September – Exercise PUNCH. Initially, it was planned that elements of the 1st Armored and 34th Infantry Divisions respectively of the US Army in Northern Ireland would be involved but in the event they did not participate. Instead, American forces were represented by paratroops of the 503rd Parachute Infantry Regiment, under the command of Lieutenant Colonel Edson Raff, 565 of whom arrived at Nutts Corner from RAF Ramsbury

Exercise PUNCH, the paratroopers check their harnesses prior to climbing on board the waiting C-47. *(Clive Moore Collection)*

Men of the 503rd Parachute Infantry Regiment board the C-47 Skytrains. *(Clive Moore Collection)*

in Wiltshire on 26th September in Douglas C-47 Skytrains[7] of the 64th Troop Carrier Group of the USAAF's 12th Air Force, involving an additional 138 officers and men, accompanied by ten American War Correspondents. At this time, intensive training was under way throughout the UK to prepare for Operation TORCH in North West Africa and PUNCH was the context of the very first appearance in Northern Ireland of US paratroops training for active service.

A large contingent from the RAF Regiment, 32 officers and 602 other ranks, drawn from 2708, 2775, 2880 and 2883 Squadrons, were attached to Nutts Corner to take part in of the exercise. The catering facilities were also reinforced by the temporary posting of Catering Officer Flying Officer A Dew from RAF Aldergrove and the Sick Bay was enhanced by the attachment of Flight Lieutenant AL Wolby from RAF Long Kesh.

The exercise took place over a wide area of Counties Antrim and Londonderry, straddling the lower River Bann. The forces participating, identified as 'Erne' and their ally 'Derry', were opposed by 'Scotia', the side which the 503rd were part of in conjunction with the Curtiss Tomahawks of No 231 Squadron, then based nearby at RAF Maghaberry. Ground forces on both sides consisted of elements of the 59th and 61st Infantry Divisions of the British Home Forces; there was no air element to the Erne/Derry side. Just as the Glider Ferry Service referred to earlier was adversely affected by bad weather so too was PUNCH. By the end of the fifth day of proceedings, 25th

---

7 C-47 was the USAAF designation for the DC-3, which would be known as the Dakota by the RAF.

Inside the aircraft, waiting for the command to jump. *(US National Archive)*

September, aerial reconnaissance by 231 Squadron indicated that ground forces were mixed up to such an extent that it was difficult to identify a 'front line' and it was at this juncture that the decision was taken to involve the 503rd PIR, two companies of which were deployed on 26th September, operating from Nutts Corner. Whether of necessity or due to faulty navigation is unclear, but the drop zone turned out to be low-lying, boggy land just north of Newferry on the western side of the River Bann, north-east of Bellaghy, 'two miles from their objective, after which bad weather prevented further jumps.' It was not an auspicious performance through no fault of the paratroops involved, some of whom landed in the river while others were caught up in trees. By the end of September, the 503rd were back in Britain and, five weeks later, these same men assaulted and capture the airfield at Tafraoui near Oran, Algeria, in the opening stages of TORCH.

Chapter 4
Army Co-operation 1943

Up until the end of 1942, the RAF squadron with the longest continuous period of wartime service in Northern Ireland was No 231 Squadron which by then had returned to Long Kesh from Maghaberry, prior to which it had been based at Newtownards and initially at Aldergrove. In September the Squadron had flown 132 sorties in support of Exercise PUNCH and had followed this up in October with Exercise BIG BINGE; the defence of Belfast in co-operation with the 1st US Armored Division and including an 'attack' on a Royal Army Service Corps trainload of supplies. At the beginning of January 1943, it was on the move again, to Nutts Corner, under the command of Wing Commander VA Pope. An Army Co-operation unit equipped with Westland Lysander and Curtiss P-40 Tomahawk aircraft, its members were by now very experienced in carrying out a wide range of related activities; including photo reconnaissance – high-level, low-level tactical, vertical and oblique, reconnaissance for the artillery and spotting for shoots (frequently held in both the Mourne and Sperrin Mountains), message dropping, smoke carpet laying, contact patrols, fighter cover, ground attack simulation and general liaison. Air to ground firing and dive-bombing skills being an essential requirement, frequent visits to the ranges on

Top: The pilot prepares to climb up into his Westland Lysander III, VM-B, of No 231 Squadron. *(Ernie Cromie Collection)*

Left: A Curtiss P-40 Tomahawk of No 231 Squadron, shown here at Sydenham with the pre-war civil terminal in the background. *(Ernie Cromie Collection)*

Lough Neagh were commonplace and readily achievable.

By now, though, operational activities were evolving and other changes were occurring in ways that suggested 231 Squadron could soon be taking on a more offensive role. Significantly, on 25th January 1943, A Flight with their Tomahawks was detached for a fortnight to Northern Ireland's premier fighter station, RAF Ballyhalbert to develop, in conjunction with the Supermarine Spitfires of No 501 (County of Gloucester) Squadron, a new aspect to training – practice 'Rhubarbs', an operational tactic in which small numbers of fighter aircraft, usually just a pair, flew at low-level into France or Belgium to shoot up targets of opportunity on the ground.

Spitfires at RAF Ballyhalbert, in this case from No 315 (Polish) Squadron. *(archives.wartimeni.com)*

For practice purposes though, RAF Andreas on the Isle of Man and RAF West Freugh in south-west Scotland served as the limit of operations for 231's Tomahawks. Time was found in a busy schedule for the Lysanders to be used in giving air experience flights to ATC cadets on 4th February. On 14th February B Flight took their Tomahawks to Ballyhalbert, to replace A Flight which had returned to Nutts Corner a few days earlier, thereby establishing a pattern of activity. One of the Flight's sadder duties was on 18th February, searching for a missing Spitfire.[1] There was also a very unfortunate accident on 24th February, when Aircraftman FJ Stagg died of injuries sustained when attending to Tomahawk AK279. While at Ballyhalbert, all of the Flight's pilots took the opportunity to fly solo in a Spitfire Vb on 27th February. These varied activities continued until mid-March when the Squadron was informed that both A and B Flights should prepare to move to England. On 20th March, No 231 Squadron's brief period of residence at Nutts Corner ended and it left for RAF Clifton in Yorkshire, where it would convert to the North American Mustang I. C Flight remained behind in Northern Ireland with its six Tomahawks, two Lysanders and a Tiger Moth on detachment at Ballyhalbert, from where a number of mock attacks were made in early March on the Battle School at Lisburn. Sadly, one of C Flight's Tomahawk IIbs, AK140, flown by Flying Officer ER Jones, was lost on 31st March.[2]

---
1 Spitfire Vb, AB960, of 501 Squadron, flown by Sergeant HW Stanley, which had impacted into a hillside.
2 Ewart Richard Jones was 19 years old. Only a few days before, he had completed his first solo in the Tomahawk.

Chapter 5

Operational Training and Heavy Conversion 1943–44

231 SQUADRON WAS REPLACED at Nutts Corner by a new unit, 104 Operational Training Unit (OTU) which was formed there on 12th March 1943, with Wing Commander M Hallam as CO. The Unit was part of No 44 Group, RAF Ferry Command which was responsible for the ferrying of new aircraft for the RAF across the North Atlantic from manufacturing plants in the USA and Canada to operational units in the UK; it was also responsible for the ferry training of aircrew as well as the preparation and despatch of aircraft to overseas commands. A little later in the month, these responsibilities were subsumed into Transport Command which, in recognition of the substantial increase in the number of transport squadrons in the RAF, was formed to be responsible for their overall control and operation throughout the world and increasing involvement in assisting combat operations.

On its formation, 104 OTU had an initial establishment of 20 Vickers Wellington bombers, not that instruction in the skills of aerial warfare was part of the training programme, bearing in mind that the Mark XV and XVI versions used by Transport Command carried no armament, the bomb-bays were sealed and the number of aircrew required was reduced accordingly, three or four being the normal complement. Unfortunately, it would appear that substantial parts of 104 OTU's Operations Record Book are missing prior to November 1943, with the result that little is known about what form the training took during the seven

The Vickers Wellington Mk IV was used by 104 Operational Training Unit at Nutts Corner. *(Joe Barr Collection)*

months until then. Generally speaking, however, much emphasis was put on long-distance navigation, day and night flying and, on completion of these training courses, many crew were posted to the British Overseas Airways Corporation (BOAC). What is known is that Wellingtons from another transport OTU, No 105 which was formed at RAF Bramcote in Warwickshire on 5th April 1943 with an establishment of 35 Wellingtons, used Nutts Corner from time to time in the course of cross-country navigation exercises and vice-versa.

By summer 1943, because construction work was getting under way to equip Nutts Corner for a new chapter in its history which we shall come to in due course, part of 104 OTU was detached on 10th July, to operate from a new airfield at Toome, on the north-eastern side of Lough Neagh. Two months later, the detachment was relocated to RAF Maghaberry and in October it moved yet again, to RAF Mullaghmore, west of Ballymoney, before rejoining the main part of the unit at Nutts Corner in January 1944, prior to disbanding there at the beginning of February 1944.

Military flying has always been a dangerous business and that applied whether on operations, during training or simply flying in adverse weather conditions. Accidents occurred frequently and there were numerous causes. Although 104 OTU experienced a considerable number of accidents between March 1943 and February 1944, the majority were of minor consequence, comparatively speaking. A high proportion occurred during the landing phase of flight, attributable to errors of judgement, usually resulting in undercarriage collapse due to overshooting or veering off the runway. On 20th July, as a result of an engine failure after taking-off from Toome, Wellington IV, Z1315, was successfully force-landed by Flight Sergeant Stapleton eight miles south-west of the airfield, near Coagh, without serious injury to himself or his crew. On 17th December, following take-off at Nutts Corner, Wellington IV Z1253 hit some trees on the south side of the airfield but the pilot, Flying Officer Henderson, immediately carried out a successful forced landing back on the runway. With few exceptions, the particular aircraft supplied to 104 OTU were hand-me-downs that had already been in service with one or more Bomber Command squadrons although there

The geodetic construction – metal lattice – of the Wellington can be seen through the plexiglass of R1515. It gave the fuselage great integral strength. *(Joe Barr Collection)*

is no evidence to suggest that associated wear and tear on the airframes was a significant cause of the mishaps.

Sadly though, at least five Wellingtons of 104 OTU were lost with much more serious consequences, including fatalities. The first of these was on 12th September, when Wellington Ic X9820 flew into a hillside three miles south of Bryansford, County Down, with the loss of all three members of the crew.[1] During the night of November 24/25th 1943 Wellington IV Z1313 was airborne on a night navigation exercise, piloted by New Zealander Flight Sergeant T Kemp with trainee Navigator Sergeant EF Lurkins and Wireless Operator/Air Gunner Sergeant AA Richardson. Carrying out a descent through cloud procedure (QGH) the Wellington was seen to pass over Nutts Corner at about 800 feet, incorrectly, and did not reappear. Not long after dawn its wreckage was discovered five miles away on the upper slopes of Divis Mountain. Tragically, Flight Sergeant Kemp had been killed on impact and his two companions suffered very serious injuries from which Sergeant Lurkins died later that day in the 24th General Hospital, Campbell College, Belfast. Despite his injuries, Sergeant Richardson survived, made a good recovery and was taken off the seriously ill list on 2nd December.[2]

A crew member on board a Vickers Wellington places night flares in position in the cramped rear fuselage. Note the Elsan chemical lavatory to the right. *(Wikimedia Commons)*

Just over a month later, on 31st December, Wellington IV R1520 was returning from a four-hour, night navigational exercise and was approaching to land when it flew into the ground close to the summit of the 945-feet high McGowan's Hill, three miles south-east of Nutts Corner, killing all three crew.[3]

Receipt of a telegram containing news of accidents was invariably grievous news for relatives and friends of subject aircrew but in one sense news of men posted as 'Missing in action' must have been even more traumatic. On 26th January 1944, Wellington IV Z1490, piloted by Flight Sergeant MJ Fletcher, did not return from a night navigation exercise and was posted as 'Missing'.[4]

---

1 Flight Sergeant John Sherlock Price, pilot, Sergeant Harold Thomas Arthur Walters, navigator, Sergeant Thomas Brewin, wireless operator.
2 Trevor Kemp, age 32 and married, from Christchurch, New Zealand, was buried in Killead Presbyterian Churchyard; Frank Lurkins, age 26 from Great Yarmouth, Norfolk, was taken there for burial, in Gorleston Cemetery.
3 They were the pilot, Flying Officer HE Massey, his Navigator, Flying Officer V Tanner and Wireless Operator/Air Gunner Sergeant JER Cote. Hugh Massey, age 21, who had trained with the RAF in Canada and whose parents were from Babbacombe, Torquay, was taken to Plymouth for cremation; Victor Tanner, age 34 and a married man whose wife was living in London, was taken to Bettws-Penpont, Breconshire for burial while Joseph Cote, age 25, from the State of Quebec in Canada was buried with full military honours in St Joseph's Roman Catholic Churchyard, Glenavy.
4 On the following day, the body of the aircraft's Wireless Operator/Air Gunner, Warrant Officer LT Erickson,

Also on 26th January, the crew of Wellington IV Z1206, piloted by Flight Sergeant Patterson on a night navigation exercise, almost suffered a similar fate. They had been airborne for 10 hours, were lost and, having experienced radio failure, were preparing to ditch at dawn when land was spotted which they thought was Norway. Just managing to reach an embayment, Patterson successfully ditched close to the beach and they waded ashore to hide among the sand dunes, fearing capture by occupying German troops, only to discover subsequently that they were at Uig Bay near Stornoway on the Isle of Lewis! Over the course of succeeding days, the aircraft was deposited on the beach by the tide. When an RAF recovery team eventually arrived, they managed to take off the wings and remove the engines but abandoned the fuselage as it was well embedded in the sand where it became something of an adventure playground for local children until they and storms removed everything above the surface.[5]

On 10th October 1943, No 1674 Heavy Conversion Unit (HCU) formed at Aldergrove to provide conversion training for crews intended for long-range patrol squadrons in Coastal Command. Between 20th February and March 18th 1944, the Liberators and Fortresses of the HCU used Nutts Corner as a substitute, while the runways at Aldergrove were being repaired. Trainees could arrive singly or as part of a crew. It is noteworthy that many aircrew had in fact completed a tour of duty on Coastal Command flying a twin-engine type of aircraft. Training sorties in this period included conversion to type, fighter affiliation, gunnery, practice bombing runs from a height of approximately 100 feet against a simulated U-boat target, night flying and navigational exercises.

A rather 'tired looking' Fortress I on delivery to Nutts Corner. *(Ernie Cromie Collection)*

Another point of interest is that senior officers undertaking refresher or conversion training could well be allocated a 'tired' aircraft for their first circuits and bumps with the resulting sweating and heaving of the control yoke. Like the Operational Training Units, the Heavy Conversion Units suffered from the dangerous mix of 'clapped-out' aircraft that had been replaced by newer ones on the squadrons, and inexperienced crews.

One of the instructors, Flight Lieutenant Keith McGonigal recalled:

---

was washed up on the island of Tiree, Inner Hebrides and just over a fortnight later the body of the Navigator, Flying Officer GG Stobie was found washed up elsewhere on the Tiree shoreline. Matthew Fletcher's body was never recovered but his name is recorded on Panel 217 of the Runnymede Memorial; he was 22 years old and from County Durham. Leif Erickson, age 21 and a member of the Royal Canadian Air Force from Montreal, was buried in Soroby Burial Ground on Tiree; Graeme Stobie, age 20 and a member of the Royal Australian Air Force from Melbourne, was buried in Pennyfuir Cemetery, Oban.

5 In 2002, the remains were uncovered by members of the Midland Aircraft Recovery Group who have conserved what they can. Before being taken on strength by 104 OTU, Z1206 had carried out 14 operational missions with 142 Squadron, Bomber Command.

'Aircraft showed near human characteristics at times. An old, black (ex-Bomber Command) Halifax at 1674 HCU was always serviceable and so gentle that it could only with difficulty be persuaded to demonstrate the briefest of stalls, and with wheels and flaps down, almost refused to stall. I think it was DG304. On a less savoury note, was a white aircraft, whose serial number is forgotten and rightly so. It could fairly be said to be a swine – it had a built in cross-wind, would remain trimmed for about half a second and could be trusted for less. I was eventually able to have it grounded and, I hope, made into saucepans.'

Sometimes tragic events were the result, as these two examples show; the first concerns Halifax II, DT642, on 29th July 1944, captained by Warrant Officer LW Lenz RCAF.[6] A few minutes after taking off on a routine training flight, the aircraft lost height and flying speed, began to turn, hit some trees near Clotworthy House and crashed south of the Six Mile Water in Antrim. There were no survivors. Then, on 23rd October 1944, when Halifax II, JB963, captained by instructor Flight Lieutenant DE Evans DFC, caught fire in the air and crashed into the ground near Dundesert Bridge whilst on approach to Aldergrove during a flying exercise, killing all on board.[7]

A Handley Page Halifax similar to the one belonging to 1674 HCU which crashed near Aldergrove on 23rd October 1944. *(Guy Warner Collection)*

---

6 Also losing their lives that day were, Flying Officer G Fraser RCAF, Flight Sergeant HV Heaton RCAF, Sergeant JH Edwards, Sergeant RW Cook, Sergeant ER Turrill, Sergeant JL Snider RCAF, Sergeant LM Hembruff RCAF and Sergeant GN Thomas (from the Met Office at Aldergrove).
7 The other crew members were Flying Officer ML Gillis RCAF, Flight Sergeant JH Saunders and Sergeant RL Dixon.

Chapter 6
Transatlantic Ferry
1943–44

To return to the reason for the construction work previously mentioned, it is necessary to firstly set the scene. On 1st July, 1942, a B-17E Flying Fortress bomber of the American 8th Air Force landed at the RAF Ferry Command Transatlantic Ferry Terminal at RAF Prestwick in Scotland, to effectively inaugurate a gigantic operation to fly across the Atlantic thousands of new combat and transport aircraft that would be required by the American 8th Air Force initially and then, successively between July 1942 and November 1943, by the 12th, 9th and 15th Air Forces as the United States built up its military aviation strength more widely in the European and Mediterranean Theatres of Operations.

By November 1942, this air delivery operation was gathering momentum and it was then that the British Air Ministry took a decision which was to have profound development implications for Nutts Corner; in fact, the consequences turned out to be more far-reaching than initially envisaged. To help facilitate the deliveries, the planners resolved that Nutts Corner would be utilised as a Transatlantic Air Ferry Terminal, to complement Prestwick

Two Boeing Fortresses on the snow covered runway at Gander, Newfoundland prior to their transatlantic crossing to Prestwick. *(Major Fred Paradie RCAF History and Heritage)*

which was now handling large numbers of aircraft for service with both the American and British military air services being delivered from the United States. In the summer of the following year, two further air terminals would be created, at RAF Valley in Wales and RAF St Mawgan in Cornwall. Notification of the decision was conveyed in a minute dated 10th December to RAF Ferry Command's 44 Group; in mid-January 1943, Nutts Corner's transfer was made official and the planning process to adapt the airfield began.

Actually, detailed surveys had already been carried out during December when a number of issues were highlighted for attention. It was noted that dedicated hard standings to park only 12 heavy, six medium and six light aircraft were available. There were three runways: 2000 yards (10-28), 1600 yards (04-22) and 1200 yards (16-34) but they were surfaced in tarmac primarily, use of stronger load-bearing concrete having been confined to the take-off and touch-down ends of the E-W runway and on the 'dumb-bell end of the NE-SW runway, which had a decided 'hump' 100 yards from the NE-end. Hangars were limited to two T1-types and two Extra-Over blisters, while work on constructing a control tower had just recently been completed. Doubt was expressed that it would be adequate for the future traffic anticipated, an observation that would prove to be prophetic. Moreover, the facilities for workshops, refuelling and aircraft salvage equipment were inadequate. Reservations were expressed about the length of the main runway although it was noted that, if necessary, the Crumlin River could be diverted to permit extension while two water towers, 120 feet in height, constituted a flying obstruction and would have to be removed. It was also noted that the boggy nature of the ground between the runways would require 'special treatment' and that the newly-aligned main public road just beyond the eastern end of the main runway might have to be closed when flying was taking place. In the event, the only shortcomings of any substance to be addressed resulted in the provision of two new T2 hangars, belatedly, a very large terminal parking apron on the eastern side of the airfield close to the control tower and additional aircraft parking space in the form of state of the art 'spectacle' hard standings which, efficiently used, would eventually prove capable of accommodating 160-200 aircraft. However, the plans formulated fell short of what was really necessary. Moreover, construction work took time and it would be well into 1944 before the work was completed, to the frustration of the airfield's prospective new American occupants, as we shall discover.

The first indication of Nutts Corner taking on its new role as a transatlantic ferry terminal was the arrival, on 19th June 1943, of an officer and 22 enlisted men of the USAAF's 69th Ferry Squadron on detachment from RAF Valley (AAF Station 1005). Three days later they were joined by five more officers from the 69th, one of whom, Major Paul E Freydig, became the detachment's first commander. They were billeted on Site 13, one of numerous widely dispersed sites that were characteristic of wartime airfields throughout the UK. For the Americans the damp conditions in the Nissen hut living accommodation, inadequate heating and lighting and the unsanitary conditions which, even by then, were little different to those experienced by the initial RAF contingent in 1941, cannot have been other than a huge culture shock.

Meanwhile on 25th July 1943 the first group of USAAF aircraft on oceanic delivery (known

An aerial view of Nutts Corner on 31st August 1943. *(Ernie Cromie Collection)*

as transats) was recorded as arriving at Nutts Corner, reportedly from RCAF Gander. All four were B-17F Flying Fortresses and on 29th July three more landed, to be followed a week later by a further six. Intriguingly, these aircraft went on to St Mawgan in Cornwall and records indicate they were destined for the 12th Air Force which in August 1942 had been activated in the USA prior to moving to the Mediterranean Theatre of Operations to be involved in Operation TORCH. Why these Fortresses were delivered by the Northern Route is strange; some records suggest that they had not been allotted to a Southern Route because of an administrative error. Perhaps that also explained the arrival, on 7th August 1943 of a B-24 Liberator which subsequently flew on to RAF Dunkeswell in Devon to join anti-submarine squadrons of the USAAF that were temporarily resident there until replaced by their US Navy counterparts during the following month. By 9th August there was no doubting the scale of the operation that was developing, when 21 C-47 and one C-53 Skytrooper[1] transports landed at Nutts Corner from Reykjavik.

They too left two days later for Cornwall. In fact, between 25th July 1943 and 31st July 1944, Nutts Corner would handle 1985 USAAF transats, comprising 1288 B-17s, 579 B-24s

---

1 The C-53 was the second major DC-3 variant operated by the USAAF.

Above: Eight C-47s can be seen in this air-to air shot. *(US National Archive)*

Above right: The C-53 Skytrooper was a transport version of the C-47 without the reinforced cargo floor, large cargo door, and hoist attachment. It was dedicated for the troop transport role and could carry 28 passengers in fixed metal seats arranged in rows in the former cargo space. This photo was not taken at Nutts Corner! *(US National Archive)*

and 118 miscellaneous, twin-engine types. During that period, the busiest month was July 1944 when 372 transats arrived. Whereas these statistics convey some idea of the logistical problems they are not the full story. Although considerable numbers of the aircraft were flown out on the day of arrival, many were not, some remaining on the airfield for two or more days, depending on weather and whether or not they required extensive maintenance or repair after the oceanic journey. In that regard, proximity to the US air depot at Langford Lodge was of benefit. So began what would turn out to be the most intensive 14-month period for transient aircraft movements during the course of the airfield's wartime history.

To return to July 1943, most of the aircraft were being flown over by replacement combat crews unfamiliar with the changeable weather conditions peculiar to the British Isles rather than by specialist USAAF ferrying personnel of Air Transport Command, who had been involved to a greater extent in the early days of the ferrying operation. Increasingly too, the aircraft themselves were being left at the ferry terminal to be picked up by crews from ferrying squadrons of the 8th Air Force who had been based in the UK since the autumn of 1942, to be flown to one or other of the American Base Air Depots (BAD) at Burtonwood and Warton in Lancashire or, less often, to Langford Lodge, where they were modified for use in the European Theatre of Operations (ETO). In November, 1943, to complement units already in Britain, three squadrons, the 311th and 312th Ferrying Squadrons and 321st Transport Squadron were activated at Maghaberry; two months later another Ferrying Squadron, the 325th, would be formed there. In May 1944, Langford Lodge replaced Maghaberry as the base of ferrying squadrons in Northern Ireland.

Early in September 1943, B-24 Liberator 42-52293, which had been assigned to the 44th Bomb Group at RAF Shipdham in Norfolk[2] and was being flown by a replacement crew who had just completed basic training in the USA took off from RCAF Goose Bay under the captaincy of 2nd Lieutenant RC Griffith.

His planned route was to Prestwick via Bluie West-1 (later known as Narsarsuaq Air Base) in Greenland and Meeks Field (Naval Air Station Keflavik) in Iceland, but on the final leg of the journey he was instructed to divert to Nutts Corner because Prestwick was

---

2 RAF Shipdham was the first US heavy bomber base in Norfolk and was also the continuous host to Consolidated B-24 Liberators longer than any other Eighth Air Force combat airfield in Britain.

closed due to weather. One of the gunners, Technical Sergeant Forrest S Clark, takes up the story,

A B-24D Liberator of the USAAF. *(newenglandaviationhistory.com)*

'I recall my first glimpse of Northern Ireland as we came over the Hebrides Islands and could see the green-clad shores approaching. We all took our combat positions in the aircraft because we were instructed that we could be inside the air space of enemy aircraft over the North Atlantic. The landing approach was hazardous because we had been informed of a hill which had to be avoided at all costs. The runways were small for a B-24 and we were warned of the boggy earth should we run off the hard surface. You won't believe this but our co-pilot 2nd Lieutenant Tinsman had never landed a B-24 before we got to Nutts Corner. We kidded him about that. We did avoid collision with the hill but after landing we got mired down in the mud and a group of WAAF girls came out in a jeep to meet us. We checked into quarters there and I recall the RAF welcomed us. Later we took a convoy to town and there the first person we met was a Scots sailor on leave who took us for what money we had, all the time warning us of the dangers of Belfast, which was blacked out at the time. We went to many pubs in the centre of the city and then to this large dance hall with a balcony around the floor near the centre of town crowded with Irish girls and men in uniform but the girls outnumbered the men. How we got back to base I don't recall. I do know that we

A USAAF B-24 Liberator and crew at USAAF Station 238, RAF Cluntoe, on the western shore of Lough Neagh and the location of No 2 Combat Crew Replacement Centre. Back Row: Technical Sergeant William Bento (Radio Operator), First Lieutenant Paul W Perry (Pilot), Flight Sergeant Joseph R Kelly (Co-Pilot), Second Lieutenant Lloyd K Randolph (Navigator), Technical Sergeant Gerald D Camp (Flight Engineer). Front Row: Staff Sergeant Jack F Towner (Nose Gunner), Staff Sergeant John F Durtsche (Ball Turret Gunner), Second Lieutenant Oliver J Rauch (Bombardier), Staff Sergeant Robert L Traeger (Waist Gunner), Staff Sergeant Arel A Bye (Tail Gunner). *(Ernie Cromie Collection)*

seemed to be very popular with the girls at the time. We all laughed at the name Nutts Corner but we were glad it was there otherwise we would have likely run out of fuel. As it was we were running low. The next day we were forced to take a C-47 to Prestwick because our B-24 got mired in the mud.'

A few days later, on 16th September, it would appear that two more B-24s exited the runway on to soft ground with resulting undercarriage damage. Records are somewhat confused but indications are that, arriving from Meeks Field within 75 minutes of each other around twilight and during darkness, respectively, the first touched down too fast and ran off the runway end while the second, approaching with landing lights inoperative, landed too close behind a preceding C-47 and had to be turned sideways off the runway to avoid a collision.

The hill referred to by Forrest Clark was undoubtedly Divis Mountain. There was a history of aircraft crashes on Divis and it was just about to become the scene of a further tragedy. During the morning of 10th October B-24 Liberator 42-40758, being ferried on assignment to the American 14th Air Force in the India-Burma Theatre, took off from Nutts Corner's main runway with 10 crew on board. Weather at the time of departure was variable with a cloud base of 1200-1500 feet and visibility four to five miles. After completing a circuit of the airfield, it set off for its next destination, St Mawgan, but flew into Divis a few minutes later at an altitude of around 1200 feet, bursting into flames. Seven of the crew, including the captain 2nd Lieutenant William O'Connell from New York died instantly; the remaining three were seriously injured and taken to the 10th Station Hospital at Musgrave Park, Belfast where two of them succumbed to their injuries within three days. The only survivor was the Radio Operator, Technical Sergeant John D Johnson, from Ohio.[3]

By 24th September 1943 the USAAF detachment referred to earlier had grown to 16 officers and 122 enlisted men, comprising air traffic controllers of the 24th Army Airways Communications Squadron, meteorologists of the 24th Weather Squadron and technical personnel. By the end of the year, they would increase in number to around 370 and their job would be to check the USAAF aircraft on arrival, remove certain equipment, temporarily store before shipping it out to USAAF air depots, refuel and service the aircraft as necessary, then provide overnight accommodation, food and care for the exhausted crews. They formed the basis of Station No 2 European Wing, Air Transport Command (No 2 EWATC) (Station 1009) which was formally activated at Nutts Corner on that date as a lodger unit, officially marking the opening of the Ferry Terminal. Inauspiciously, however, during the course of the three months since June it had become evident to the Americans, who had arrived in anticipation of working harmoniously alongside their RAF counterparts in handling the transatlantic traffic that things were not working out entirely as expected, much to their dissatisfaction. There were several contributory factors including the cramped,

---

3   2nd Lieutenant William J O'Connell (pilot), 2nd Lieutenant Roy VA Haho, Flight Officer Saul G Spilker, Staff Sergeant Abraham G Eddy, Staff Sergeant Paul H Jones, Jr, Staff Sergeant Oscar W Nelson, Staff Sergeant William B Whitehurst, Staff Sergeant Rice.

unsatisfactory nature of the living quarters and communal facilities available for both them and the transient USAAF personnel, disruption caused by the far from complete airfield construction works, as well as insufficient hangar accommodation and aircraft parking facilities, which the RAF's resident 104 OTU also required. Fortunately, 104 OTU would be disbanded in February 1944.

But what concerned the Americans most of all was that their personnel were not being permitted to control the arrival and departure of transient aircraft to the extent they felt necessary. Initially, the Americans had wanted two airfields in the UK to be handed over exclusively for use by the USAAF, but they were persuaded to compromise on that and what was agreed was that while US communications services and procedures would be established throughout the Northern Route and that Air Transport Command would develop its own weather service, they accepted there would be joint tenancy and control at the ferry terminals on the basis of close co-operation between the RAF, RCAF and USAAF. The joint control that was agreed then was not, in the view of the USAAF personnel, being effectively implemented by the RAF at Nutts Corner. For example, in the control tower the only space that was provided for American approach controllers and log clerks was one room approximately five feet square affording no view of the airfield, while local, for example, airfield control, was conducted from the upper deck of the tower by an RAF controller whose British accent and terminology was often misunderstood by American pilots. Worst of all, USAAF controllers were not being permitted to sit alongside their RAF counterparts. As a result, misunderstandings and mishaps were occurring, with implications for the safety of personnel and aircraft. The issue was the subject of much contention for months, involving numerous references to higher authorities, meetings and inspections and was not resolved to the satisfaction of both sides until April, 1944.

A US Army sentry guards new Boeing B-17Fs on the Boeing airfield at Seattle before being flown across the USA and onwards to the ETO. *(Wikimedia Commons)*

In that context, as traffic on the Northern Ferry Route continued to increase, given the combat replacement crews' unfamiliarity with the route, the inherent navigation difficulties, the ever-present possibility of technical failure and the onset of winter weather, it is not surprising that the USAAF would increasingly experience aircraft losses on oceanic delivery just as the RAF continued to do. There had been a tragic instance of that in Northern Ireland as early as 3rd October 1942 when B-17F, 41-24451, en route from Gander to Prestwick, flew into Slieveanorra Mountain, 30 feet below the summit, 12 miles east of Ballymoney, in very poor visibility and burst into flames.

Five of the ten men on board died in the wreckage and of the five who were thrown clear by the force of impact, only two survived.[4] Before leaving the USA, 41-24451 had been assigned to the 91st Bomb Group whose aircraft were in the process of being delivered to RAF Kimbolton in Cambridgeshire and it was being flown by a newly trained and inexperienced combat crew.

A further regular visitor was added in late 1943. In March 1942, the US Navy Courier Service had commenced a connection between London (Hendon) and Londonderry (Eglinton), calling at Long Kesh to drop or collect passengers, light freight and mail, using Cessna JRC-1 Bobcats, Lockheed Model 12s and Douglas R4D-4s. This transferred to Nutts Corner on 1st November.

Each accident was a manifestation of the risks inherent to the ferrying operation but

Above: In the utility role the Cessna Bobcat could carry four passengers. Its nickname was the 'Bamboo Bomber.' *(US National Archive)*

Above right: A United States Navy R4D-4, which developed from the Douglas DC-3S. *(Dave Welch Collection)*

the outcome of a ferry flight by a large group of B-17s in early December 1943 was an especially stark reminder of the scope and scale of potential consequences of the hazards that were experienced on a daily basis. On 8th December, 21 Fortresses were assembled at Goose Bay awaiting clearance to leave for Prestwick at one minute intervals starting at 21.00 hours (01.00 GMT) on 9th December. 2nd Lieutenant Clarence 'Kit' Carson was the co-pilot on one of them and, after the war ended, he committed to paper his recollections of the circumstances and the outcome.

'The North Atlantic Wing's navigation expert gave us a final briefing on the route after the weather briefer told us it would be ceiling and visibility unrestricted (CAVU) all the way across with a 50-60 knot tailwind. The route briefer stated that with wind and weather being so favourable we should be over our destination approximately eight and a half hours after take-off. A communications briefer gave us the information on radio procedures. He warned us that although we could tune

---

4 1st Lieutenant John A McLean, Pilot, Captain Dale Laselle, Co-Pilot, 2nd Lieutenant Robert N Allen, Navigator, 2nd Lieutenant Leonard Koebel, Bombardier, Sergeant Robert J Vaughan, Gunner, Corporal John Gibson, Radio Operator, Captain George C Wassell, Passenger/Doctor, Private Justin C Hamblin, Passenger, all lost their lives apart from: Corporal Leon R Harrison, Gunner and Private First Class Norman E Wickes, Radio Operator.

in the powerful radio beacon located at Stornoway, Scotland on our radio compass halfway across the Atlantic, the compass bearing obtained at that distance could be in error as much as 30 degrees. He also warned us that the Germans had a powerful radio transmitter on the coast of France with communicators speaking with a British accent who would give you false QDMs (magnetic headings) to lead you around the British Isles into France.

After a final word from our Group Commander, 21 crews headed for their aircraft in the bitter cold, crisp night. The stars were very bright and Bob Schmidt was happily anticipating the chance to use all of the celestial navigation practice he had soaked up during phase training. Little did he know that it wasn't to be. The 21 B-17s lined up on the taxi strip to take off at one-minute intervals, starting at 21.00 hours. Our position was somewhere in the middle of the pack. We were pretty close to our maximum gross weight of 64,500 pounds when we took off. Our fuel tanks were all full of fuel so we had 2780 gallons for the eight and a half hour flight. If we used good cruise control we could make it with 800 gallons to spare. All went well until we were about an hour out of Goose Bay. It was then that we ran into clouds and snow. Joe and I looked at each other. 'I thought the weather guy said CAVU!' was Joe's comment, 'we can't do celestial navigation in this stuff. We'll have to climb on top, I guess.'

Joe advanced the throttles as I set 2300 rpm on the props and we started to climb. We were still in the soup at 15,000 feet and I noticed that we were beginning to ice up on the wing leading edges. I turned on the wing de-icer boots after ice had built up about an inch thick. It was then that I noticed something very disquieting. My oxygen pressure gauge was down to 150 psi from the normal 400 psi that had been in the system when we left Goose. Normally the tanks would provide enough oxygen for about 15 hours of normal usage with the diluter switches in the MIX position. We shouldn't have used any oxygen until we climbed above 10,000 feet so it could mean only one thing – a leak! I tapped Joe on the arm and pointed to the oxygen gauge. He immediately levelled off, stopping our climb at about 18,000 feet. After thinking a bit, he made his decision. 'Pilot to crew', he said on the interphone, 'we are losing our oxygen. All positions, check your mixer switch and your emergency flow valves. Make sure you are in MIX position and that emergency flow valves are closed. I want a report from every position.'

The reports came back and though no obvious leaks were discovered the decision was made to descend to a low altitude so that oxygen would not be necessary and possibly we could reach a level where icing would not increase our fuel consumption. The icing made me nervous and even though we were operating the propeller anti-ice system, the inboard props were slinging chunks of ice against the fuselage right under the cockpit occasionally and each time the loud bangs caused me to jump nervously.

We descended to about 3000 feet by the altimeter, not daring to go any lower in the darkness as we couldn't be sure how accurate the altimeters were since we had obviously flown into an area of lower pressure which could affect altitude indications. At 3000 feet we were still in the clouds but were picking up only rime ice since it was snowing moderately. We flew on for several hours and since we couldn't do celestial navigation our navigator could only figure our position by dead reckoning, not a very precise method when you have no idea what the wind direction or velocity might be… The bearings I was getting on the Stornoway beacon indicated that we were still a long way from Ireland. I asked a British radio station for a QDM but the one he gave me would have required an 80-degree turn to the right. This didn't sound reasonable and didn't correlate with the bearing I was getting from Stornoway. I concluded I was in contact with the German radio station we had been warned about so we ignored his directions and continued to drive on into the grey soup.

When we had been airborne for about nine and a half hours we really began to get worried. The ice we had picked up had increased our fuel consumption and, after some discussion, Joe and I decided to ease down through the overcast to try to get under the clouds so that when we did come to land we would be able to see it. We edged down and finally broke out at about 400 feet. The altimeters were indicating 1000 feet when we levelled off but we were obviously only about 200 feet above the water so we reset our altimeters to that altitude. It was at that point that we saw a huge armada of cargo ships, escorted by a number of destroyers. When we saw the

A Boeing B-17 Flying Fortress, as flown by 2nd Lieutenant Clarence 'Kit' Carson from Goose Bay to Nutts Corner in December 1943. *(Wikimedia Commons)*

destroyers swivelling their guns to bear on us we did a sudden steep climb back up into the overcast, levelling off and flying for a few minutes to be sure we were past the convoy, after which we descended again until we were under the clouds. About 20 minutes after we passed the convoy I began picking up a radio beacon from a station in Northern Ireland.[5] The signal was fairly strong so I tried the frequency of the Nutts Corner Radio Range and heaved a big sigh of relief when the 'dit-dah' 'A' signal of the west quadrant of the range came clearly in my ear. I listened only long enough to pick up the Morse Code identifier 'HU' that was broadcast every 30 seconds. Joe turned the airplane about ten degrees left to zero the needle on the radio compass and as he rolled out of the turn we spotted land ahead of us. Since the clouds were lower than the hills and mountains near the Irish coast we had to climb to 5000 feet to make sure we would clear everything and put us on an odd thousand feet altitude that our easterly heading called for under instrument flight rules. As we approached Nutts Corner I called them to declare a low-fuel emergency and request an immediate clearance to do an instrument let-down on the range. I was told that there were four aircraft ahead of us in the stack and we were cleared to 3500 feet to enter a holding pattern on the North-West leg of the range to await further clearance. I was keying the mike to tell them we might have to bail out if we were forced to stay airborne much longer when we spotted a fairly large hole in the overcast. 'Hang on everybody, we're going down through this hole', Joe said on interphone as he put the B-17 in a tight descending spiral through the hole in the clouds. I could see green fields below us and when we rolled out of our turn and levelled off under the clouds we saw the airfield about seven miles in front of us. We were lined up with the runway that had another airplane just touching down on it. I called the tower for clearance to make a straight-in approach, insisting that we didn't have enough fuel for a go-around. 'You'll have to take it around' the tower informed me, 'we have an aircraft over the low cone on an instrument final approach. Report on downwind leg and space yourself to land behind that aircraft.'

With our fingers crossed and a prayer that we had enough fuel left, we maintained 800 feet as we overflew the runway and turned left on the crosswind leg of the traffic pattern. After turning on the downwind leg we could see the other aircraft, another B-17, about four miles out on final approach with his landing gear and flaps down. Extending our downwind leg a bit to give us adequate clearance behind him, we made our left turn on base leg as I dropped the landing gear. I had held off completing the landing checklist, wanting to wait until we were ready to turn final to lower the gear, increase the rpm to 2300 and lower one-third flaps in order to save every drop of fuel I could. About two miles from the end of the runway at about 300 feet Joe called for full flaps and eased back on the throttles. He set the ship down

---

5   To facilitate transatlantic navigation there was a non-directional beacon, coded UU7, at Derrynacross in Co Fermanagh and two four-course radio ranges at Magherameenagh, UU, also in Co Fermanagh and between Nutts Corner and Aldergrove, HU, which was associated with a fan marker at Langford Lodge.

Boeing B-17s at the USAAF 3rd Base Air Depot, Langford Lodge, on the shore of Lough Neagh, not far from Nutts Corner and Aldergrove. *(Ernie Cromie Collection)*

three-point at the end of the runway and we were on the ground, safe!

We were taken to Quonsets[6] that would be our overnight quarters and were told that we would depart the next day for Stone in England, the transit camp where we would be processed for assignment to a bomb group. We learned later that as a result of the bad forecast we had been given at Goose Bay, seven of the 21 aircraft were lost.'

Happily, six B-17s, including Lieutenant Carson's aircraft, made it to Nutts Corner on 9th December. Two more landed at Toome, one at RAF Cluntoe in Co Tyrone, two at RNAS Maydown in Co Londonderry and four at Langford Lodge although one of those which made it to Langford, 42-31491, touched down half way along the east-west runway, overshot the end and crashed, caught fire and was subsequently pronounced a write-off.

Fortunately, the crew escaped with only minor injury and shock. Although the aircraft's fuel gauges had become unserviceable over the Atlantic and its Nutts Corner approach control radio was inoperative, aircraft captain 2nd Lieutenant Martin Borchert managed to make VHF radio contact and was cleared for an instrument let-down on the radio range but, knowing his fuel state was critical he opted for a straight-in landing on the first airfield and runway he saw. Of the seven Fortresses that Lieutenant Carson was told later failed to complete the journey, two others crashed in Ireland during mid to late afternoon. Both had been in radio contact with Nutts Corner prior to crashing. One, Fortress 42-31468, named

---

6 A Quonset hut – a lightweight prefabricated structure of corrugated galvanized steel having a semi cylindrical cross-section; similar to the British Nissen hut.

'Galley Uncle' and almost out of fuel, was attempting to reach St Angelo but by the time the crew broke through cloud above the airfield three of its engines had stopped and the aircraft failed to make it, crashing in the grounds of the Passionist Monastery at the Graan, three miles to the south west of St Angelo and two and a half miles north west of Enniskillen. Seven of the 11 crew on board were killed and the remaining four were seriously injured.[7] Somewhat later, in fog and failing light, the other Fortress, 42-31420, flew into high ground close to the summit of Truskmore Mountain across the border in County Sligo. Two of the 10-man crew died on impact, one four days later in hospital, the remainder being seriously injured. Two airmen, 2nd Lieutenants Walch and Grim, struggled down the mountain to find help in Ballintrillick.[8]

This was followed on 16th December by an incident with a happier outcome. Flight Lieutenant EJ Woosley, was a pilot with 1402 Met Flight at Aldergrove.

On the day in question, flying Gloster Gladiator II, N5592, he had completed the midday met climb through thick cloud and found clear air at 24,000 feet; he also found two B-17s circling 3000 feet above him and clearly lost. He could not communicate with the Americans by radio and his controller was unable to provide guidance. Tired of waiting, and with one B-17 already following him closely, he guided the bomber through the cloud to Nutts Corner, then repeated the process with the second aircraft. The cloud base at Nutts Corner was less than 1000 feet and the visibility less than a mile. Having guided the second Fortress down safely, Woosley was asked to locate a Cessna JRC-1 Bobcat light transport that had been sent to assist the two aircraft. Unfortunately, by that time he was short of fuel and had to land.[9]

Gloster Gladiator, N5900, of the Met Flight at RAF Aldergrove. *(Guy Warner Collection)*

Accidents notwithstanding, the pace of deliveries increased, as already indicated. On 13th January 1944 in very bad weather, about 40 American aircraft were scheduled to arrive from Goose Bay after transatlantic flights. One came in too low while attempting a touchdown

---

7 Lieutenant Joseph R Rudolph, Pilot, Lieutenant Aloysius J Rodeo, Bombardier, Sergeant Edward J Mankowski, Flight engineer/top turret gunner, Lieutenant Earl W. Simpson, Radio Operator, Sergeant John Morton, passenger, Sergeant Myrl E Youngs, Lieutenant Melvin Skerpon all lost their lives, Lieutenant Robert M Phillips, Co-pilot, Lieutenant Earl Simpson, Navigator, Sergeant Stanley C Thomas, William C Simpson, returned to duty.

8 2nd Lieutenant Richard E Fox, Bombardier, 2nd Lieutenant William F Wallace, Navigator, Sergeant Adam J Latecki all perished, 2nd Lieutenant RC Walch, Pilot, 2nd Lieutenant M Grim, Co-Pilot, Staff Sergeant ML Mendoza, Engineer, Staff Sergeant RA Smith, Radio Operator, Sergeant WNG Vincent, Gunner, Sergeant EC Drake, Gunner and Sergeant CW Williamson, Gunner, survived. Local people from the homes below the mountain hurried to the crash to provide assistance to the aircraft's crew, being joined later by personnel from the nearby Irish Army barracks. After many hours of struggling, the injured men were taken down the mountain and brought to Sligo County Hospital. All survivors were later taken across to Northern Ireland. (ww2irishaviation.com)

9 Details from the No 2 EWATC Operations Book, signed by Major Norman F Timper.

and a large portion of one wing was torn off. The pilot and co-pilot managed to maintain control and climb the aircraft to permit the crew to bail out safely by parachute before the pilots successfully landed the Fortress. Eight B-17s in total succeeded in finding Nutts Corner while another eight landed at St Angelo, two at RAF Belfast (Sydenham), and one each at Aldergrove, Cluntoe and Ballyhalbert. One was unable to find an airfield but, fuel just about exhausted, made a successful forced-landing on farmland about half a mile north east of Eden, Carrickfergus, with no injuries to the crew. It was a particularly notable month for incidents at the Station. On 23rd January, during a showery spell of weather mid-afternoon, 2nd Lieutenant Tracy E Geiger and his crew of B-17, 42-97459 were approaching at the end of a flight from Goose Bay. They were cleared to land on runway 28 but for an unknown reason, possibly related to the joint control issue referred to earlier, Geiger chose the shorter runway 22. The surface was wet with the result that, after landing, the aircraft was unable to stop and skidded off the end into a ditch, breaking its back, causing severe damage to propellers and engines and injuring two members of the crew, fortunately not badly. On the same day, the crew of B-17, 42-31570, on approach to Nutts Corner with a reported engine fire, decided they couldn't make it safely and bailed out successfully. Amazingly, the aircraft carried on flying, crossed the border into neutral Ireland and ended up crashing into a bog near Johnstown in County Kilkenny with no loss of life.

In addition to the usual stream of transat deliveries, there were some uncommon diversionary movements during February and March. On 26th February a Douglas C-54 Skymaster[10] landed from Goose Bay during a blizzard, low on fuel and took off again for Prestwick after the weather cleared.

It was followed by another on the following day and exactly one month later a further two of the same type landed from Casablanca, before flying on to Prestwick. Considerable

The Douglas C-54 Skymaster could carry up to 50 troops or 32,000 lbs of freight. This one is at Lagens in the Azores. *(National Museum of Naval Aviation, Pensacola)*

---

10 The C-54 was a militarised version of the pressurised, four-engine DC-4E civil airliner.

numbers of C-54s were in service with Air Transport Command's Atlantic Wing although whether or not these particular aircraft were in transit with passengers or on delivery is unclear. Most likely, they were on Air Transport Command duties.

As the pace of deliveries quickened, the job of the USAAF personnel at ATC Station 1009 wasn't made any easier by the erratic nature of the arrivals. On 11th March 40 aircraft arrived while 58 and 83 aircraft, respectively, landed on two different days in April, out of a total of 356 for the month as a whole. Also in April, gliders made a brief return, with two Horsas[11] being towed across by Dakotas from the Air Transport Training and Development Unit at RAF Netheravon.

On 18th June, within a two-hour period between 19.55 and 21.55 hours, 35 aircraft landed from Goose Bay, comprising 16 B-17s and 19 B-24s. And it wasn't just the USAAF personnel who had to contend with unexpected arrivals. On 9th June, 18 Avro Lancaster and seven Handley Page Halifax bombers of RAF Bomber Command, returning from operations over France in bad weather, were diverted to Nutts Corner from their home bases in England. On the following day, a further 12 Lancasters arrived in similar circumstances.

An Airspeed Horsa; two of these large gliders made a brief visit to Nutts Corner in April 1944. *(Museum of Army Flying)*

A Halifax is refuelled from an AEC Matador fuel bowser. *(D Petty)*

---

11 The AS.51 Horsa was much larger than the Hotspur and had a crew of two plus 20-25 troops.

Chapter 7
The Coronados of Sandy Bay
1944

Meanwhile, by the end of May, the controllers at Station No 2 EWATC were having to contend with an additional and novel aspect of American transatlantic operations that had not been envisaged at the time of the Station's activation. It did not involve the delivery of aircraft; rather, it was a passenger, cargo and mail carrying service linking, via Botwood in Newfoundland and New York with Lough Neagh and onwards to North Africa. The parties primarily involved, as well as No 2 EWATC, were the US Naval Air Transport Service (USNATS), Pan American Airways (Pan Am), American Export Airlines (AEA), the US Naval Operating Base at Londonderry (USNOB, code-named Base One Europe), USAAF Air Transport Command, RAF Transport Command, No 1 Armament Training Camp (No 1 ATC) and RAF Flying Control, Aldergrove. In a supporting capacity, it also involved the USAAF's 27th Air Transport Group and the neighbouring American Air Depot/Storage and Experimental Station at Langford Lodge – which gives an indication of the importance placed on the operation.

This service, even though it was destined to be comparatively short-lived, had its origins in March 1944 when the London office of the Commander of US Naval Forces in Europe, Admiral Harold R Stark, requested information from Air Transport Command at Nutts Corner about flying boat alighting facilities on Lough Neagh. It would appear this was after the Admiral had been informed by the somewhat uncooperative British Air Ministry that nothing was available. At that time, the US Navy was urgently seeking ways of increasing naval capacity for the forthcoming European offensive, it being the Admiral's desire that a facility should commence operations in mid-May, with four-engine Consolidated PB2Y Coronado flying boats that would be contract-flown by civilian Pan Am crews. In response, he was informed that at Sandy Bay there was an auxiliary seaplane base consisting of moorings and slips under the control of RAF Aldergrove. Sandy Bay, the area of sheltered water between Ram's Island and the eastern shore of Lough Neagh, had been rudimentarily developed in the early stages of the war to provide moorings and basic onshore facilities for use by flying boats when visiting Aldergrove or training on the extensive bombing and gunnery ranges on the lough which were in continuous use throughout the war by aircraft of the RAF, Fleet Air Arm and USAAF under the auspices of No 15 Group's No 1 Armament

Training Camp, Aldergrove. RAF marine craft were of course on hand to provide a service between the flying boats and lough shore.

Evidently, Admiral Stark quickly perceived Sandy Bay as the solution to his problem with the result that US Navy and Pan American representatives visited Nutts Corner in April for communications and weather information. Three weeks later, they returned to discuss detailed arrangements relating to air traffic control, briefing and debriefing of flying boat crews, living accommodation and messing. In the event, transatlantic and approach control was exercised from Prestwick while Nutts Corner controlled the local let-down, in liaison with RAF Aldergrove, as well as briefings and debriefings of the Coronado crews; including receipt of classified materials and en route weather reports from incoming crews and provision of call signs, codes, colours of the day and route manuals to outgoing crews. It took two months before all these provisions were formally agreed but, meanwhile, such was the urgency on the part of the US Navy that, on 17th May, a communication was received from Botwood, Newfoundland that a Coronado was already on its way! On the following day, Thursday 18th May at 11.50, Captain Audrey D Durst, the Chief Pilot of Pan Am's Atlantic Division, flying Coronado 7219, alighted on the ruffled surface of Sandy Bay to inaugurate the new service.

The weather, according to the Operations Record Book for No 1 ATC, was fair but with occasional thundery showers. Coronado 7219 was one of 14 specified in a contract between the US Navy and the civilian airlines for use on the Atlantic service, that had been signed early in 1943 but in the event only the Bureau Numbers (Bu No/Serial Numbers) for 11 of the 'boats were recorded by various sources as having visited Sandy Bay: 7077, 7086, 7092, 7094, 7100, 7101, 7216, 7219, 7223, 7226 and 7230. Initially, it was planned that the service would operate on to Port Lyautey in Morocco but because of the inadequacy of facilities at Sandy Bay, traffic on this leg of the route did not commence until 8th June.

Sandy Bay, an area of sheltered water between Ram's Island and the eastern shore of Lough Neagh, where facilities were established to receive flying boats. *(Ernie Cromie Collection)*

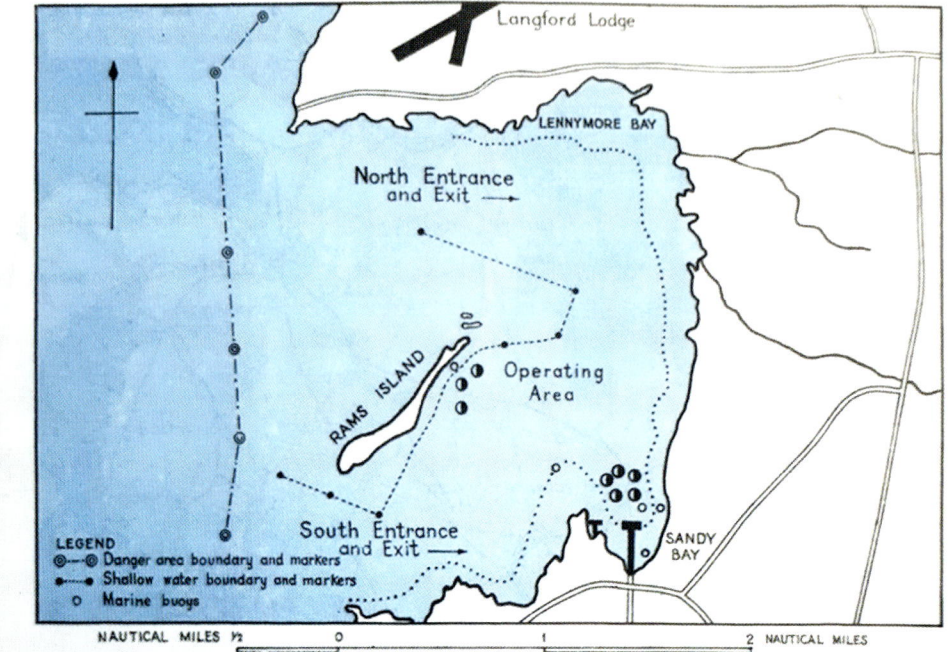

A page from the 1945 edition of the Captain's Route Book for North Atlantic Crossing concerning Lough Neagh. *(Darrell Hillier Collection)*

So urgently had planning been carried out, that on the evidence of correspondence during April and early May between some very senior officers of the Air Ministry, RAF Transport Command, USNOB, Station 2 EWATC and Royal Air Force Northern Ireland, there was not a little bewilderment about what was happening and there had not been time to construct the necessary onshore facilities at Sandy Bay! This task was quickly assigned to the US Navy's 97th Construction Battalion, which left Londonderry on 17th May and set up camp in the grounds of Ben Neagh, a former large residence on the edge of Crumlin and site of an erstwhile anti-aircraft gun battery, four miles from Sandy Bay. At Ben Neagh and Sandy Bay, the Battalion proceeded to construct accommodation, mess facilities, storehouses, improved pier and other buildings for the permanent staff of the base and the transit personnel passing through. Funds were made available from the British Admiralty under reciprocal aid arrangements and authorisation was given for about 150 local civilians to be employed to help set up and maintain the operation, consisting mainly of labourers, tradesmen, mess attendants and some cooks. Initially, these civilians were under the charge of James Monaghan who was succeeded in July by T Harper. Lieutenant Commander Theodore T Ludlum was posted from USNOB to take command of 'Camp Ben Neagh' where he established his Headquarters.

As mentioned earlier, the purpose of this USNATS service was the carriage of passengers, freight and mail and, from mid-August, purpose-designed litter installations were stored at Sandy Bay to facilitate the carriage of medical patients, the first instance of which occurred on 13th August when several were transported from Lough Neagh to New York.

Not surprisingly, USNOB in Londonderry played a significant role in various aspects of the service. Daily, in the Postal Office there, pouches containing outgoing mail were made ready by 15.30 hours when the Base Secretary would be informed of the exact weight and he would hand over any additional items to be posted, priority being given to Air Mail and V-Mail letters.[1] The total package would then be given to a mail clerk who would be met at 16.00 by a driver with a jeep or truck as appropriate and driven to Ben Neagh where both would remain overnight to effect an exchange the following morning. Driver and clerk would then travel to Langford Lodge, there to receive any additional mail for USNOB following which they would telephone for further orders before driving back to Londonderry as quickly as possible. Flying boat passengers travelling overland to/from bases in the UK were flown on a connecting shuttle service provided by the ferrying squadrons of the USAAF's 27th Air Transport Group based at Langford Lodge.

At the outset, the USNATS service schedule for Sandy Bay anticipated that an average of two flying boats would arrive and depart each day (four movements). The schedule was of course subject to various constraints including aircraft serviceability as well as the emergence of sudden unforeseen requirements and was often influenced by weather conditions. Interestingly, for reasons that are unclear, six Coronados arrived at Sandy Bay on 21st June and only three left. Within a few days however, any upset to the usual schedule seems to have been resolved. Throughout the lifespan of the service, the maximum number of movements recorded daily was 11, which occurred on only two occasions, on 23th and 29th August. On the basis of available records, disruption due to engine trouble was a comparatively rare occurrence. It was the cause of a Coronado having to return to Sandy Bay on three occasions not long after taking-off, on 7th July, 26th August and 2nd September. Remarkably, there were few serious incidents or mishaps. The most consequential happened on 17th July when Coronado 7223 was holed on some rocks, while being manoeuvred by an AEA crew. It was quickly re-floated by the McGarry organisation based two miles to the north at Ardmore Boatyard, towed to shallows, repaired and returned to service. Since the 1930s, this small civilian company was well experienced, not only in maintaining the Lough

A Coronado in flight. Originally designed as a patrol bomber, in the transport role it could carry up to 44 passengers or 25 stretcher cases, though on a transatlantic flight the capacity was lower. (NHHC 80-G-359435)

---

1 V-mail, short for Victory Mail, was a hybrid mail process used by the United States during the Second World War as the primary and secure method to correspond with soldiers stationed abroad. To reduce the cost of transferring an original letter through the military postal system, a V-mail letter would be censored, copied to film, and printed back to paper upon arrival at its destination, thus freeing up room and weight for other valuable supplies.

Naval officer passengers seated in the somewhat spartan accommodation of a Coronado's after section. *(NHHC 80-G-K-1141)*

Neagh targets and moorings but also in recovering sunken or damaged aircraft. During the years it was under contract to the Air Ministry, the company raised 10 aircraft or substantial portions of them from Lough Neagh, of which the Coronado was the only one capable of being restored to service. For all of this work, the McGarry family and its employees have never received the degree of recognition deserved.

On an unspecified date in August, Coronado 7230 was delayed at Sandy Bay due to the failure of a propeller unit and the lack of spare parts. Initially, it was thought two days would be required to fly them from New York but the USAAF came to the rescue (almost certainly from Langford Lodge) and the delay was reduced to one day. During the previous month, although it did not cause a delay, Coronado 7101 was returning to New York from Sandy Bay when Captain GC George, reported that several passengers had become ill due to fumes which had collected in the aft compartments, the trouble being traced to a crack in the exhaust line of one of the four Stewart-Warner heaters installed in the aircraft. Subsequent engineering investigation established it would be susceptible to cracking because of the layout employed and work immediately began to redesign the heating system. As a temporary expedient, blankets and flying suits were used!

Whereas few records are available for the number of passenger carried by the Coronados, an entry in the RAF Nutts Corner ORB for the month of June indicates a total of 280 from Botwood and Port Lyautey, equating to about one third of available seat capacity. During July and August, the average number of aircraft movements increased to about six daily but on 12th September the invariably less busy Port Lyautey-Lough Neagh link was discontinued and for the remainder of the month the average returned to what it had been initially. The New York-Sandy Bay link had always been the busier of the two and it was on 22nd September that a new record was achieved for the cargo payload carried when Coronado 7226, flown

by Captain AE Matlack, arrived from Botwood carrying 10,487 pounds of freight, including 15 pounds of company mail.

The Coronado was a large and impressive aircraft, about the size of a Sunderland flying boat, and could carry 18 passengers plus nine crew. Painted in a navy blue colour scheme from August onwards, they displayed standard US national markings and the 'Contract Carrier' endorsement beside the NATS emblem on the nose or forward part of the hull. They normally cruised at 140mph and one, 7230, piloted by Captain Olaf Abrahamson on 21/22nd July, flew from Lough Neagh to Shediac, Prince Edward Island in a record time of 14 hours 18 minutes, taking a further 3 hours 57 minutes to reach the Marine Air Terminal at La Guardia, New York. On 12th October, 1944 the Northern Ireland Prime Minister, Sir Basil Brooke, was invited to Sandy Bay by Commander Ludlum to witness the departure of some of the last to leave. In his diary he commented,

Above left: In the cockpit, or more properly, the spacious flightdeck of a Coronado. The navigator, flight engineer and radio operator would also occupy this area. *(NHHC 80-G-K-1156)*

Above: Unloading the mail from the portside forward door of a Coronado. *(US National Archive)*

'Went to Lough Neagh to see the departure of five Clipper ships for the USA. This is the end of the season. It was a great thrill to see these ships going off into the night and to think that by 11 o'clock tomorrow morning they will be in The States. I dined with Commander Ludlum, US Navy, where we said goodbye.'

A very rare image of a Consolidated PB2Y Coronado on Lough Neagh. *(Clive Moore Collection)*

Naval Air Transport Service (NATS) Coronado 02745 on its mooring in calm waters.
(US National Archive)

Evidently, Sir Basil was no stranger to American aviation terminology!

On 2nd October scheduled operations between New York and Sandy Bay had been cut back from two trips to one per day and on 15th October, coincident with the onset of winter weather conditions came the announcement that the contract between USNATS and the contract carriers would officially terminate on 31st December.

On 16th October Coronado 7086, which had been delayed at Sandy Bay for three days due to weather and maintenance requirements, became the last to leave Lough Neagh for New York. Ironically, it flew via the Southern Route due to the possibility of unfavourable weather over the North Atlantic. Cessation of the Sandy Bay operation resulted in a welcome easing of pressure on RAF Controllers at Nutts Corner and their Air Transport Command counterparts, indeed all USAAF personnel at Nutts Corner.

Some Statistics

Throughout 1944 up until the beginning of September the total USAAF complement at the Station had been steady at around 370, around half of the total number of RAF personnel on the station and well below the USAAF establishment figure of around 600 which appears to have been contemplated at the time of the disbandment of the RAF's 104 OTU. By October, the number was diminishing as arrivals of ferried aircraft had reduced to a trickle, with only 17 in September. It had been a markedly different story during the previous three months when a total of 862 aircraft had arrived – 209 in June followed by an all-time monthly record of 372 in July and 281 in August. Up until the end of June 1944, Nutts Corner had handled 1613 transat deliveries, consisting of 1042 B-17s, 489 B-24s and 82 miscellaneous types. To gain a better idea of the intensity and efficiency of effort that was required in the handling of such numbers it is helpful to consider a further break-down of the statistics. Those for July will suffice.

Of the 372 transatlantic arrivals, consisting of 246 B-17s, 90 B-24s, 18 Martin B-26 Marauders and 24 C-47s, 171 flew in from Gander, 21 from Goose Bay and 180 from Meeks Field, Iceland. 134 of those aircraft were ferried out of Nutts Corner on the day of arrival, 176 were ferried out on the following day (most of which had arrived late the previous day), 41 remained as long as two days and 21 remained longer as they required prolonged servicing or repairs. It should be borne in mind that all the foregoing figures in this paragraph are exclusive of Coronados as well as aircraft of RAF Transport Command and USAAF Air

Transport Command on flights internal to the UK. In circumstances such as these, the work of maintenance personnel to refuel the aircraft and attend to their servicing and maintenance needs was anything but easy. At times, in fact, they were temporarily overwhelmed. That also applied to those personnel whose responsibility it was to debrief, feed and find overnight accommodation for the transient aircrew after stressful and exhausting flights and take care of any medical ailments. In July alone, the total number of transient aircrew was 3339, 35 of whom required treatment in the station sick quarters.

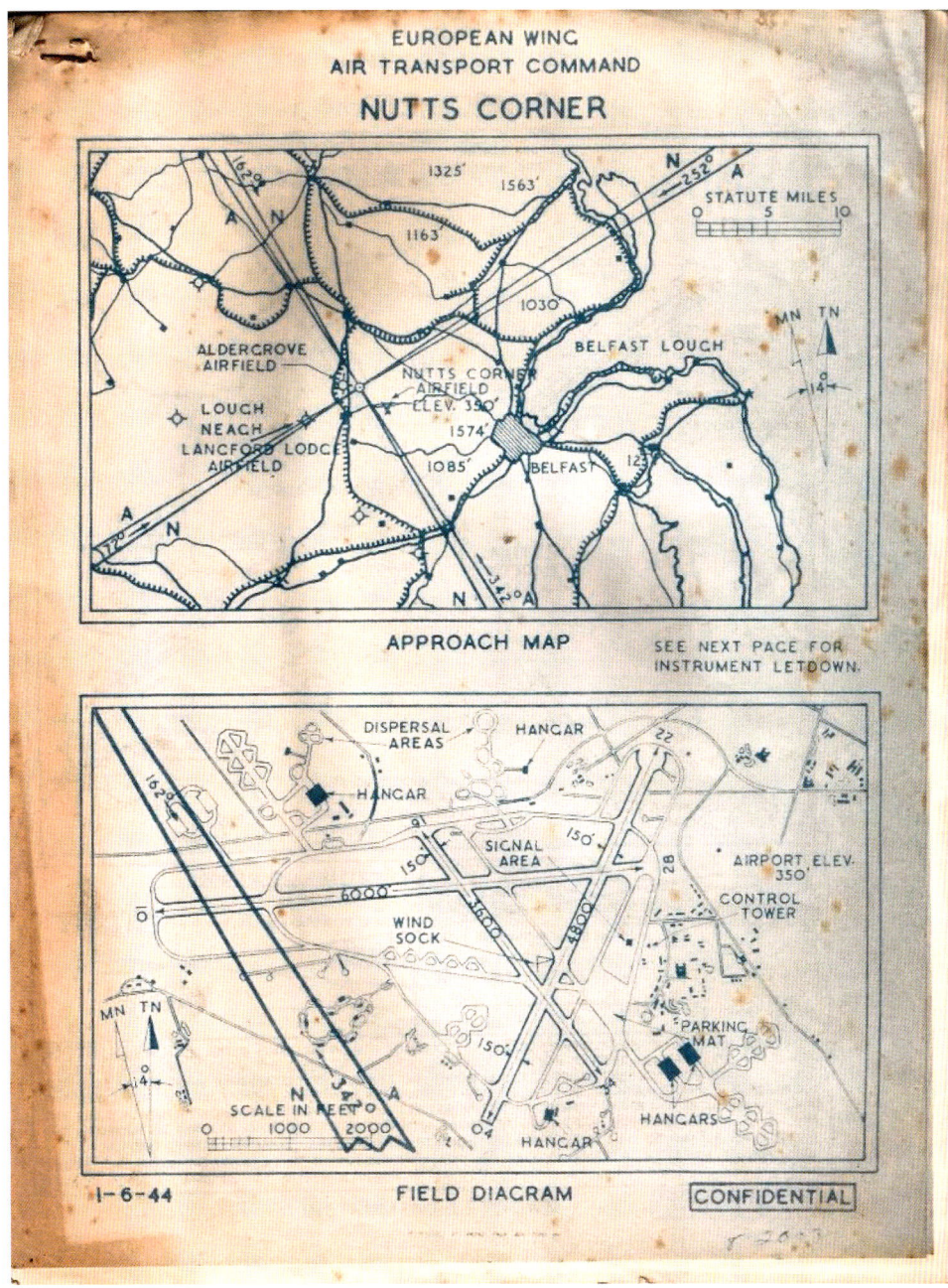

The European Air Wing Air Transport Command Approach Map and Field Diagram for Nutts Corner, dated 1st June 1944. Note that it also shows the nearby airfields at Aldergrove and Langford Lodge. *(Guy Warner Collection)*

Chapter 8
B-17G Flying Fortress 42-97862
1944

In June 1944, exhaustion at the conclusion of a long and demanding flight could have been a causal factor in respect of one especially tragic crash, about which much has been written and conjectured. Around midnight on 31st May/1st June 1944, B-17G Flying Fortress 42-97862 took off from Gander bound for RAF Valley. On board were 10 crew captained by Flight Officer Lester Brooks, a 23-year-old from Ohio. They were a mixed-age bunch, from the youngest, 20-year-old Flight Officer Leighton B McKenzie, bombardier, from California, to the eldest, Staff Sergeant Lawrence E Dundon, radio operator, who was from Kentucky and just twelve days short of his 32nd birthday (little did any of them realise that the tragedy of which they were soon to become victims would, 60 years later, inspire the production of a film entitled 'Closing the Ring' which was directed by Lord Richard Attenborough and premiered at the Toronto Film Festival in 2007 although in the event the film bore only a passing resemblance to the facts of the story).

Somewhere over the Atlantic, in the small hours of 1st June, for reasons that require further investigation but which probably reflected the aircraft's fuel state, the decision was taken that it would divert to Nutts Corner. Around the time of its arrival there, weather conditions included ten tenths cloud cover at 1000-2000 feet and between four and six tenths stratus cloud at 600 feet. As if that wasn't sufficiently worrying, Lester was also advised that there were already 15 aircraft flying holding patterns on the radio range and he was instructed to join them. Inevitably, that would have put both pilots under considerable stress because although a radio range enabled an aircraft to approach directly overhead in nil visibility, observance of the correct procedures necessary to put it in visual contact with the airfield required the utmost concentration by the pilots which in this particular case would be a prolonged process. First, 42-97862 would have to take up and patiently fly an oval-shaped holding pattern above the other aircraft, one end of which was defined by the cone of silence of the radio range and continue to do so at gradually lowering altitude until its turn came to commence the airfield approach procedure. The radio range transmitted a signal along four 'legs' emanating from the range transmitter and the approach procedure for Nutts Corner at this time involved bringing the aircraft directly overhead at an altitude of 4000 feet, flying outward along the 072° leg for a distance of six miles (normally equated to flying time of about three minutes) towards Lyle's Hill, then making a left hand 180-degree turn at 2500 feet on to the reciprocal heading of 252° before continuing its descent to pass over the range at 1500 feet. If visual contact with the ground was not established by then, the aircraft could continue to descend beyond the range on the same heading out over Lough Neagh in hope that the pilots would become visual with the surface whereupon they would again turn the aircraft on to the reciprocal heading prior to making a further course correction towards the airfield and a landing. If, however, visual contact was not made by 552 feet altitude or within three minutes of passing over the range they would have to climb straight ahead to begin the process again or seek an alternate elsewhere.

USAAF Boeing B-17s at Langford Lodge on 13th April 1944. *(US National Archive)*

The fact that, prior to 10.30am on 1st June, several people in Belfast observed and subsequently testified that they saw 42-97862 fly from the direction of the village of Mossley towards Belfast Lough, strongly suggests that Lester Brooks had been in the process of attempting the procedural approach just described but that he had flown too far on the 072° leg and failed to make the turn on to the reciprocal heading. The aircraft, which was below the cloud base and well below the obscured summit of Cave Hill, was then seen to make two very wide left hand orbits over Belfast Lough, the city, the Castlereagh Hills and Holywood, during the course of which in the last radio contact between the aircraft and Nutts Corner control tower the crew reported they had 'contact over a lake'. The aircraft was then seen to fly off in the direction of Nutts Corner with landing gear extended and fly into the precipitous, wooded slopes above Ben Madigan Park whereupon it exploded, killing all 10 crew members.[1] Poignantly, the bodies of all ten crew were buried in the American Military Cemetery at Lisnabreeny, over which it would appear they had flown earlier and which was within sight of the impact location. This and the Cushleake Mountain disaster[2] on 12th September 1943 were the worst aircraft crashes experienced by the USAAF in Northern Ireland during the War.

---

1 Flying Officer Lester B Brooks, Pilot, Flying Officer Jeremiah C Murphy, Pilot, 2nd Lieutenant Joseph V Nobilione, Navigator, Flying Officer Leighton B McKenzie, Bomb Aimer, Staff Sergeant Lawrence E Dundon, Radio Operator, Staff Sergeant Edward E McGill, Air Gunner, Sergeant Robert L Graves, Air Gunner, Sergeant Howard A Hibbler, Air Gunner, Corporal Lawrence R McCrane, Air Gunner.
2 Boeing B-17, 42-30675, crashed six miles NW of Cushendall, en route to Prestwick.

Chapter 9
Accommodation, Food and Welfare
1944

By July 1944, fortunately, facilities at Nutts Corner were a great deal better than what the Americans had experienced on arrival 14 months earlier. Living accommodation, food and welfare conditions generally were much improved and spare time recreational activities were thriving, as a result of which morale was at an all-time high. Organised games were well catered for, including softball, baseball, football, soccer, volleyball, badminton and boxing. Special Services personnel were also very active organising other activities. Sunday trips were especially popular to places of special interest including Portrush, Giant's Causeway, Londonderry, Bangor, Newcastle and Armagh. Trips were facilitated by a well-equipped Transportation Section which had a total of 60 vehicles including 15 jeeps, 10 command cars, five Chevrolet trucks and four buses which were used to maintain the Sunday trips as well as a regular shuttle service between working sites, living quarters and messes, continuous shuttle service to all sites when transient aircrew were on station and a liberty return bus service to Belfast four evenings per week, leaving at 18.30 hours and returning at 23.00. For the less physically energetic and those disinclined to roam far from base there was a small cinema and a library with day room which was well patronised.

In July, the American Red Cross (ARC) officially opened its Coffee Club, named 'Do-Nutts Corner'. In charge was Miss Carol Lee Davis from Lewisburg, Pennsylvania, ably and enthusiastically assisted by Crumlin resident Elizabeth Harrison. The hours of opening were normally 14.30 to 22.30 but on days that transient crews arrived late the club opened for their convenience. Its popularity is evident from the records for July, 'The good old American custom of dunking was indulged in to the tune of 6587 cups of coffee and 17,500 doughnuts'. Coffee was made and supplied by the mess hall on the base, the doughnuts being made in Belfast by the Red Cross Club there and brought to the airfield by ARC personnel who assisted the 'Do-Nutts Corner' staff.

There was also a thriving NCO Club, run by a seven-member Board of Directors and five staff which was located on the RAF Communal Site by arrangement with the RAF Station Commander. There were 95 members in July. It consisted of two large rooms, one a lounge with bar serving beer and soft drinks but no hard liquor and the other a dance hall, with two small rest rooms. Dances were organised twice monthly, to which local girls were invited from the ARC Club, Belfast, British Services, local colleges and businesses. The Club's rooms were also available to officers upon request, for parties.

Members of the US Forces stationed in or visiting Northern Ireland were issued with this annotated map of Belfast. *(Guy Warner Collection)*

Chapter 10

Weather Forecasting and Area Flying Control 1944–45

As mentioned earlier, trustworthy weather forecasting was one of the factors of vital importance to ensuring the safety of aircraft flying between the USA and the UK, especially on the Northern Route. To a weather forecaster, precise knowledge of meteorological conditions in the atmosphere including the winds aloft is essential and throughout the war, various means of obtaining and processing the information required were continuously being developed. Initially, USAAF Weather Squadron detachments in the UK were very dependent on British weather services but, as with the air traffic control aspect referred to earlier, some differences between the American and British methods of processing meteorological data led to confusion and eventual separation of services, by joint agreement. It was in that context that an American RAWIN (RAdio WINds) station was established at Nutts Corner in July 1944.

This was a state-of-the art refinement of the long-established practice of releasing gas-filled balloons into the upper atmosphere carrying telemetry equipment capable of measuring air pressure, temperature and humidity. Initially, the balloons were tracked visually by theodolite, a method of limited use given the prevailing weather conditions over the British Isles but in 1944 the US Army introduced the SCR-658 radio direction finder which was developed in conjunction with SCR-268 radar. This enabled the balloon to be tracked and speed determined whatever the weather. The trained weather forecasters manning the Nutts Corner Station (five or six personnel usually) were primarily concerned with the speed and direction of winds in the upper atmosphere, to which end a hydrogen-filled balloon capable of ascending

A USAAF serviceman using a Rawin weather device to measure wind velocity at different altitudes. On the reverse was typed: "A weather 'rawin' in operation. It is a weather device used by the weather men of the US Army Air Forces for visual observation of a balloon, called a 'pibal' which is released to determine wind velocity at different altitudes. The 'rawin' principle is based on radio 'triangulation', a method of direction finding well understood by all amateur radio 'hams'. By timing the ascent of the balloon and computing the speed with which it drifts with the wind, 'rawin' is able to tell at any given moment the altitude it has reached. It gives to weather men a clear picture of what is happening above the earth's surface." *(Official Photograph US Army Air Corps)*

to very high level (50,000 feet plus) was released twice daily, at midday and midnight initially, carrying battery-powered telemetry equipment (known as a radiosonde) to measure and transmit back to the station details of temperature, pressure and humidity. Throughout the ascent, until atmospheric pressure reduction caused it to burst, the balloon was tracked and wind data computed using the SCR-658 set at the RAWIN Station. At Nutts Corner, the Station was initially under the command of 2nd Lieutenant Augustus N Hill, a professionally qualified meteorologist who with one of his enlisted men, Private First Class George Panchak was also thoroughly trained in the operation and maintenance of the radio direction finder. No official Operations Record has been found for the Nutts Corner facility; fortunately, however, for his own convenience and use a detailed personal diary was commenced in November 1944 by the commanding officer who incorporated some records from a previous log. Maintained by successive commanding officers until the station closed in June 1945, it is a revealing account of RAWIN Station activities. Left behind when the Americans departed, it would appear that the small note book came into the possession of Air Ministry meteorologists and at some stage was taken to the Air Ministry Radiosonde Unit at Long Kesh from where it was rescued following the Unit's closure.

The first test run with the new equipment was made on 20th July and although initial results were satisfactory subsequent tests showed up defects which took time to eliminate. The Americans had a close relationship with colleagues manning the RAWIN Station at Stornoway and also with British meteorologists at RAF Nutts Corner which fortunately was not adversely affected as a result of the Station being broken into on 10th October. Two days later, some of the equipment and tools that had been stolen were returned by British personnel on the airfield who admitted the break-in, following which it is evident from the record that co-operation between the American and British meteorological personnel was of a high order and mutually beneficial.

Area Flying Control

By the summer of 1944, Air Transport Command had become a huge organisation that was truly worldwide in its scope and what had been the European Wing became the European Division. One result was that Station No 2 EWATC was re-designated as the 1404th Army Air Force Base Unit on 18th July, at which time, as already mentioned, transat traffic through the ferry terminal was at its peak. By October, the torrent of transat deliveries had become a trickle, resulting in the disestablishment of 1404 AAFBU mid-month. So began the final chapter in the military history of Nutts Corner even though it would be June 1945 before the last USAAF personnel would depart.

Meanwhile, although the decreasing numbers of transats being delivered to the UK were now arriving almost exclusively at the terminals in Great Britain, Nutts Corner continued to play a role in regard to Air Transport Command's shuttle service for passengers and freight within the UK and exercise an especially significant function regarding the control of and provision of meteorological data to transatlantic traffic in general. One aspect of this was the associated need for and continuing development of aids to radio navigation

Unit patch of Army Airways Communication System, United States Army Air Corps. *(Guy Warner Collection)*

and communication. In fact, during this chapter of its history, Nutts Corner became the nerve centre of an emerging Area Flying Control system assisting air traffic over the North-East Atlantic and northern part of the British Isles which relied on a network of radio aids. One American unit which played a significant role in that regard was the Northern Ireland detachment of the 132nd Army Airways Communication Squadron. This unit arrived at Nutts Corner in mid-May, 1944, with a complement of just under 100 personnel, most of whom were enlisted men in the charge of a handful of officers. On arrival, they took over responsibility for ATC approach control equipment in the tower, the radio ranges at Nutts Corner and Belleek, a DF Station at Mullaghmore airfield south of Coleraine and a fan marker at Cushendall. The fan marker, which was within half a mile of the village, was on the south west leg (256°) of the Prestwick Radio Range. It transmitted a radio signal vertically to form a narrow fan-shaped pattern, which was only heard when an aircraft was directly overhead, thus indicating to the pilot his exact position which in this case was 63 miles from Prestwick. It was the detachment's job to maintain these installations and improve the network where necessary, one of the first tasks being the installation of an additional fan marker, at Langford Lodge. Sited on that airfield between its control tower and Lough Neagh and just north of Langford Lodge house, on the south-west leg (252°) of and 5.3 miles from the Nutts Corner Radio Range, it was put into operation on 25th July 1944. The facility at Mullaghmore, which was just becoming operational round about the time of 132nd Squadron's arrival, consisted of three units manned by a small number of AACS personnel who were accommodated in RAF quarters at Mullaghmore. Their job was to take bearings on aircraft flying on the Southern and Northern Transatlantic Routes and transmit the information to Prestwick and RAF Transport Command Headquarters at Gloucester.

The hardback cover of the Captain's Route Book for North Atlantic Crossing. *(Darrell Hillier Collection)*

In the 132nd Squadron History, it is recorded that, on 25th September 1944, the small number of AACS personnel who had been manning the Cushendall fan marker checked out of the nearby hotel in which they had been billeted and the facility was deactivated. Apparently though, it was put into care and maintenance because in April 1945 the building was cleaned up and repainted and new Blackstone generators were installed. The Belleek and Nutts Corner Radio Ranges were also well maintained and still very much active as was Mullaghmore DF Station. The value of this network of facilities was demonstrated on at least two occasions. Detachment 206 stationed at RAF Mullaghmore was retained until the beginning of 1946.

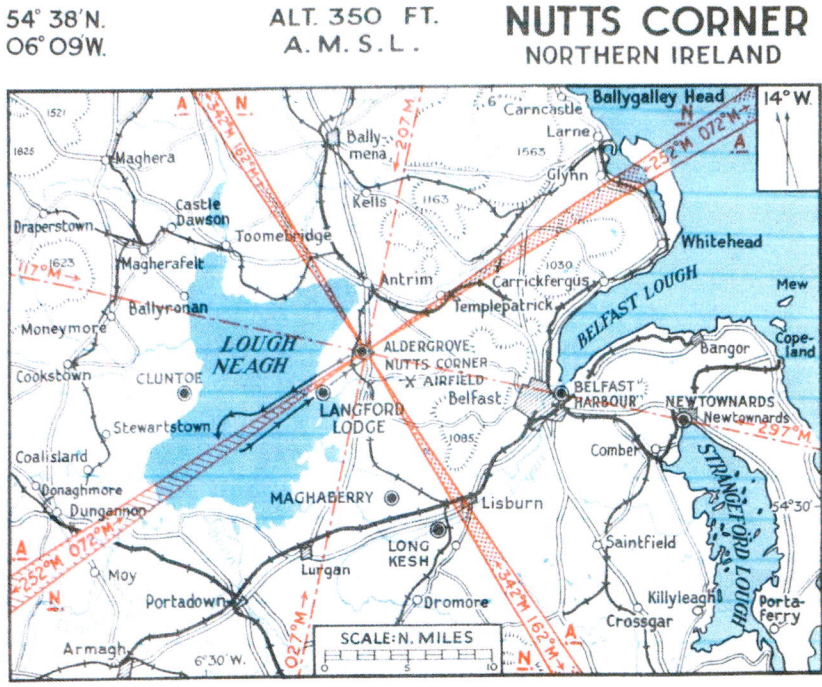
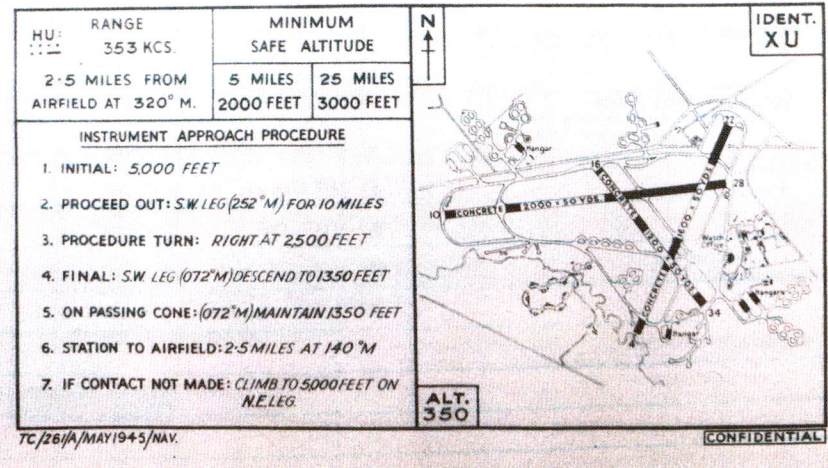

The page from the 1945 edition of the Route Book concerning Nutts Corner.
(Darrell Hillier Collection)

Chapter 11

Heavy Conversion
1944–45

No 1332 (Transport) Heavy Conversion Unit (HCU) was formed on 5th September 1944 at RAF Longtown, Cumberland, in No 44 Group, Transport Command. It moved to Nutts Corner on 7th October 1944 (training commencing on 17th October 1944), with an establishment of 15 Short Stirlings, four Liberators, and five Avro Yorks.

Five aircrew who served with the Unit at Nutts Corner, pilots, Flight Lieutenant JS Ross and Flying Officer George Mackie DFC, WOp/AG, Warrant Officer JA Doxsey and flight engineers, Flying Officers Reg Miles and Thomas Jones DFC, recorded in their logbooks flying variously in Yorks, Stirlings and Liberators – night flying, cross-country exercises, circuits and landings, some on three-engines.[1]

Reg Miles later recalled:

Top: Fifteen Short Stirlings were on the strength of No 1332 (Transport) Heavy Conversion Unit at Nutts Corner in 1944-45. *(Ernie Cromie Collection)*

Above: To which could be added five Avro Yorks, including MW149. *(Guy Warner Collection)*

'I was posted to No 1332, HCU at Nutts Corner, where I crewed up with Flight Lieutenant Poore, a navigator and a wireless operator, all of us being officers and had completed at least one tour on bombers. We were being trained to fly Avro Yorks on the main trunk routes from UK to India and Ceylon. We started the flying part of the course on 8th April 1945 and completed it on 17th of the same month. My flight log of my time there showed ten flights totalling just over 23 hours. The Avro York interior layout was much as the Lancaster. The pilot, flight engineer Nav and WOp were together in a small group, the flight engineer acting as second pilot even if untrained.'

1 ibccdigitlarchive.lincoln.ac.uk

From there he was posted to No 242 Squadron at RAF Stoney Cross, in Hampshire, but not before 'thumbing a lift to England from Nutts Corner to marry on 28th April.'

George Mackie recorded three incidents in his logbook, the first just after he had arrived on 30th November 1944. While flying Stirling LK537, he and his crew were tasked to search for Stirling LJ470, which had been on a navigation exercise and was last plotted on radar as being off Stornoway but had not returned to base. Sadly the 'rough trip' noted in his logbook

Two pages from George Mackie's log book were illustrated with photos of Stirling LK687's mishap. *(IBCC Digital Archive, University of Lincoln)*

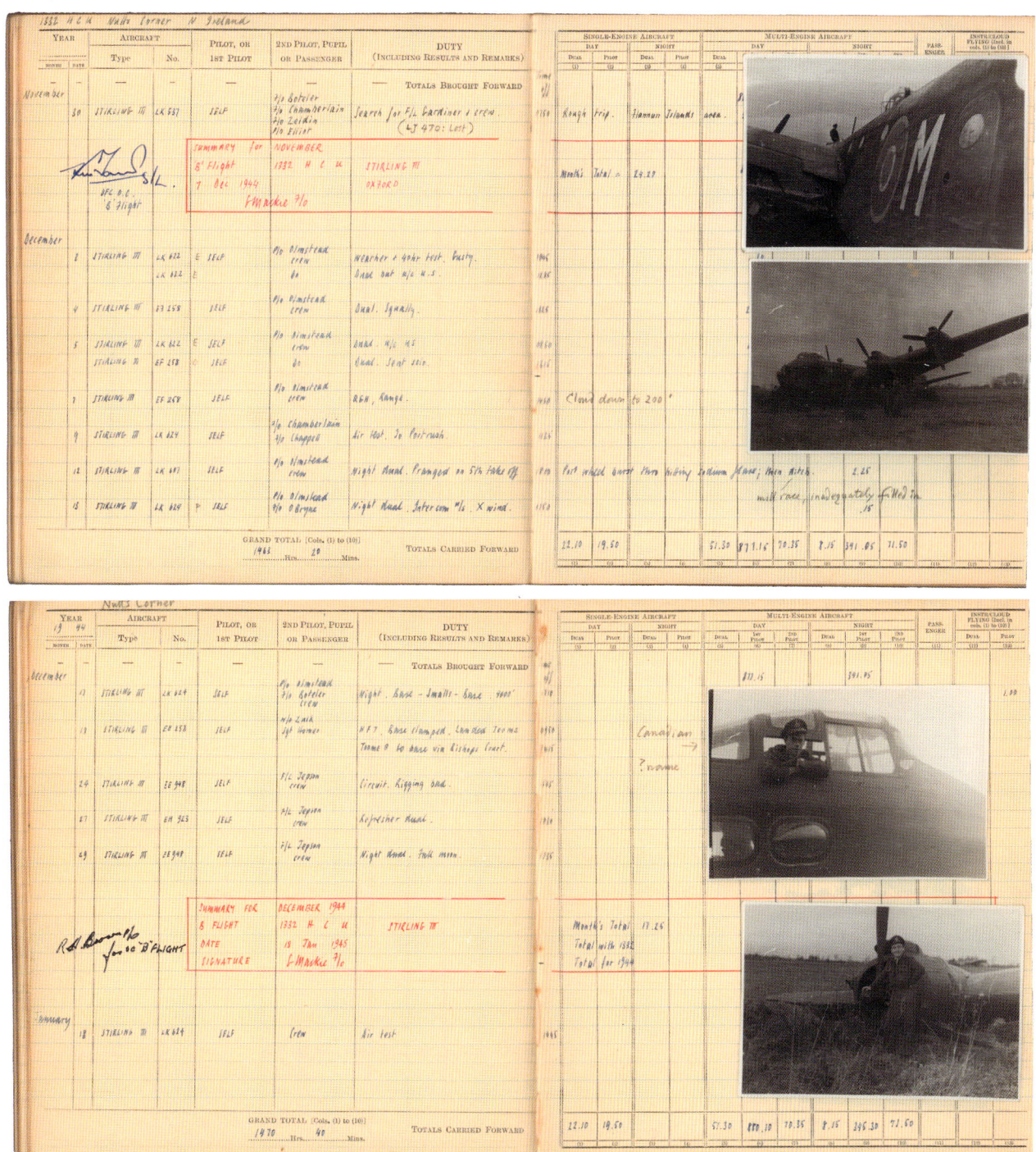

was unsuccessful in finding any trace.[2] Then on 18th October, while flying Stirling, PW262, from Nutts Corner to Prestwick in a half gale, 'narrowly missed Ailsa Craig.'[3]

He suffered a further mishap on 12th December, when taking off on for night exercise in Stirling LK687, when, 'the port wheel burst on hitting a sodium flare and then a ditch, a millrace inadequately filled in.'

Thomas Jones, later wrote an account of his time with 1332 HCU:

Flying Officer Thomas John Jones DFC is on the left with his friend Roy Baker to the right. *(Peter Jones Collection)*

'In September 1944 we were declared Ops Expired, having completed 64 Ops as a crew. A few days later we were posted to RAF Brackla, on the shores of the Moray Firth, from where we were posted our separate ways. We wished each other luck, shook hands, and parted; never to meet again. In November I was posted to RAF Nutts Corner, near Belfast. No 1332 Heavy Conversion Unit, Transport Command was stationed there; and I was to fly in Stirlings once again. A lot of the student pilots were foreign. They were very enthusiastic and eager to convert to heavy bombers, their over-enthusiasm and language difficulties made for an interesting time. It was disconcerting to be on the final approach with wheels up and red flares going up like a firework display from the caravan below.

My nights and weekends were spent in Belfast with Tommy Thompson, Mac MacDonald, and Roy Baker visiting the Four Hundred Club and the Grand Central Hotel. Mr and Mrs Cree of Cliftonville Circus invited me to spend Christmas 1944 with them, I was treated like a member of the family. A wonderful thing to do for a lad so far from home at Christmas.

I remember watching an incident involving my pal Roy Baker. A Stirling was coming into land when a tyre burst, the undercarriage collapsed as the aircraft went into a ground loop at over 100 knots. When it came to a halt all the crew rapidly emerged from various escape hatched except Roy Baker, the Flight Engineer. He was still inside the badly damaged aircraft diligently carrying out his emergency drill, turning fuel cocks off, electrics off, closing engine cooling grills etc. He was cheered when he finally emerged.[4]

---

2 The crew of the missing Stirling was: Flight Lieutenant FES Gardner, Flight Sergeants JA Hitchcock, EW Wright, JEC Buttle and Corporal GW Palmer.

3 Also known familiarly as 'Paddy's Milestone' this granite outcrop can be seen on the ferry route between Larne and Cairnryan.

4 In all probability this was either Stirling III LK497 on 4th January or LK621 on 26th January 1945 which both had accidents of this nature while making a night landing.

Nothing ever eclipsed the beauty of Northern Ireland from the air. With its patchwork of fields of brown, straw yellow, and the most brilliant green it was truly magical. I have never forgotten the generous, warm hearted people I met there, and I was sad when I received the news that I was being posted to RAF Riccall in North Yorkshire.'[5]

It was noted in February 1945 that a new use had been found for empty four-gallon kerosene drums; about 1000 had been painted white, filled with sand and placed at intervals by the side of the perimeter and taxi tracks. The identity letters 'XU' were also painted at either end of the main east-west runway and illuminated at night. The pilots thought that these innovations were of considerable help. The HCU moved to Riccall beginning on 27th April 1945, with Dakotas from 108 and 109 (Transport) OTUs assisting with the movement of personnel and equipment.

In the air the Stirling was an imposing sight, in this case, the Belfast-built Mk III BF509. *(Guy Warner Collection)*

---

5 His son, Peter Jones, a Collections Archivist at the International Bomber Command Centre, Lincoln, adds, 'He flew on operations with No 622 Squadron in Stirlings and Lancasters, then No 7 Squadron Pathfinder Force in Lancasters, completing 64 operations with the same crew. When he was alive he wouldn't talk about his time with Bomber Command. He would only relate humorous stories. However, 24 hours after he died, I discovered a WH Smith notebook amongst all the paperwork I needed to attend to. Fifty years after the war he completed a memoir and hid it with his will etc. I read it that evening, He was a wonderful, modest man, I am very proud of him.

Chapter 12
Fleet Air Arm
1945–46

At the end of May a party of naval officers visited to inspect the facilities and were followed by an advance party in the middle of June. On 11th July 1945 the airfield was transferred on loan from RAFNI and was commissioned as a Fleet Air Arm station, HMS *Pintail*. At 12.00, Guards-of-Honour from the RAF and the RAF were mounted as the RAF Ensign was lowered from the flagstaff, on what would henceforth be known as the quarter-deck and replaced by the Naval Ensign, raised by the Yeoman of Signals. The necessary signatures on the 'receipt books' were provided by the out-going and in-coming Station Commanders, Wing Commander RAC Barclay AFC and Commander JH Swain DSO, DFC. *Pintail* was equipped to handle first line fighter squadrons with a capacity for 60 aircraft but with the end of the war at hand it was used principally for the disbandment of Supermarine Seafire, Grumman F6F Hellcat and Vought F4U Corsair squadrons.

Sadly, there were a number of accidents both fatal and otherwise in the course of the following months. 1837 NAS moved to Nutts Corner on 31st July. Tragedy struck on 8th

Naval personnel surround a Seafire at Nutts Corner in 1945.
(Guy Warner Collection)

August when Sub Lieutenant Ian MacAllister RNVR was killed shortly after take-off. He attempted to return to base after smoke began pouring from the engine of Corsair JS593 but the aircraft dived into the ground and burst into flames. He was just 20 years old.

There were two more incidents with less unhappy results; on the following day, Sub Lieutenant NE Phillips RNVR, bounced while landing on Corsair JSS40 causing the port wing tip to strike the ground, while, on 13th, Lieutenant AW Watson RNVR made a forced landing at RAF Mullaghmore after his aircraft, Corsair JS812, developed engine trouble. The Squadron disbanded at Nutts Corner on August 18th.

On 3rd September Grumman Hellcat II, JZ921, of 891 NAS had a mishap from which the pilot was fortunate to survive. During aerodrome dummy deck landings, the aircraft stalled on approach, struck the runway with its port wing, rolled onto its back and crashed.

The pilot, Sub Lieutenant (A) GW Worner RNZN was injured and had to be rescued from the cockpit. On the same day, Hellcat JZ912 also had an accident, followed by JZ903 on 4th. Apparently in this last incident, the pilot had failed to lower the flaps before landing, with the result that the Hellcat ended up on its nose.

The Vought F4U Corsair was widely regarded as one of the best carrier-born fighters of the war. Corsair Mk 1, JT108/7C, is seen here in the USA in 1943. *(Guy Warner Collection)*

The pilot was fortunate to survive this accident, involving Hellcat, JZ921, on 3rd September 1945. *(Gill and Gerald Worner Collection)*

Hellcat, JZ912, of 891 NAS had a less dramatic accident on 3rd September 1945 at HMS Pintail. *(Gill and Gerald Worner Collection)*

Followed by Hellcat, JZ903, also of 891 NAS, on 4th September 1945. *(Gill and Gerald Worner Collection)*

803 NAS, which was equipped with twelve Seafire F.XVs, arrived at Nutts Corner on 23rd September. It suffered a loss on 2nd October, when Seafire SR482, flown by Sub Lieutenant (A) Leonard Wade RNVR, age 23 and from British Columbia, collided with Seafire SW850 while flying in formation and crashed on Slievenanee Mountain near Cushendall on the North Antrim coast.

Then, on 5th November, Seafire SW849, impacted on Aughrim Hill, Co Down, with fatal injury to another Canadian pilot, Sub Lieutenant (A) William Nash RNVR.

This was followed by another accident on 19th December and involved two Seafire F.17s, SX126 and SX128, of 809 NAS, which collided just off the north coast. The *Belfast Telegraph* of 24th December 1945 reported:

'Pilots Missing off North Antrim After Air Collision

There is still no trace of the bodies of the pilots, who in their two single-seater aircraft crashed into the sea off the North Antrim

Possibly the last naval landing accident at Nutts Corner was in February 1946, involving a Seafire F.XV of 883 NAS. *(G Standley Collection)*

coast on Wednesday last, after colliding in mid-air over Dunseverick harbour. The missing airmen are Sub Lieutenant (A) David Lees-Jones DSC, RNVR (21) and Sub Lieutenant (A) Thomas Siddall RNVR (20). Two fishermen, Daniel McMullan and Robert McClelland, who were engaged in fishing operations in the harbour, observed the crash. Debris showered all over the harbour, but although the fishermen found the backs of two seats and a glove bearing the name of Sub Lieutenant Lees-Jones, neither body was found. A further search by an Air-Sea Rescue launch from Portrush proved of no avail.'

Between August 1945 and March 1946 aircraft from eleven naval air squadrons passed through. A number of these had been destined for the British Pacific Fleet, if Japan had not capitulated.

Postscript
A New Life
1946

The site was reduced to care and maintenance status on the books of HMS *Gadwall*, Belfast on 14th November 1945, being paid off on 1st April 1946 to No 4 Group, RAF Transport Command. However, on 25th February 1946, a Dakota, flown by Flight Lieutenant D Baker, of No 1680 (Transport) Flight landed from Prague, after a five and a half hour flight, with 25 young Jewish refugees, who had arrived for resettlement.[1]

They were mostly from Ruthenia, a province of Czechoslovakia which had been annexed by Hungary in 1938. After the German occupation of Hungary in 1944, the Jews of Ruthenia had been confined to ghettos and from there shipped to Auschwitz. The navigator of the Dakota, FZ670, Warrant Officer Denzil Jacobs[2], was surprised and delighted by the warm welcome given to the passengers and aircrew at Nutts Corner, where a splendid tea had been

Boys' group of the refugees, some of whom would be coming to Millisle, at the Jan Hus memorial in Old Town Square Prague in 1945. (*'45 Aid Society*)

1 Air 29/881 National Archive
2 Jacobs (1921–2013) served in the St John's Wood Home Guard in 1941, where his sergeant was Eric Blair (the author George Orwell).

laid on, 'It did my ego a lot of good because all the ladies of the community, quite undeservedly treated us like conquering heroes.' Another Dakota, in the hands of Flight Lieutenant Alex Appleby and on the same mission, had taken off earlier that week, from Ruzyně (Prague) and landed at Sydenham, the location of *Gadwall*. All the children were taken by bus to 'The Farm' – Ballyrolly House, Millisle, on the Ards Peninsula, where the process of starting a new life would begin with, 'a meal of soup, fried egg, potato, cabbage, pudding, and coffee.' Victor Greenberg was one of the boys:

Refugees arriving at Eastleigh, Southampton in a Dakota of No 1680 (Transport) Flight. *('45 Aid Society)*

'Our routine was to have prayers each morning, followed by a hearty breakfast. We had English tuition in the mornings and in the afternoons, we had recreation and games in the playing fields, while some of us did gardening. The good food and exercise helped to develop our bodies, which we desperately needed. We were given half-a-crown a week pocket money. We used this for going into Donaghadee to the cinema, at a reduced entry fee, and the amusement arcade.'

The centre closed in 1948, having helped some 300 young people to make a fresh start in life. Some would remain in Northern Ireland, while others would put down roots further afield.

Some of the children at 'The Farm' – Ballyrolly House, Millisle. *(Robert Neill Collection)*

Appendix
Nutts Corner – A Military Timeline

264 Squadron (Det)	Defiant	8th May 1941 to 20th May 1941
120 Squadron	Liberator	2nd June 1941 to 21st July 1942
220 Squadron	Hudson, Fortress	4th January 1942 to 23rd June 1942
160 Squadron	Liberator	7th May 1942 to 8th June 1942
44 Squadron (Det)	Lancaster	12th June 1942 to 19th July 1942
224 Squadron (Det)	Liberator	19th September 1942 to 26th September 1942
231 Squadron	Tomahawk, Lysander	2nd January 1943 to 20th March 1943
Ferry Command (later Transport Command)		19th January 1943
104 OTU	Wellington	15th March 1943 to 31st January 1944
69th Ferry Squadron USAAF		19th June 1943
24th Army Airways Communications Squadron		by 24th September 1943
24th Weather Squadron		ditto
1149th Military Police Company		ditto
Station No 2 EWATC (Station 1009)		24th September 1943 to 18th July 1944
1674 HCU	Fortress, Liberator	19th February 1944 to 18th March 1944
USNATS, Pan Am, AEA	Coronado	18th May 1944 to 16th October 1944
132nd Army Airways Communication Squadron		May 1944 to 25th September 1944
RAWIN		July 1944 to June 1945
1404th Army Air Force Base Unit		18th July 1944 to October 1944
1332 (Transport) HCU	Stirling, York, Liberator	7th October 1944 to 25th April 1945
HMS *Pintail*		11th July 1945 to 31st March 1946
1837 NAS	Corsair	31st July 1945 to 18th August 1945
891 NAS	Hellcat	11th August 1945 to 24th September 1945

1835 NAS	Corsair	23rd August 1945 to 3rd September 1945
1852 NAS	Corsair	August 1945
803 NAS	Seafire	23rd September 1945 to 28th February 1946
809 NAS	Seafire	21st October 1945 to 11th January 1946
807 NAS	Seafire	31st October 1945 to 16th February 1946
883 NAS	Seafire	7th November 1945 to 21st February 1946
879 NAS	Seafire	10th November 1945 to 7th January 1946
802 NAS	Seafire	10th January 1946 to 26th February 1946
772 NAS (Det)	Wildcat	February 1946 to March 1946
No 4 Group RAF Transport Command		1st April 1946 then to the Ministry of Civil Aviation

Nutts Corner Part 2
The Civil Airport For Northern Ireland

Chapter 13
Introduction

As previously noted, Nutts Corner was taken over by No 4 Group RAF Transport Command from the Royal Navy on 31st March 1946 (by this time there were no RAF or RN aircraft based there, with the RAF Flying Control detachment having departed at the end of February) and then opened as the civil airport for Northern Ireland on 1st December

Nutts Corner in 1945, clearly showing the three runways. *(Ernie Cromie Collection)*

1946, replacing Belfast Harbour Airport at Sydenham. Because the airfield had been developed with large Coastal Command and USAAF cargo aircraft in mind, there were relatively long runways (6000, 4800 and 3700 feet in length) and concrete parking aprons available for the bigger commercial aircraft which were anticipated.

Other reasons for the move included the limited space available at Belfast for expansion and the danger associated with the obstacles present around Belfast Harbour, for example cranes. Other sites had been studied as possible alternative civil airports, for example RAF Long Kesh, Lisburn, but rejected. The former RAF station then became known as Belfast-Nutts Corner Airport.

Not everyone welcomed the move. On 13th May 1946, a lunch was held in Belfast, hosted by Scottish Airways and Railway Air Services (RAS). In its report on the event, *Aeroplane* magazine noted that reference was made to 'the controversy raging over this airport.' Sir Stephen Bilsland, the Chairman of Scottish Airways said that the Ministry of Civil Aviation should 'pay the closest attention to local opinion and local wishes.' It was the opinion of RAS that it would be greatly disadvantageous to the business community if the air services should be diverted a long way from the centre of Belfast. He would go further and add that, 'such a move would be deplorable.' He appealed to the Ministry to give serious attention to the point of view held by the present operators. He was supported by Sir Frederick Rebbeck, the Chief Executive of Harland and Wolff, who said that after watching a Dakota make a perfect landing, he could not help thinking about the stories of the unsuitability of Sydenham. He reinforced what Sir Stephen had said:

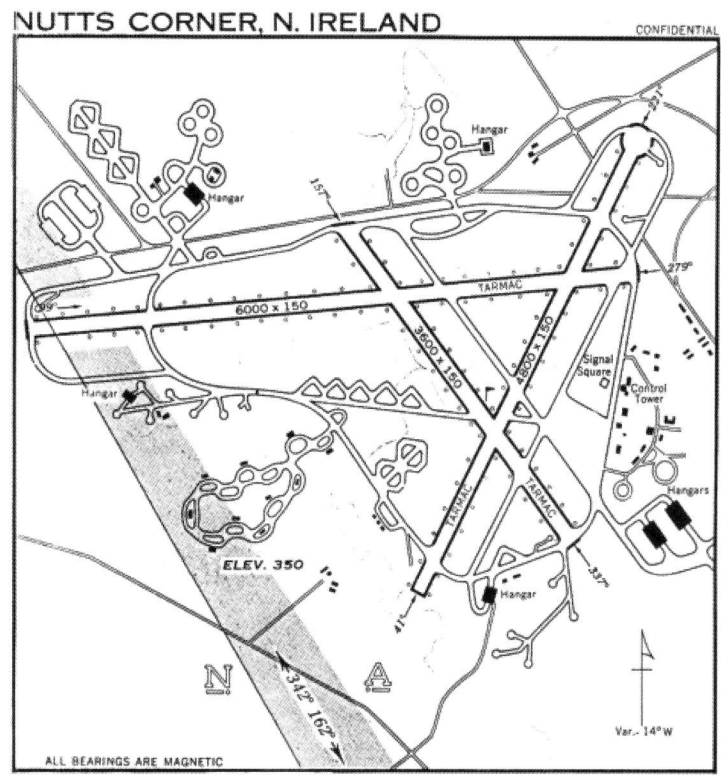

A plan of the site. *(Ernie Cromie Collection)*

Sydenham should not be done away with because some planner had said they must have Nutts Corner. If they must have Nutts Corner, let them also have Sydenham. There was as much reason why they should retain Sydenham as Scotland should retain Prestwick.

On the same day Belfast Corporation passed a unanimous resolution that the General Purposes Committee, 'expressed deep concern' about the transfer of the regular scheduled services from Belfast Harbour Airport to Nutts Corner.

During the year of 1945/6 that Railway Air Services operated from the Harbour Airport to London (Croydon), Liverpool, Manchester, Glasgow (Renfrew), Prestwick and the Isle of Man, in excess of 40,000 passengers were handled, an impressive total given the relatively small size of the aircraft and the fairly basic nature of the facilities. However, the die was cast and the transfer of services went ahead.

BEA had commenced operations on 1st August 1946, along with the two other newly created government owned corporations, the British Overseas Airways Corporation (BOAC) and British South American Airways (BSAA). BEA assumed full responsibility for scheduled civil air transport in the United Kingdom. The management of the new corporation was adamant that scheduled passenger services should cease at Belfast Harbour and transfer to Nutts Corner. Until the end of January 1947 and the formation of the Corporation's English and Scottish Divisions BEA's schedules at Nutts Corner would be maintained by the existing operators at Belfast Harbour: Railway Air Services (RAS) to Croydon, Liverpool and Manchester and Scottish Airways to Glasgow.

The Avro 19, G-AHIB, the civil version of the Anson, of Railway Air Services. RAS operated 15 of this type, most of which were passed on to BEA. *(via John Stroud)*

On a Sunday morning in late 1946, a de Havilland DH89 Rapide, an Avro Nineteen and a Ju52/3m left Belfast Harbour Airport for Nutts Corner, laden with all the office equipment, desks, chairs and files – RAS booking clerk Bert Hutchinson flew in the Ju52, which he said was a little noisy, not as smooth as the DH89 in which he had flown from Sydenham at wave top height to the Isle of Man. One of the staff, W Gamble, British European Airways' (BEA) Personnel Officer in Belfast, later wrote:

> It was, perhaps, unfortunate that the transfer to Nutts Corner took place in the middle of what proved to be a very severe winter and the staff had to endure many hardships. The task was, however, tackled with vigour and enthusiasm and after some hard work and the liberal application of grey and red paint, the old service huts and buildings were quickly-transformed into offices and passenger accommodation which provided a reasonable degree of comfort. The local staff were augmented by several English members posted from London, many of them from the BEA Training School at Northolt.

The Avro 19's rather utilitarian interior. An effort was made to enhance passenger comfort by lining the cabin walls in an attempt at soundproofing. *(via John Stroud)*

One of the staff later remembered:

Most of us can recall that winter of '46/47, certainly those involved in the transfer to Nutts Corner will never forget it. Lorries carrying heavy equipment had to be dug out of six-foot drifts, pipes were frozen, roads ice-bound and conditions generally severe. Despite all these hardships the move was completed, and with the arrival of the thaw the staff hoped they would never again have to endure such a winter.[1]

The popular and successful DH89 Rapide at Nutts Corner, in this case, G-ALPK of, Carlisle-based, Air Taxi (Cumberland) Ltd. *(Ernie Cromie Collection)*

---

1 Senior officials at Nutts Corner in 1946-47 included W Coen the Airport Managers, AE Slocombe and W Kearney, Air Traffic Control Officer, JW Dunn, Tels Officer, Ralph Thurley, BEA Station Superintendent and S Harvey, Met Officer.

Chapter 14

Nutts Corner in the 1940s

BEA absorbed RAS on 1st February 1947. The first non-stop service flown by BEA from Croydon to Belfast was on 20th March 1947 by the Junkers Ju52/3m, G-AHOF, one of a fleet of these veteran tri-motors taken from Germany as war reparations and used briefly without conspicuous success. (Ju52s had been operating on the Croydon-Liverpool-Belfast Harbour route since November 1946, with the first service on 18th by RAS Ju52, G-AHOG, which was painted in BEA colours. They were named the *Jupiter* Class.) The pilots were Captains DG Moynihan and Derek Yapp, also on board was one of Britain's most respected aviation journalists and authors, John Stroud, who had begun his working life in 1933, in the employ of Imperial Airways. During the 350-mile flight, of two hours and 51 minutes duration, 'OF trundled along at a steady 125 mph and John Stroud, to his delight, was permitted to take the controls for half the journey. On arrival, he was given free rein to photograph the aircraft and the airport.

Having taken a spot of lunch at the airfield, John clambered back aboard G-AHOF for the return flight to Croydon, the trimotor departing Nutts Corner at 13.43, the crew once again allowing him to pilot the aircraft, this time for 50 minutes. The *Jupiter's* wheels touched down at Croydon at 16.04 after two hours 21 minutes airborne.

The Ju52s had been constructed during the war to much lower standards than pre-war machines, in the realistic expectation of a much shorter active life. They had been modified by Short & Harland in Belfast with a smart royal blue interior and seating for 17 passengers, at a cost of between £10,000 and £12,500 each. Despite being easy to fly, light on the controls, sedate and having the capability to lift a good payload, this type had only limited success,

British European Airways staff gather beside G-AHOF on the day of the inaugural non-stop London–Belfast service. The colour scheme was natural metal overall with the name of the airline in red and the BEA "Speedkey" logo reversed out within a red circle on the fin. *(John Stroud/The Aviation Historian)*

A view of Nutts Corner from a port-side window of G-AHOF, with G-AHOE on the ramp below. *(John Stroud/The Aviation Historian)*

chiefly due to a lack of useable spares. Passengers were also caused some alarm as the coiled springs of its undercarriage jangled noisily when taxying and the heating system gave a loud shriek when it was turned on, quickly followed by a blast of hot air through the floor vents. It also had an unfortunate tendency to shed its nose engine cowling in flight and more than once, the airline's office received a call from an irate inhabitant or two of Co Down who had found a foreign object in their field. The greater size of the aircraft did, however, allow the provision of one of the earliest attractive innovations for passengers, an in-flight tea and coffee service. The well-known aviation author and historian, AJ Jackson, described the aircraft thus:

> The cabin had been furnished in a light and artistic decor with airline seats complete with folding tables, and there was a toilet compartment in the rear which still boasted a light switch marked 'Ein' and 'Aus'. The breakfast of sandwiches, biscuits and hot coffee was more than welcome in view of a serious malfunction in the cabin heating system.

On 19th May 1947 Douglas DC-3 Dakotas replaced the Ju52s and the London terminal changed from Croydon to Northolt. (BEA services from Croydon ceased altogether on 1st November 1947.) The renowned Dakota could carry 20 passengers and was more reliable and faster.

The summer programme featured 19 flights a week from Belfast to Northolt. Some of the early routes, which in 1947 included Liverpool, Manchester, the Isle of Man, Glasgow, Carlisle and Newcastle, were flown by BEA using the long-serving DH89 Rapide biplanes, which could carry a maximum of eight passengers, as well as Avro Nineteens, another type inherited from RAS and a civil version of the famous Anson, with accommodation for seven passengers. (The Avro Nineteen has its own place in the aviation history of the Province as the type which flew the first non-stop Belfast to London schedule, operated by RAS from Sydenham to Croydon on 3rd December 1945. It had rather a narrow passenger cabin. Moving about the cabin was not made any easier by the main wing spar having to be climbed over. The comfort facility was rather basic, an Elsan toilet aft, secreted behind a curtain.) The service to Carlisle and Newcastle was briefly described by *Flight* magazine:

> The BEA service between Newcastle, Carlisle and Belfast will operate twice daily, excluding Sundays, from July 1st. There will be a minimum capacity of 520 seats a month, and fares for the single journey will be: Newcastle-Carlisle, £1 5s: Carlisle-Belfast, £3; Newcastle-Belfast, £5 19s; Newcastle-Isle of Man, £2 19s 6d.

Top: BEA's inaugural DC-3 flight to Nutts Corner on 19th May 1947. *(Guy Warner Collection)*

Center: A DH89A Rapide, G-AGLP, in BEA livery. *(Guy Warner Collection)*

Lower: An Avro 19 of Railway Air Services at Speke, Liverpool. *(via Bert Hutchinson)*

They were flown by DH89s, but lasted only a few months as destinations, as the load factors were not sufficient to sustain the services, both being terminated in October.

A very unusual type was used between 16th December 1946 and 10th August 1947 by Scottish Airlines (a subsidiary of Scottish Aviation) from Prestwick; the four-engine, high winged, 22 seat, 1935 vintage Fokker F.XXII G-AFZP, a former KLM aircraft, which had been purchased by Scottish Aviation in August 1939 and must have made quite a sight in its orange and silver livery. [1]

---

1 PH-AJP Papagaai (Parrot) was reregistered as G-AFZP, impressed into the RAF as HM160 and used for a variety of tasks, including transport, training, communications and supply dropping. In 1944 was returned to the owners and overhauled. After returning from Nutts Corner for the last time, it was used for a just a few local joy-riding flights and thereafter remained in storage until scrapped in 1952.

The striking Fokker F.XXII, G-AFZP, of Scottish Airlines. *(Richard Riding Collection)*

In July 1947 *Flight* reported, with considerable attention to technical details:

Belfast's airport is now Nutts Corner, as British European Airways (BEA) have made a firm stand in condemning Sydenham airport on the east side of Belfast docks for operating Dakotas. The Corporation made it quite clear that unless alternative accommodation could be provided, air services to Belfast would have to be cancelled; consequently, Nutts Corner was selected. The airport lies nine miles west-by-north of the centre of Belfast and only three miles from the shore of Lough Neagh. The Lough consequently provides an excellent area for letting-down in bad weather. It is rather interesting to note that the weather in the area, although invariably wet, seldom clamps down completely, and there is usually a sufficiently high ceiling to allow descent through cloud over the Lough and a visual approach to be made. The DH89 Rapides flying into Belfast do a normal QGH (Controlled Descent through Clouds) in these conditions as they are not fitted with SBA (Standard Beam Approach – blind landing radio navigation system); in fact, only a few are so fitted, and they are on the London services. The Dakotas, of course, are equipped with SBA. I was given to understand that Trans-Canada Airlines have already surveyed the airfield for possible diversion of transatlantic traffic. Nutts Corner is an ex-RAF airfield, but has several peculiarities and is certainly well equipped with flying facilities, but the accommodation is quite inadequate. The present arrangement for passengers involves a coach drive of several hundred yards around the perimeter.

An early view of the control tower and terminal at Nutts Corner, taken in 1948. *(L Engelen)*

The flying facilities include SBA, MF/DF (medium frequency direction finding), HF R/T (high frequency radio telephony), VHF R/T (very high frequency radio telephony); VHF DF (very high frequency direction finding) is being installed, and there is the possibility that SCS 51 (instrument landing system), VHF Cathode Ray DF, GCA (Ground Controlled Approach) and a second channel on MF/DF will be installed. There are sodium approach lights to all the runways and full contact lighting on the main runway in the east-west direction of 2,000 yards. The north-east south-west runway is 1,600 yards and the south-east north-west runway 1,250 yards. The airfield has been built with special taxying tracks with lighting controlled in sections from the tower. The taxi tracks are designed to allow aircraft to follow different routes to reach the same destination. The result is that at night-time only the route which the aircraft is to follow need be lighted, and if there is an obstruction on one section the alternative section may be used. There are now fifty BEA scheduled services passing through Nutts Corner each day. These are summer schedules, and by August there will probably be more than sixty, owing to the additional Aer Lingus service which is starting up on August 1st and will fly from Dublin through Belfast to Liverpool. During May 6,346 passengers were handled at the airport. As already mentioned, ex-RAF buildings are in use for passenger handling and office accommodation; there is, however, a plan to build a semi-permanent hut near the tarmac. All the buildings used by the Ministry and BEA have been painted white with red roofs, and one's first impression is rather that of a National Fire Service headquarters, especially with the three bright-red fire tenders and three ambulances outside the control tower; the whole effect, however, is clean and tidy, and although accommodation is cramped, the organization is most certainly efficient. The coach run to Belfast takes about twenty minutes. The new BEA premises in Imperial House, Donegall Square East, were opened on May 15th by HE the Earl Granville, Governor of Northern Ireland. They comprise a large double-fronted office and booking centre on the ground floor, and a waiting room in the rear of the building. On the ground floor there are additional offices, including the office of the Area Manager, who is responsible for BEA operations in Northern Ireland.

The BEA Booking Office in Donegall Square, Belfast in 1948. One of the junior members of staff was shorthand-typist, Miss Ruby Black, the mother of co-author, Guy Warner.
(L Engelen)

W Gamble was able to give further insight:

> Before these were ready the administrative staff worked temporarily in three rooms on the first

An Ulster Transport Authority (UTA) Leyland Tiger PS1, painted in BEA livery, loading passengers outside the BEA terminal, Glengall Street, Belfast. The Grand Opera House can be seen to the left and behind the bus. *(Guy Warner Collection)*

floor and it is interesting to recall now the morning when Mr RH Murphy, his secretary, Miss ME Cupples, Mr FA Robinson, Miss D Millar, and the writer settled down there among heaps of wood shavings and tins of paint. In the centre of the office was a table, borrowed from the LMS, piled high with BEA Routine Orders and copies of the many miscellaneous instructions that were so popular at that time. The big increase in passenger traffic during the year has imposed a heavy strain on the Booking Office staff who, being the first contact with the public, must always keep smiling. Many amusing stories could be told concerning the situations which arise in the Booking Office from time to time. There was, for instance, the old lady who, having never flown before, decided to try it, and called in the month of October to ask what the weather would be like on the 12th December as she wished to fly to Manchester on that date. Then there was the woman who asked for accommodation to be reserved to Glasgow on a particular day. The clerk, having completed the booking, collected the appropriate fare and when handing the ticket to her advised her of the time the coach departed for the Airport. He was rather taken aback when the woman, with an astonished look on her face, exclaimed, 'The coach? The Airport? I want to go by boat!'

With the end of the Second World War, Aer Lingus planned an ambitious expansion of its network and services, and it was envisaged that Belfast would play a key role in this development. In mid-January 1947 Aer Lingus officials carried out an inspection of Nutts Corner to review the facilities and make preliminary arrangements for the start of operations there later in the year. It was planned to open an Aer Lingus branch office in Belfast to handle passengers travelling on its services to Dublin and to the planned new destinations in the UK, as well as bookings for a transatlantic service.

The first Aer Lingus service on the route Dublin – Belfast – Glasgow commenced on 29th July 1947. This was followed by Dublin – Belfast – Liverpool on 6th October 1947. It is likely that most schedules were operated using DC-3s, of which the company had nine in its fleet. It is possible that Vickers Vikings were also used, as seven of these entered service in the summer and autumn of that year. The routes via Belfast did not prosper and were terminated on 10th March 1948.

The invaluable W Gamble once more noted:

> At the peak there were sixty aircraft movements per day and 13,750 passengers passed through Nutts Corner in the month of July. The forwarding of mail increased greatly in the Autumn of 1947 when the Post Office made arrangements to dovetail the air mail facilities into ordinary surface transmission services and the special fee was abolished.

During September and October 1947 (and again in the autumn of 1948), a considerable civil air operation took place. Because of severe milk shortages in England which was matched by a surplus in Northern Ireland, an airlift from Nutts Corner to Speke Airport in Liverpool and Squire's Gate, Blackpool was organised. The advantage over using sea transport was that the milk would arrive fresh and not sour. In 1947 the main effort was made by the Avro Lancastrians of Skyways Ltd, with BEA acting as agents. Each aircraft was tasked to fly four round trips daily, with a target of 14,000 gallons a day to be transported. The milk itself was carried in aluminium ten-gallon churns. On 3rd October 1947 one of the milk carriers came to grief, fortunately without any loss of life. It was a very foggy morning when the Avro Lancastrian, G-AHBU, *Sky Path* of Skyways Ltd attempted to take-off with a full load of 1000 gallons of milk in churns. It failed to gain height and tore through a boundary fence, crossed a rough field and struck the bank of a stream, before disintegrating and burning out. The pilot, Captain Ralph Stokes, navigator, Leonard Purvis and radio officer, William Bruce, were saved by Skyways' milk loaders and the airport crash crew, who had rushed to the scene. One of the crew suffered a broken ankle and head injuries, the others just shock.

In the March 1948 issue of *BEA Magazine*, W Gamble wrote:

> We have been busy recently with the organisation of the new booking system which has been introduced throughout the Division. Our Freight Section is now getting back to normal following the 'turkey invasion' at Christmas. The office on occasion resembles a miniature zoo

An Aer Lingus DC-3, EI-ACE, St Colmcille, being refuelled at Dublin Airport in the late 1940s. Note the fire extinguisher to the left. The vehicle is a Tweed 1200-gallon, 2-compartment refueller. *(Aer Rianta)*

A sister ship of the ill-fated G-AHBU, Avro Lancastrian, G-AHBZ, Sky Ambassador of Skyways Ltd. *(via Peter Myers)*

as the special 'attractions' carried include tropical fish, a goat, live turkeys and a Siamese cat.[2] It is also said that our Cargo Assistant was observed parading the City Hall grounds with a rather frightened greyhound bearing a BEA label! Irish linen has always been a vital dollar-earning material and is now playing an important part in the drive for increased exports. Many of the leading Northern Ireland linen firms are using our services for forwarding packages and samples to all parts of the world, particularly to North and South America. During the past weeks both Airport and Town Office staff have taken advantage of the facilities for an educational flight in order to gain experience of actual conditions. Work is proceeding on the new Terminal buildings at the Airport but they are not expected to be ready for occupation for some months yet. The first Annual Staff Dance at Belfast was held on Wednesday 17th December last, in the Carlton Ballroom in Donegall Place and proved a huge success. Our staff has been reduced recently by the departure of Mr AH Absolom, posted to Manchester, and Mr B Henderson, Personnel Representative, who had resigned to take up a similar position with a local firm. Genial John Dooley, the Aer Lingus representative in Belfast, has been posted to Liverpool. John was a great favourite at Belfast and delighted everyone with his pleasant personality and true Irish 'gift of the gab'.

A further article appeared in *Flight* magazine in August 1948,

After discussion with the Northern Ireland Advisory Council during his recent visit to Northern Ireland, Lord Pakenham, Minister of Civil Aviation, confirmed the decision to use Nutts Corner airfield as the air terminal for Belfast. In a subsequent statement giving reasons which prompted the decision, the Minister said that Nutts Corner had been chosen, after a survey of numerous RAF airfields in Northern Ireland, for its superiority in runway length, buildings, meteorological record, and in its possibilities for further extension. The rival claims of Sydenham airport as a terminal, situated as it was within the town of Belfast and built to serve the town, had also been seriously considered against Nutts Comer, which was situated nine miles from the town. Several operational reasons however, had led to the conclusion that the move to Nutts Corner from Sydenham was an urgent necessity for post-war scheduled services. Chief among those was the inadequacy of runway lengths at Sydenham for aircraft types being used, or rapidly being brought into use; the inadequacy of the runway layout for various wind directions, especially for smaller aircraft; and the obstructions to the approaches caused by distant high ground to the East and West, and, in the case of the nearer approaches, by dockyard gantries and shipping to the north-west, and by several obstacles including a high tension power line and pylon to the south-west. An additional drawback to Sydenham was that

---

2 On the subject of unusual passengers, is said that Lady Londonderry would habitually fly accompanied by her parrot in its cage.

during the winter, visibility was less than 2,000 yards on 18 per cent of occasions, as compared with five per cent at Nutts Corner. Further, as a result of the short runways and poor approaches the use of instrument approach aids would constitute a danger. For the same reasons night flying at Sydenham would be dangerous. The Minister pointed out that the MCA intended that Belfast should become a terminal for direct services to the Continent, and as the chosen airport had to be developed to international standards it was inadvisable to continue services into Sydenham.[3]

By the summer of 1948, as shown in a contemporary timetable, the airport was serving four destinations, London Northolt, Glasgow, Liverpool and Manchester, all by BEA Dakota. The monthly return fares were advertised as: £11 to London, £5.10.0 to Manchester and Liverpool and £4 to Glasgow.

In August 1948 the following short item appeared in *Flight*, with a somewhat provocative heading,

DOG IN THE MANGER
It is understood that the government of Eire has refused permission for Ulster Aviation Ltd to operate a scheduled air service between Belfast and Dublin. The Eire Department of Industry and Commerce is sheltering under the agreement between the United Kingdom government and the government of Ireland made in 1946 that the right to operate certain scheduled services should be reserved to Aer Lingus, which was reconstituted with British interests. The route at present between Dublin and Belfast was one of these so reserved, but Aer Lingus are operating no services. The Minister has considered it desirable, however, that the position of the government-sponsored company should not be jeopardized by granting permission to any other company for operating scheduled services on that route. Certain routes in England and Scotland have been granted to independent operators by the British Ministry of Civil Aviation on the recommendation of BEA. The British Corporation, however, has no jurisdiction over the Irish route and can do nothing to influence the Irish government's decision.

For the 1948 Milk Lift a Ground-controlled Approach (GCA) unit was installed at Speke and also at Nutts Corner. Extra air traffic control staff were brought in to handle the additional traffic. Bill Eames, who was a controller at the airport for many years, recalled that a Non-Directional Beacon was set up on Mew Island (which lies at the mouth of Belfast Lough) to assist the flow of traffic and that a 'Baltic Exchange' was set up in an airfield hut to allocate jobs to aircrew and aircraft. More charter companies were involved, using Handley Page Halifaxes, Douglas Dakotas and Consolidated Liberators. The Liberator and Halifaxes could each carry 110 ten-gallon milk churns, the Dakotas 56. There were no palletised,

---

3 Frank Pakenham's tour had included visits to Glasgow Renfrew, the Western Isles and Dublin. He succeeded to the title Earl of Longford in 1961.

mechanised loading systems in those days, each churn had to be manually lifted on board. The Massereene Hotel in Antrim town was taken over for the period of the Milk Lift and 100 aircrew and maintenance personnel were based in Belfast to support the operation. The airlift resumed on Tuesday 31st August 1948 and for the next six weeks, Nutts Corner became Britain's busiest airfield. Each day, around the clock, the 13 aircraft involved were scheduled to complete 60-70 round trips in an effort to maintain the two and a half pints per person, per week, milk ration. The target for each seven day period, to the end of October was 350,000 gallons. In an all-out effort, hundreds of workers toiled ceaselessly at Belfast on the first day of the airlift to get as near as possible to their target of clearing 50,000 gallons during the first 24 hours. The weather had taken a turn for the worse during the night and from 3 am to dawn, flights into Belfast had to be cancelled due to a 300 foot cloud-base. Two Dakotas tried to land, but had to divert back to Liverpool. The bad weather continued for the next few days, with a consequent reduction in flights. On 2nd September only 30,000 of the proposed 50,000 gallons got away, as during the night heavy rain meant that only eight flights could operate instead of the planned 16. Gradually however, the operation settled down, and most of the milk reached its destination on time. Sadly, in that year, a fatal accident occurred. A Halifax C.VIII, G-AJNZ, of World Air Freight Ltd departed Nutts Corner on the morning of 28th September 1948 carrying 1140 gallons of milk. This was the last of six round trips to and from Speke that it was scheduled to make during the period 27/28th September. The aircraft left Nutts Corner at 09.30 and had been in contact by radio until passing into the Northern Flight Information Region where contact was made with the Northern area controller. This was followed by further contact at 09.59 which ended abruptly mid-sentence with, 'I am over or abeam Isle of Man'. All subsequent attempts to contact the aircraft met with no response. A search was begun immediately and at about 12.30 the Commandant of Ronaldsway airport reported that the wreckage had been located. It had crashed into high ground, with the loss of all four crew members.[4] At the subsequent enquiry it was concluded:

> In the opinion of Air Commodore Vernon Brown CB, OBE[5], the Ministry of Civil Aviation's Chief Inspector of Accidents, the accident was due to the aircraft colliding with the summit of the mountain when being flown in cloud and was considered to be the result of an error of airmanship on the part of the Captain.

On 13th October the Scottish Airlines Liberator, G-AHZP, while on final approach to Liverpool, undershot the runway, hitting two approach lighting poles, stalled and crashed short of the runway threshold. All four crew members were slightly injured, while the aircraft

---

4 Pilot, Captain John Savage, navigator, Richard Miller, radio operator, Oswald Hiscock and flight engineer, Albert Noon.
5 Vernon Brown is regarded as being largely responsible for the increased safety of air transport as a result of his efforts in the development of air crash investigation between 1937 and 1952. During his tenure he laid the foundations of an effective organisation, using techniques which would eventually be more concerned with preventing future accidents as opposed to simply determining the causes. He received a knighthood in 1952. (rafweb.org)

was written off, together with a considerable amount of spilled milk.

The scheme continued until early November, when with the approach of even worse winter weather, coupled with demand falling as England recovered from the shortage, meant that lesser quantities of milk (7,000 gallons a day) could be transported by ship to meet the demand.

At its peak the Ulster Milk Lift resulted

Consolidated LB-30 Liberator 1, G-AGZI, of Scottish Airlines. *(Barry Friend Collection)*

Handley Page Halifax C.VIII, G-AKEC, of Lancashire Aircraft Corporation at Nutts Corner, with milk churns in the foreground. *(Ernie Cromie Collection)*

in up to 30,000 gallons of milk a day being transported by air. The cost to the consumer was subsidised by the government by about two or three pence a pint. There is no doubt that some of the skills learned on this operation were soon applied in the more testing circumstances of the Berlin Airlift.[6]

---

6 Operators involved in the Ulster Milk Lift:
1947: Skyways with three Avro Lancastrians at Belfast. Drawn from: G-AGLV, G-AHBT, G-AHBU, G-AHBZ, G-AHCC. Lost G-AHBU w/o.
1948: Scottish Airlines with two Liberators at Belfast. Drawn from: G-AGZH, G-AHZP & G-AHZR. Lost G-AHZP w/o.
Scottish Airlines with two Dakotas at Belfast. Drawn from: G-AGWS, G-AGZF, G-AGZG, G-AKNM.
Lancashire Aircraft Corporation, two Halifax at Blackpool. Had around 12 a/c, known to have used G-AKEC.
British American Air Services, two Halifax at Blackpool. Likely G-AKBB & G-AKGN.
Bond Air Service, one Halifax at Blackpool. Drawn from: G-AIOI, G-AIWW.
World Air Freight, one Halifax at Liverpool. Only had one, & lost G-AJNZ w/o.
Air Transport Charter, two Dakotas at Liverpool. Drawn from: G-AJBH, G-AJVZ, G-AKIL.
Ciro's Aviation, one Dakota at Liverpool. Drawn from: G-AIJD, G-AKJN.
VIP Services, one Halifax used by other operators, G-AJPK.

Taken in 1947 at Ards, this photograph shows a Ford Prefect being loaded for the first car-carrying flight to the Isle of Man in the Miles Aerovan, G-AJTD. Mr RE Hamilton, appears in the photograph with Wing Commander TWT McComb OBE, Managing Director of Ulster Aviation. The car had been sold to an antique dealer on the Isle of Man. *(Ernie Cromie Collection)*

In the 1940s Northern Ireland had its own fledgling airline, which occasionally used Nutts Corner. Ulster Aviation Ltd had been formed at Newtownards as Londonderry Air Charter in November 1946 by the Marquis of Londonderry. It had a fleet of six Miles Aerovans. They were employed from 1947-49 on tourist traffic to the Isle of Man and Blackpool. Freight was charged at three shillings (15p) per ton mile. A return trip from Newtownards to the Isle of Man for a party of nine passengers would have cost 37 shillings (£1.85) per head, while the return fare to Blackpool was £4. The first car-carrying flight in an Aerovan between Newtownards and the Isle of Man was in 1947. A Ford Prefect had been sold to an antique dealer on the island and was airlifted there in G-AJTD. In the summer of 1948, the company was granted a BEA Associate Agreement for regular tourist flights between Newtownards and Aberdeen. A contemporary newspaper advert offered pleasure flights from Nutts Corner on Saturdays and Sundays at a cost of ten shillings, under the slogan, 'See your home from the air.' Ulster Aviation also operated an Airspeed Consul, a pair of Rapides, a Miles Falcon Six, two Miles Gemini Mk1As and two Miles Messenger Mk.2As. On 26th February 1949 Ulster Aviation and Mannin Airways established North-West Airlines (IOM) as a joint venture, with Rapides and an Aerovan, as well as several Geminis and Messengers. In 1950-51 the company operated a scheduled service to Blackpool and Leeds but was bought out by the Lancashire Aircraft Corporation which was based at Blackpool.[7]

Meanwhile, the indefatigable W Gamble described further enhancements to passenger booking:

> Business increased at such a rate that it was found that the waiting room accommodation at Imperial House was inadequate and, in addition, there was considerable traffic congestion outside the premises. Consequently, through the good offices of Mr GB Howden and Mr HS Knott of the Great Northern Railway, arrangements were made for the erection of temporary buildings on that Company's

---

7 Aircraft operated by Londonderry Air Charter/Ulster Aviation Ltd included: Miles Aerovans Mk.2 G-AGWO and the Mk.4s G-AJKJ, 'KU, 'OB, 'TD and 'HD, Airspeed Consul G-AIKT, a pair of DH Rapides G-AGIF and G-AHLN, a Miles Falcon Six G-AECC, Miles Gemini Mk1As G-AIHM and G-AKEJ and two Miles Messenger Mk.2As, G-AJFH and 'KL.

property at Glengall Street, in a position close to the City centre and beside the main terminus of the line from Dublin. These premises comprise an entrance lobby, spacious passenger waiting room, left luggage office, traffic counter and office and a freight office. They were opened by the Lord Mayor of Belfast on 1st September 1948. The boys at Glengall Street often act as a buffer between frustrated passengers and Airport officials and their job requires a high degree of courtesy and tact. Facilities for handling freight traffic at the Donegall Square East premises were rather limited and since the opening of the Terminal at Glengall Street this section has really come into its own.

In December *Flight* magazine devoted another article to Nutts Corner:

The new terminal buildings at Nutts Corner airport were officially opened jointly by Mr GS Lindgren MP, Parliamentary Secretary to the Ministry of Civil Aviation, and Mr G D'Erlanger CBE, chairman of BEA, on November 26th 1948. The opening ceremony was attended by the Governor of Northern Ireland, His Excellency Vice-Admiral the Earl of Granville KCVO, CB, DSO; the Minister of Commerce, Senator Major the Rt Hon Sir Roland Nugent DL; the Lord Mayor of Belfast, Sir William Neill MP; and chairman of the Northern Ireland Civil Aviation Advisory Council, Mr WA Edmenson CBE. Mr Lindgren reported on the work that had been done to Belfast Airport in the past two years, during which time the sum of £163,000 had been spent. The new terminal is a semi-permanent structure which will be replaced by permanent buildings. It has been made up of a number of prefabricated hut sections recovered from military camps used during the war. Approximately £30,000 a year would be allocated to maintain the facilities and when fully complete the permanent landing installation would be up to the standard required at a first class airport. Mr Lindgren said that expansion and continuation of existing services would be dependent upon the load factor and demand from the people of Ulster.

Upper: A lovely composite of the cafe, entrance, control tower and apron. *(Mike Charlton Airportpostcards.com)*

Lower: Cars belonging to the staff park by the control tower, a Viking can just be made out in the background. *(Mike Charlton Airportpostcards.com)*

The recent Milk Lift showed the capability of the airport to handle heavy traffic in all weather conditions to be considerably in excess of the present traffic. During a period of eight weeks while Nutts Corner was handling the milk run traffic in addition to normal scheduled services and charter flights, the total number of landings and take-offs amounted to 4,779; the maximum in any one period of 24 hours was 118 movements. During September Nutts Corner was the third busiest airport in the UK, after Northolt and London Airport; actual figures of aircraft movements during the month being Northolt 4,708, London Airport 3,176 and Nutts Corner 2,995.

The work of transforming an ex-RAF station into a first class civil airport has been proceeding continuously since December 1946. This has entailed grouping all buildings in one compact area rather than dispersing them as is necessary for military purposes. Structurally, the new passenger buildings have made little demand on the supplies of building materials since they are made up from a number of prefabricated hutments recovered from wartime military camps. These have been masked by gables to give the buildings an individualistic appearance. The likelihood of direct communications between Ulster and the Continent has been borne in mind when laying out the arrangement of facilities for Customs services, immigration clearance and public health formalities. Large numbers of travellers have been envisaged and rooms have been planned so that in-coming and outgoing passenger flows are led clear of each other so as to avoid congestion. It is hoped that the restaurant, primarily intended for the convenience of air passengers, will become popular with motorists, and the management have provided a public enclosure with buffet for the convenience of visitors. Mr D'Erlanger, who received the key of the buildings from Mr Lindgren, stressed that these buildings, though a progressive step, were not meant to be regarded as more than an interim measure. He quoted figures illustrating the growth of the service in and out of Belfast and said that although in the light of present requirements the new buildings might appear commodious they might well be insufficient for traffic in a few years' time.

The reference to the various arrival formalities above is of particular interest as a contemporary BEA timetable advised:

Passengers are reminded that for entry into Northern Ireland passports or travel permits are required and these should be carried with them and not packed in their luggage. They are advised to verify the validity and accuracy of such documents, as BEA cannot accept any responsibility for the consequences of non-compliance with regulations.

A further enhancement was noted in *Flight* in April 1949 and harks back to the days when a trip to the airport was a popular family outing:

Two BEA Dakotas in front of the spectators' terrace at Nutts Corner. *(via Jim Rankin)*

Public enclosures at civil airfields have in recent years done much to increase national interest in air affairs, especially when combined with an informative loudspeaker system. With the advent of better weather, a number of Ministry of Civil Aviation enclosures all over the country are being opened. Among those now open are Birmingham, Bristol (Whitchurch), Cardiff, Croydon, Hurn, Weston, Prestwick, Yeadon and Renfrew. The public will be admitted to London Airport and Northolt from April 13th, and other enclosures opening soon are Belfast (Nutts Corner), May 7th; Blackpool, April 14th; Liverpool, May 26th. Facilities for joyriding will be arranged at all airfields, but are restricted by traffic congestion at Northolt, Croydon and London Airport.

Another relatively short-lived service to Northern Ireland was flown by Air France. On 13th June 1949 it began a direct link between Nutts Corner and Paris, Le Bourget, using 33-seat, four-engine SE.161 Languedoc airliners. It operated three days per week, on Mondays, Wednesdays and Saturdays from Belfast, with a return fare of £28.16.0, with a cheaper rate at the weekend and provided a summer schedule in 1949 and 1950. *Flight* magazine added:

The nose section of the graceful SNCASE SE.161 Languedoc, F-BCUP. *(Guy Warner Collection)*

The service will be an extension of the direct Glasgow-Paris route which has been operated since 1946. It will take three hours, stopping for a short time at Prestwick, and reaching Paris before midday, in time to connect with services to the French Riviera, Switzerland, Corsica, New York and Cairo. By stopping overnight in Paris, connections can be made with Rome, North and West Africa, South America, India and the Far East. It is significant as the first scheduled service to operate from Northern Ireland to the European mainland.

In an interesting footnote to this part of the story, the author received an email from Sam Kenny, a retired Station Manager at Vancouver Airport, British Columbia. He began working in the airport business at Nutts Corner in July 1957, when he was twenty-one years old:

> I was sitting in a BEA crew-car making its way over the mountain out of Belfast before arriving at Nutts Corner. On arrival, I noticed something rather odd. Not the funny little buildings or the few aircraft sitting on the tarmac but a long, wooden ship's gangway sitting out on the grass in front of the little flower garden with the flags. I knew a ship's gangway when I saw one, I had walked up one many times at Donegall Quay, boarding the Liverpool boat on my way to visit relatives in England. I could not wait to find out more about this gangway. The answers I got ranged from, 'I have no idea' to 'who cares.' Finally, I found someone who did tell me the story of the gangway. It appeared that Air France had operated a short-lived service from Belfast to Paris. There were no aircraft steps at the airport long enough for passengers to board their Languedoc aircraft so the airport authority at that time borrowed a gangway from the Belfast Docks. Air France and their Languedoc service were now long gone. The gangway remained rotting away on the airport lawn.

Airport Commandant HP Finch, with DH Dove, G-ALFT of the Civil Aviation Flying Unit behind. *(Public Record Office NI)*

Brian Finch was the son of the Airport Commandant, HP Finch. He kept a detailed log of the aircraft which he spotted at Nutts Corner, which yields much interesting information about the traffic over a period of about 10 years from the late 1940s onwards. He noted many of the Languedocs and also in those early years, something of a rarity, an Avio Linee Italiane tri-motor Fiat G.212, bringing in a cargo of motorbikes.

The last year of the decade brought a tragic event. On the morning of 19th August 1949, the BEA Dakota G-AHCY, under the command Captain Frank Pinkerton, took off from Nutts Corner on a scheduled flight to Manchester with twenty-six passengers and three crew members on board. Most of this flight was under Instrument Flight Rules due to cloud cover. As with wartime flights, navigation was aided by radio navigation with the crew utilising their GEE receiver to gain a positional fix while off Blackpool at 12.40 and subsequently D/F fixes from the ground stations at Blackpool Squires Gate and Manchester Ringway. The co-pilot, First Officer Holt, was acting as navigator during the flight and recorded their positions and other notes in the navigation log. This was found in the wreckage and was the only useful item from onboard the aircraft to aid the investigation and subsequent Court of Inquiry. At 12.45 Holt noted a change of course by seven degrees to starboard as they were north of their intended track, however the Court of Inquiry concluded that this change of course was not made as at the time the pilot reported crossing the Standard Beam Approach radio beam the aircraft was some 11 nautical miles NE of where it should have been. At 12.49 the pilot contacted the duty controller at Ringway to state that they were, 'Approaching from NW at 3,500 feet, descending to 1,500 flying under IFR, ETA 11.57' (the time was recorded as GMT). When the aircraft passed through the radio beam the pilot turned to fly along the beam before making a procedural turn to turn the aircraft through 180 degrees and end up flying back down the beam towards Ringway.

An hour after take-off, at 12.59, the last radio contact with the crew occurred and about one minute later the aircraft crashed. It was flying at approximately 1,350 feet when it hit a mist-covered hill at Wimberry Stones on Saddleworth Moor, near Oldham, 15 miles from Manchester Airport. The aircraft was flying with the undercarriage lowered in preparation for landing but was further east than it should have been. The normal procedure for landing at Ringway in IFR conditions was that the aircraft should over-fly the 'cone of silence' in the radio beam that was directly overhead the transmitter station on the airfield but this was not done and was considered to be one of the three factors that caused the accident.

The ill-fated Dakota, G-AHCY, of BEA at Manchester Ringway Airport in 1949. *(Guy Warner Collection)*

The rescue was hampered by bad weather and the remote location of the crash site. Workers from a paper mill approximately three-quarters of a mile away formed a human chain to carry the injured from the hillside to lower ground and a doctor at the scene said:

> I found bodies scattered all over the place. There were a few survivors lying groaning on the hillside but some of them died before I could attend to them. I have been a doctor since 1914 and served in both wars, but this was the worst sight that I have ever seen.

In all, eight of the passengers survived, with 21 fatalities. The cause of the accident was an error in navigation, incorrect approach procedure and failure to check the position of the aircraft accurately before the descent from a safe height.

To conclude this chapter concerning the early post-war years at Nutts Corner, the following is another extract from the article written by W Gamble, which appeared in the November 1949 issue of *British European Airways Magazine*:

> We have combined the duties of Loader and Truck driver and the arrangement has worked very satisfactorily. Mr Norman Thompson, Head Loader-Driver, was originally in railway transport while another Loader-Driver, Danny McAuley, has practically grown up with the job, having commenced as a boy porter in 1942. The MT section consists of Senior Driver WHC Stevenson, and three other drivers. Fitters A Mathers and N Logan keep the vehicles in trim. The three BEA minibus "Crewcar" drivers, who conveyed flight crew members to hotel in Belfast, in addition to Bill Stevenson were; Bob Adams, Charlie Cable and Fred Porteous[8].
>
> During the time the services were operated from Sydenham the aircraft maintenance was undertaken by Messrs Short Bros & Harland Ltd, whose factory in Belfast is located alongside Sydenham Airport, and with the amalgamation of the various companies into British European Airways the maintenance staff employed there were given the opportunity to transfer to BEA. Mr JR Kennedy, Station Engineer, commenced his career with Airwork Ltd in 1933 and joined Shorts in 1939. He gained experience at many places in Great Britain during the war years in the course of his duties with the Civil Repair Organisation.

BEA Assistant Foreman CA Blackstock, Station Engineer John Kennedy, assistant Foreman R Wylie and Radio Maintenance Engineer L Engelen. *(WS Crawford and the BA Archive)*

---

8 Now and again, they gave young aircraft enthusiast, Joe Brown, lifts if no crew were on board.

He has under his supervision a fine staff, who take a pride in their standard of aircraft maintenance. Malcolm Templeton, one of our engineers, is a well-known motor cycle racing enthusiast who competes regularly in the Isle of Man. He has won many awards in Northern Ireland, including first place in the Cookstown 100 in 1948. Radio Mechanic L Engelen is a keen photographer and took two of the photographs published with this article.

Passengers are conveyed between the Airport and the City Terminal by buses hired from the Ulster Transport Authority and which have been painted in BEA colours. The route covers part of the famous Ulster Grand Prix Clady Circuit motor cycle race course and many cross-channel visitors use BEA services when coming to see the race each year. Travellers find the bus journey interesting from the sight-seeing angle and on a clear day there are extensive views, not only over the city and the sea, but across Lough Neagh to the hills of Tyrone and Londonderry or over the Lagan Valley and across County Down to the Mourne Mountains.

In the same issue JRP O'Neill contributed a brief piece entitled, Ulster Exile:

The British Services passenger building is full of people; there is plenty of talk and a thrill of excitement in the air, for these are no ordinary passengers, they are the exiles returning to Ulster. Every Bank Holiday you see them filling the Belfast service, and the homely accents of the North of Ireland are in evidence all around. What a change from the tiresome train and boat journey of the old days, off which one arrived exhausted at home and usually had to start travelling back the next day. Now after an easy trip of two hours we are practically on our own doorstep. We are a miscellaneous lot; the serious-looking young curate from a local suburb, a married couple with two young children who look as if they will keep the steward busy, a rather pretty girl with auburn hair who might be a mannequin, with her fiancé; two engineering students who are discussing their lectures. Then comes the welcome call from the Tannoy, and we walk briskly across the tarmac to the waiting 28-seater Dakota. The steward on the Belfast run has a busy time looking after us, but he is in good form, and from his voice hails from the North of Ireland himself. Conversation now flows freely in the aircraft, and some of the stouter passengers have difficulty in turning round in their safety belts to speak to friends in the seats behind. In a few minutes we are airborne, and the steward comes round with his appetising dinner boxes and coffee. Soon we are over Birmingham, then Rhyl, and then speeding across the Irish Sea. How small the occasional ship looks below. We have a lovely view of the Isle of Man, and then, but never soon enough, the County Down coast and Strangford Lough. The view of the Ards Peninsula and the compact whitewashed cottages and larger farm houses are a lovely introduction to the Ulster scene and are like manna to the exile. On disembarking we notice it has been raining heavily, and there is a stiff breeze blowing. Typical Northern Ireland weather! Still,

A UTA Leyland Tiger PS1, painted in BEA livery, at Nutts Corner, with BEA Dakota, G-AGHM, Edward Maitland, in the background. *(Guy Warner Collection)*

we would not have it any other way, for the soft moisture gives those varying hues of green to the landscape. I get a handshake from Mr Thurley, the Station Superintendent, and climb into the bus. We all crane our necks until we see our own baggage on board, extraordinary habit, but natural.

Outside, the bus is painted the familiar BEA grey, but inside it retains its original green coachwork, which to the returning exile is another symbol that he is home. At the Great Northern Railway Station in Belfast, the cheery Mr Pollock greets us. Friends gather round the bus, a clergyman meets the girl with the auburn hair and her fiancé, an elderly lady collects the curate, the two engineering students go off in a taxi, and those of us who have not been met at the Airport disperse our various ways. I collect my bag and walk a few yards to catch a tram, and am on my own doorstep by ten o'clock, having left my office at six. Good smooth going, BEA!

In 1949, BEA issued a timetable for Northern Ireland. *(Guy Warner Collection)*

Chapter 15

Nutts Corner in the 1950s

A LINK WITH THE airport's military past was made and, as reported in *Flight*,

With effect from 1st May 1950, Air Commodore NAP Pritchett has been appointed Air Officer Commanding No 67 (Northern Ireland) Reserve Group and Senior Air Force Officer in Northern Ireland. He previously served in his new command in 1941-42, when he formed, and became CO of, the Coastal Command Station at Nutts Corner. Most of his war service was spent with Coastal Command. Born in 1903, he was commissioned from Cranwell in 1923 and served with the Fleet Air Arm for some years before the war, in the carriers *Argus*, *Furious* and *Glorious*.

It was also reported that 7913 passengers had arrived or departed from the airport in April, making it the third busiest in the UK after Glasgow, Renfrew and London, Northolt. Birmingham was added to the BEA Nutts Corner route structure in May 1950. In this period Nutts Corner and BEA handled nearly all of the Province's airline traffic, using Dakotas. These were renamed the *Pionair* Class after being converted by Scottish Aviation at Prestwick to 32-passenger configuration with built-in airstairs. New British cockpit instrumentation allowed the radio operator to be dispensed with, thus freeing up the extra cabin space. Some of the conversions retained the rear double door and could be speedily reconfigured for either cargo or passenger work, being known as Pionair Leopards. All the upgraded aircraft were renamed after British aviation pioneers and entered service in January 1951. From 12th March 1951 an all-freight, six times weekly, night mail service was flown by Pionair Leopards from Manchester to Belfast. In the same year the Pionairs were joined on the service to Northolt by Vickers Vikings, which was a tubby 29-seater based on the Wellington bomber.

This time the bus is attending the arrival of a BEA Viking. (Guy Warner Collection)

These would be converted to 36 seat configuration, with more modern instrumentation, again allowing for the

A striking in-flight study of the BEA Viking 1B, G-AJBR, Sir Bertram Ramsay, in the new company livery. *(Guy Warner Collection)*

Dakota, G-ALXN, Henry Royce, in the new BEA colour scheme. *(Guy Warner Collection)*

radio officer's position to be deleted. The first of these, named the *Admiral* Class, was delivered to BEA in 1952.

Another development for the airline at this time was the change of aircraft livery from the original bare metal finish to an attractive scheme with the upper fuselage painted white with a burgundy cheatline above the cabin windows.

On 27th March 1951 the Dakota, G-AJVZ, of Air Transport Charter departed from Manchester on a mail flight to Nutts Corner. Just after take-off from Runway 06, 'VZ was unable to gain height and hit a tree half a mile from the runway threshold. It stalled, crashed in a field and was destroyed upon impact. Two crew members were killed while the third occupant was seriously injured. The probable cause was loss of engine power caused by ice formation in the carburettor intakes, attributable to the captain's failure to make use of the heat controls. An extended undercarriage and the presence of snow on the wings may have been contributory factors.

In May 1951, an article appeared in the *Belfast Telegraph*,

> I sat forward in my seat to watch the rapidly changing scenery below. The sheen of Lough Neagh first caught my eye. Then I saw the airport, a broad expanse of country criss-crossed by long runways and a tidy collection of red-roofed, white-walled buildings, bordered by a great lawn. After an excellent meal in the restaurant, we began our guided tour. In the main hall comfortable settees and armchairs help to make the lounge a friendly, cosy place in which to wait. The Airport, including its restaurant and buffet, is open to visitors. Conducted tours for schools, clubs etc can generally be arranged by application to the Airport management. A novel feature on the lawn almost in front of the terminal building is a map of the British Isles laid out in heather and turf and in correct geographical orientation. It is designed to show the main air routes between Belfast and the main airports of England and Scotland. Another attractive feature in the layout is the number of young trees donated by various groups, professional, scientific, industrial and social, as mementos of their visit.

One such Belfast-based organisation was the Woodvale Presbyterian Church Women's Missionary Association. The church magazine, the *Woodvale Record*, noted in October 1950:

> In August members and friends enjoyed a bus run to Belfast Airport at Nutts Corner, where they were entertained and shown round by some BEA staff. Some of the adventuresome members also enjoyed short flights over Lough Neagh, and all voted the visit a success.

A tree being planted at Nutts Corner by Mrs Martha Greer of Woodvale Women's Missionary Association. *(Mrs Mavis Riley)*

The writer went on to list and praise the radio and radar aids. He (or she) also noted the provision of medical and customs officers:

> Who are always available in the event of a Continental flight and the Immigration officers constantly on duty to examine travel permits of passengers travelling to and from other parts of the British Isles – and beyond. I was privileged to be taken behind the scenes to see at work the people who are directly responsible for the safety and regularity of air traffic. In the Control Tower ATC staff were transmitting instructions and advice by radio telephone to pilots in flight. On the desk nearby, girl radio telephonists, with their headphones on, were taking down the radio messages. Into the Teleprinter Office, operators were clacking away on their machines, informing distant airports of aircraft arrivals and departures. Further along the corridor of the operations building were the navigational and meteorological briefing offices. I eavesdropped here for a few minutes and heard airline pilots being briefed about the latest flight conditions along their routes. As we came out of the building, I saw, on the far side of the airfield, a collection of vivid orange-and-white painted caravans that looked like a small 'one-night-only' circus. It was, however, more interesting

The Ground Control Approach Radar Unit. The vehicles are a Hillman Husky and a Leyland Cub.
(John Douglas)

and even more thrilling than a circus, for it was the Ground Control Approach Radar Unit.

The unit, being necessarily self-contained, has its own small power station. One caravan serves as a restroom for the crew when off duty, and other caravans and trucks house the generating, radio and radar equipment. I was invited into the Radar Caravan to see the 'pictures.' It was dark inside – purposely so – to permit the dim, electronically-lit radar screens to be scanned for aircraft by the Radar Controllers. We were almost hemmed in by the mysterious radar and radio apparatus. The Controller pointed out an outline map of Nutts Corner airport superimposed, as it were, on the radar screen. Suddenly there appeared a small dot of light moving into the outer lines of the circular screen map. This was an approaching aircraft. In technical jargon the moving light is called a 'blip'. As we watched the movement of a blip, the Controller was able to tell me the height, direction and distance of the aircraft from the Airport. Hence the derivation of the composite term, RADAR, RA-dio, D-irection A-nd R-ange. Aircraft can be seen over thirty miles away, even in the thickest fog or darkest night. They are then guided to the approaches of the Airport and almost to the beginning of the landing runway. An ingenious runway lighting system further assists the pilot to steer the aircraft right up to the terminal building. Time was getting on so I had to conclude my most interesting tour and catch the city-bound airport coach.

That summer brought an imposing sight to Ulster skies, as witnessed by local enthusiast, Bob Wilson, who was a regular visitor to Nutts Corner and other local airfields:

Saturday 25th August 1951, Bristol 167 Brabazon I, G-AGPW, seen overhead Bangor at 2000 feet, the massive silver aircraft made a left turn to head back to the Sydenham Air Show. The eight Centaurus engines, each coupled to four contra-rotating propellers, made a very strange deep whirring sound which seemed to hang in the air after the aircraft had passed. It had first flown on 4th September 1949 but the second prototype was not completed and the entire project for BOAC North Atlantic services was scrapped in 1953.

The Brabazon was indeed an overly ambitious white elephant. However, Bob Wilson's Spotter's Log for the 1950s and 1960s was anything but! This was Nutts Corner's heyday and Bob was no ordinary spotter. He researched the background to the aircraft he logged, added

The mighty Bristol 167 Brabazon I, G-AGPW, seen overhead Bangor by Bob Wilson on 25th August 1951. *(Barry Friend Collection)*

Miles Gemini, G-AJWH, with the notable racing driver, Prince Bira. *(Peter Amos Collection)*

his thoughts and impressions, so compiling a record which remains very useful to posterity and also gives a flavour of the times. In the course of this narrative, further quotes will be made from Bob's records.

In the same year Brian Finch logged the variety of smaller aircraft which had brought in spectators for the TT race on the nearby new Dundrod Circuit. These included a pair of Miles Geminis, an Avro Anson, a DH 89 Dragon Rapide, a Percival Proctor, a Taylorcraft Plus D, a Miles Messenger and a General Aircraft Cygnet II. He added that three Ferrari cars taking part in the race were brought in by an Avro York of Skyways. One of the Geminis, G-AJWH, belonged to the famous racing driver, Prince Bira of Siam,[1] who competed in the Ulster Trophy in 1952.[2]

Developed from the famous Lancaster bomber, Avro 685 York C1, G-AHEY, of Skyways of London. *(Ralf Manteufel)*

---

1 Prince Birabongse Bhanudej Bhanubandh (1914-1985) raced in Formula One and Grand Prix races for the Maserati, Gordini, and Connaught teams. In 1946, when the race was held on the Ballyclare Circuit, he had been the winner.
2 A full-size replica racing car sculpture, designed by Skelton Rainey and manufactured by Knight Design Engineering, was unveiled by the Mayor of Newtownabbey at Ballyrobert in 2014 to commemorate Prince Bira and his English Racing Automobiles car.

Chapter 16

Northern Ireland's Worst Air Disaster

THE YEAR 1953 OPENED with a tragic loss of life. On 5th January, the Viking 1B, G-AJDL, *Lord St Vincent*, crashed at Nutts Corner on arrival from Northolt, with four crew, 31 passengers and 925 lbs of baggage and cargo on board. Twenty-four of the passengers and three members of the crew died.

The BEA Viking 1B, G-AJDL, Lord St Vincent, which crashed at Nutts Corner on 5th January 1953. *(Richard Riding Collection)*

G-AJDL had departed from Northolt at 19.27, about 25 minutes late. Two hours later it was on approach to Nutts Corner. It was a moonless, cold night but it should have been a routine landing. By 20.53 the Viking was crossing the Irish coast at a height of 5500 feet and came under the control of Nutts Corner's ATC. At 21.26 Captain Hartley[1] was advised that he would be landing on Runway 28. When the aircraft was three miles out from the runway threshold it was 90 feet above the glide-slope. Rain clutter on the screen at Nutts Corner obscured the image received by ATC. Captain Hartley was advised that he could opt to overshoot.

Joe Brown recalls:

> My mother was making supper at the kitchen window directly below the centre-line threequarters of a mile from touchdown, and shouted 'that's really low' before it started to hit the poles.

Some 30 seconds later Captain Hartley replied that he could see the runway lights. The aircraft could be seen from the ground as it broke cloud and it appeared to be at a steeper

---

1 Gordon Hartley had served in Bomber and Transport Commands during the war, had attained the rank of Squadron Leader and been awarded the DFC.

angle of descent than usual. It then rapidly lost height and hit the pole supporting an approach light a short distance from the runway. It was normal for aircraft to approach low over the Killead to Dundrod road, so much so that the control tower operated traffic lights on the road to stop traffic when aircraft were on their final approach. Following the initial impact the aircraft hit five further poles, knocking off the tops of three of them. It was now flying 113 feet below its glidepath and well short of the runway threshold. It touched down in a field and skidded on before colliding with a mobile standard beam approach van and then striking a brick building, housing equipment operating the instrument landing system, about 760 feet from the runway. This impact caused the aircraft to break up. It was now 21.38.

Bill Eames, in the centre, was the talk down air traffic controller at the time of the crash. *(Ernie Cromie Collection)*

The *Belfast Telegraph* reported:

> From the visitors' lounge in the airport building, where friends and relatives were waiting, the hum of the plane's engines could be heard growing louder. The aircraft glistened under the glare of the runway lights, coming in low. Then, only 200 yards away there was a deafening roar, two blinding flashes and the aircraft 'split up into two balls of fire'. One of its engines was hurled over 40 yards and pieces of flaming wreckage were strewn over a wide area as rescue squads rushed out.

An ambulance crew's experience has been recorded. It is graphic in content:

> There was no warning to the crew of Paddy O'Hanlon, Tommy and Lilly of the impending disaster. It was during the evening that they received the call to Nutts Corner for an aircraft crash, as they went over the Ligoniel hill towards Ballyhill they could see, in the darkness, the glow of the fire from the direction of the airport, they realised that this was going to be a bad one.[2]
>
> On arrival they parked on the road which leads to Dundrod, along with the other emergency vehicles. The crash site was lit by the floodlights from the airport fire tenders but beyond the range of the lights it was very dark indeed. Paddy and Tommy took a stretcher and some equipment into the fields accompanied by Lilly, the field was a mess and with the darkness it made it very difficult to make good

---

2 Paddy O'Hanlon (1923–2016) was also one of the last links from the emergency services to the *Princess Victoria* disaster of January 1953. His first experience of helping in a major emergency was as a volunteer firefighter while still a teenager during the Belfast Blitz. He joined the Northern Ireland Hospital Authority in 1950 and began a long career based in Ardoyne, initially operating out of its fire station. He was much admired by his colleagues and was regarded as a true gentleman.

progress. Before they got close to the scene they were approached by a fireman carrying the lifeless body of a 9-10 year old girl, Lilly and the fireman took the body back to the ambulance and Paddy and Tommy carried on towards the aircraft. There they placed the body of a man on the stretcher and assisted by firemen they made their way back towards the road and the ambulance. As they made their way in darkness over the muddy fields Tommy tripped and stumbled over what he thought was the branch of a tree, by the light of the fireman's torch they discovered that some of the contents of the patient's abdominal cavity was trailing on the ground and this caused Tommy to trip, an indication of the extent of the man's injuries and the types of jobs that ambulance men are expected to undertake.

On arriving back at the ambulance, they discovered that both stretchers contained bodies and Lilly was sitting on the attendant's seat which was fixed to the bulkhead of the vehicle with the child on her knees, they placed their patient on the floor of the ambulance and took all four casualties to hospital for certification. They returned to the scene and Paddy remembers that the firemen were trying to release the body of one of the pilots from the flight deck of the aircraft, he was heavily entrapped. The crew were no longer required at the scene and returned to Ardoyne; only the crew of Bertie Crawford and Bill Chasty remained at the scene. A night to remember or perhaps forget.'[3]

A Board of Inquiry was formed to investigate the accident, chaired by Sir David Cairns, QC. It opened in London on 14th April 1953. After hearing evidence, the board found no indication of mechanical failure. The documentation of the aircraft was in order, the crew were properly qualified, and control procedures were correctly carried out. It concluded that, on the evidence available there existed such conditions as could properly be described as deceptive to the pilot, and that Captain Hartley made 'errors of judgement' but that no 'moral blame' was to be attached to him regarding the accident. The board mentioned that hitting the van stopped any chance of the aircraft reaching the runway, and then hitting the building made a tragedy inevitable. The approach lights were found to not be at the top of the poles, to ease maintenance; although that was not judged a factor in the crash, the lights were moved to the top of the poles following the accident. It was also recommended that when the ILS building was rebuilt that it should be offset from the approach path, or that it should be sited underground.

---

3 *The survivors:* Mr Jack Brower, Miss Kathleen Browne, Mr Roy Fairclough, Mrs TGW Haughton, Master Daniel Hill, Mrs Prescott, Mr P Scarlett, Mr James Young (Cabin Steward)
The passengers who died were: Mrs Patricia Auld, Mr AC Barnes, Miss Naomi Brudno, Miss G Clutsom, Miss Eida Duerken, Mr RC Easterbrook, Miss Dolores Griffin, Father Patrick Joseph Hackett CC, Captain TGW Haughton, Mrs Jane Hill, Mrs Patricia Kavanagh, Frances Kavanagh (16 month old child of previous) Mr J Lawrence, Mr Douglas J Maw, Mr GH Mishon, Miss Agnes McConville, Mrs PJ McGarvey, Miss Irene McKibbin, Mrs Elizabeth Pawlicz, Mr LA Rees, Mrs Greta Tweed, Master Brian Tweed (10 year old son of previous), Mr E Wiggins, Mr Jeffrey Wilks.
Members of the crew who died were: Captain GH Hartley DFC, First Officer RD Hayes, Radio Officer TRA Merry.

This remains the worst single air disaster to occur in Northern Ireland. Nearly 70 years later the events of that tragic night still wake memories, as in this letter to the *Belfast Telegraph* of 13th January 2022 from Gordon Harper:

> January 5th will be, for me, a stark reminder of the appalling Nutts Corner Air disaster. Among those who perished was Mrs Greta Tweed, with her young son, Brian, on their 1952 Christmas visit to Croydon. Mrs Tweed's husband was Manager of the original Greyhound in Croydon. I was a member of the dining room staff and would serve Mrs Tweed and her son many times during their stay which they always seemed to be enjoying so much. There is bitter irony in my recalling Mrs Tweed telling me how Brian was looking forward to his airplane journey and how much better air travel was compared to the old Belfast to Heysham boat. I shall never forget the numb feeling of shock felt when a tearful staff member broke the news that dark, chilly morning – now so long ago that the terrible event is described as the forgotten tragedy. A particularly vivid memory of their departing day from the hotel is that of Brian, with his autograph book, collecting all of our signatures. With such a personal memory how can I regard it as a forgotten tragedy?

In an email to the author, he added:

> Regarding my association with the Tweed family; back in 1950, when Mr Tweed was Assistant Manager of the old City Hotel here in Derry, which, incidentally, was one of six hotels owned by the Ulster Transport Authority, he interviewed and engaged me as a trainee commis waiter. I was there until 1952. When Mr Mann, the General Manager, moved over to England to take up his post as manager of the Greyhound, Mr Tweed went with him. Mr Mann offered me a similar move, which I gladly accepted. Coming up to Christmas, Mrs Tweed and young Brian arrived. A vivid memory I have of Mr and Mrs Tweed is that of New Year's Eve, when I served them drinks in their room. That's when Mrs Tweed asked me if I would be going to Derry for a holiday and, very difficult this part, stressed to me the comfortable way of travel was by air. It all happened so long ago and I was only 18, but from when Mrs Tweed arrived until that dreadful morning when the news came through – it is etched deeply in my memory.

Chapter 17

Transatlantic Travel

A COUPLE OF MONTHS later, just before midnight on Sunday, 22nd March 1953, BOAC Constellation G-AKCE departed Nutts Corner on a scheduled commercial flight: 24 of the passengers were rugby players from Queen's University, Belfast who were travelling to North America for a club tour. The flight originated in London and arrived at Nutts Corner from Prestwick, the intention being that it would fly on to New York via Gander, Newfoundland. However, weather conditions caused a delay at Prestwick and, in turn, after 'CE left Nutts Corner, it needed to refuel at Shannon before going on to New York. The team played five games in British Columbia, then travelled 20 hours by train to California where they played a further five matches, winning all ten.

BOAC Lockheed Constellation, G-AKCE, photographed at London Airport on 12th September 1954. *(RA Scholefield)*

The return trip to Nutts Corner was scheduled for Tuesday, 28th April. All was fine until about an hour out from the Irish coast, one of the engines developed a fault and had to be shut down. Rather than fly to Nutts Corner, the captain decided to go straight to the maintenance base at London Airport. This proved to be a good decision because, prior to arrival, a second engine gave trouble and they were met at London with fire engines and ambulances. The result was that the team returned to Nutts Corner on Wednesday, on another BOAC Constellation en route to New York. It is believed these were the first planned commercial trans-Atlantic flights from/to Nutts Corner. There were at least two other BOAC Constellations at Nutts Corner in 1953 as there were two earlier instances of diversions. The first was in January 1953 and the next was the Montreal to Prestwick flight on 15th March 1953 when, as a precautionary measure, fire engines and ambulances were alerted to its early morning unscheduled arrival. From records kept by Brian Finch three registrations are recorded – G-AHEJ, G-AHEL and the above, G-AKCE.

Other unusual visitors at about this time were Douglas C-54 Skymaster of the Indian carrier, Bharat Airways and a Douglas DC-6B of the Dutch airline KLM. The reason for their arrival at Nutts Corner is not known.

DC-6B, PH-DFA, of KLM, Royal Dutch Airlines, founded in 1919, at Nutts Corner. *(Ernie Cromie Collection)*

Douglas C-54, VT-CZT, of Indian carrier Bharat Airways, one of eight airlines nationalised to form Indian Airlines in 1953, at a rain-swept Nutts Corner. *(Ernie Cromie Collection)*

Later that year came the first BEA Airspeed Ambassador service between Nutts Corner and Heathrow. A very elegant looking aircraft, the Ambassador had the BEA class name *Elizabethan*. It could carry between 47 and 60 passengers and was the largest piston-engine aircraft ever operated by BEA. It was a perfectly good aeroplane of its type with passenger appeal, due to its high wing and excellent view from the large cabin windows but was somewhat overshadowed by the success of the world-beating Vickers Viscount.

Within a few months, this very significant type made its debut at the airport. The Vickers Viscount holds the distinction of being the world's first turboprop airliner, so offering a faster, smoother ride; G-AMOD initiating the all first class, 47-seat *Ulster Flyer* service to London Heathrow on 1st November 1953. The schedule provided for an evening departure from Heathrow with the aircraft night-stopping at Nutts Corner and returning to London early the next morning. The Viscount's flight time was one hour and thirty-five minutes, the Ambassador's was a comparable one hour forty minutes. (Viscounts were also used on mixed class services while *Elizabethans* also operated the *Ulster Flyer*).

In April 1954 *Flight* magazine published a most unusual article:

BEA Ambassador, G-ALZU, *Lord Burghley*, at London, Heathrow. *(Stephen Finney Collection)*

A press advertisement for BEA's Ulster Flyer first class service. *(Guy Warner Collection)*

BROADCAST FROM A VISCOUNT

Listeners to the BBC Home Service on April 20th were taken aboard that day's *Ulster Flyer*, the daily BEA Viscount service which leaves London Airport at 7.20 pm. and is scheduled to arrive at Nutts Corner, Belfast, at 9.05 pm. On this occasion the aircraft was G-AMOA *George Vancouver*, commanded by Captain A Caesar-Gordon DFC, DFM. It carried a full complement of 47 passengers, one of whom was BBC commentator Raymond Baxter[1], broadcasting via the Viscount's normal Standard Telephones VHF radio (using an off-airways frequency). Mr Baxter gave regular reports on the progress of the flight. The quality of reception was such that he might well have been speaking from a studio, only a faint rush of air being audible in the background. The programme opened at 8.01 pm, with the aircraft over Daventry and nearing the top of its climb to 21,000 feet, and concluded 59 minutes later as it entered the circuit at Nutts Corner.

BEA Vickers Viscount, G-AOJA, *Sir Samuel White Baker*, coming in to land. *(Ray Rimell Collection)*

The Vikings continued to fly to London Northolt, the last schedule to Belfast being flown on 30th October 1954. Henceforth all London flights were to Heathrow. Remarkably, Pionairs flew some of these schedules until 1956, outlasting the Ambassador, though taking two hours and twenty-five minutes for the flight.

BEA Vickers Viking 1B, G-AMGG, *Sir Robert Calder*. *(Guy Warner Collection)*

A pair of BEA Pionairs at Nutts Corner, in the foreground is G-AGJZ. *(Ernie Cromie Collection)*

Following the relaxation of the state corporation's monopoly, Hunting-Clan Air Transport maintained a service from Newcastle upon Tyne with Vikings in the mid-1950s. *Flight* magazine noted as follows in 1954:

---

1 The author and his wife had the pleasure, a number of years ago, of hosting Raymond Baxter on a visit to Northern Ireland. He was a charming and fascinating guest.

Vickers Viking 1, G-AHPJ, Hunting-Clan Air Transport, which began trading on 1st January 1946 at Bovingdon Airport in Hertfordshire. *(Dave Welch Collection)*

The Minister of Transport and Civil Aviation has given his conditional approval to the operation of an internal service between Newcastle (Woolsington) and Belfast (Nutts Corner) via an optional stop at Glasgow (Renfrew) by Hunting-Clan Air Transport, Ltd, until 31st March 1960. No traffic is to be carried between Glasgow and Belfast except in agreement with British European Airways.

In the middle of the decade a new control tower was built, followed by an improved runway lighting system. The restaurant and passenger lounge were refurbished but the buildings remained, in the opinion of the *Belfast Newsletter*, 'still basically a collection of former RAF huts and past the end of their official lives.' Though, to be fair, some of the original Nutts Corner huts had been replaced by other buildings.

Brian Finch noted a pair of unusual, twin-tail boom aircraft arriving on 1st May 1955, US Air Force Fairchild C-119 Flying Boxcars, bringing 80 USAF bandsmen. To emphasise the fact that he was a dedicated 'spotter', he annotated the entry with the information

The new control tower at Nutts Corner. *(John Douglas)*

The Visual Control Room in the Nutts Corner control tower, the controller in the white shirt is Ivor Ray, later Chief Civil Officer at Ulster Radar. *(John Douglas)*

A USAF C-47 at Nutts Corner, with a BEA Viscount in the background. *(Ernie Cromie Collection)*

that they had ventral fins and a double nosewheel – distinguishing them from the similar Fairchild C-82 Packet. Many USAF and USN transport aircraft passed through Nutts Corner in the 1950s, some to clear customs and others in connection with the US Navy Communication Station in Londonderry. On the same page he logged some more military aircraft – a pair of RAF DH Vampire FB5s had landed on Runway 22 as they were low on fuel, a USAF Douglas A-26C Invader[2] light attack bomber, painted completely black, which had flown in from France and a Lockheed T-33a Silver Star two-seat trainer, which had arrived from West Germany.

Brian also spotted a considerable number of flights bringing in daily newspapers; Avro Yorks of Hunting-Clan, Skyways and Dan-Air, an Avro Tudor 4B Super Trader of Air Charter London, a Bristol Freighter from Silver City Airways, Dakotas of BKS Air Transport, Starways, Air Kruise and the Lancashire Aircraft Corporation and a very unusual Pan-American Airways DC-4 'testing the airport for PAA Atlantic alternate.' A little later he recorded that a Transocean Airlines DC-4 had taken 31 Ulster Boy Scouts to the 8th Boy Scout World Jamboree, which was held in Canada, at Niagara-on-the-Lake in August 1955.

BKS DC-3, G-AMVC, one of eight operated by the company between 1952 and 1967. *(Richard Riding Collection)*

A regular visitor to Nutts Corner, Bristol Type 170 Freighter, G-ACIS, of the Lancashire Aircraft Corporation, which was merged into Silver City Airways in 1958. *(Ernie Cromie Collection)*

---

2 Having discovered that the Invader logged by Brian Finch was part of the collection of the New England Air Museum, I e-mailed the Curator, Nick Hurley, and received this very helpful reply from him: 'Based on the surviving documentation in our curatorial file on the A-26C, I can tell you that the aircraft, after a number of assignments, was eventually allocated to the 7373rd Maintenance Group in Chateauroux, France, effective 12 October 1954. In October of 1955 it was flown to Fairey Aviation Co of Manchester, England for contract modification and was then subsequently transferred to storage at Davis-Monthan AFB, Arizona. Based on these details it seems likely that the landing at Nutts Corner took place during the aircraft's flight from Chateauroux to Manchester in the fall of 1955. As far as the black paint scheme and identification of BC499, however, I cannot help.'

To return to Bob Wilson's Spotter's Log:

> Saturday, 20th August 1955. Dakota G-AJHZ – BEA Dakotas with white upper fuselage, red cheat lines and silver undersides were the most frequent visitors to Nutts Corner in the mid-fifties, with G-AGIP, G-AGZB, G-AGNK and G-AIWD all noted. Parking on the apron was self-manoeuvring with aircraft being marshalled along the top facing down and along the sides facing inwards unless wind conditions dictated otherwise. Back through the mists of time, the throaty rumble of Twin Wasps and the gentle squealing of brakes as a Dakota taxied down the slight incline to Runway-28 is a lasting memory. With red and white checkerboard markings on the twin water towers on the Belfast Road, similar markings on the Ground-Controlled Approach (GCA) caravans out on the airfield and black and white marker boards alongside the runways, Nutts Corner was a colourful icon of the fifties.

Bob was not the only young man to have fond memories of that summer. The following is an extract from an article which appeared in the *Coleraine Chronicle* on 10th September, 1955:

> Patrol Leader George Lyons, 3rd Coleraine Troop (Killowen) and Patrol Leader Billy Connor, 1st Coleraine Troop, both Queen's Scouts, have just returned from the Boy Scout World Jamboree in Canada. They were chosen to represent County Londonderry in the party of Scouts from Ulster. The British contingent comprised some 1000 Scouts who flew to Canada in fourteen aircraft. They camped with 12,000 other Scouts from fifty nations. In the following article, Billy Connor relates the outstanding features of their memorable experience:

> The Ulster contingent met in Belfast on 16th August, thirty-one boys in all. There was a farewell dinner in Belfast which was attended by the Lord Mayor of Belfast and Ulster Scout officials. After dinner we travelled to Nutts Corner by special bus. On arrival at the airport, we had to go through the usual procedure such as customs, etc. At 8:30 pm our aircraft appeared in the northern sky and within a few moments it had landed. At 9:30 we were shown on board the aircraft. Five minutes later we were ready for take off. Our engines burst into life and the aircraft turned into the wind. Slowly we moved forward towards the main runway. The entire airfield was

Based in Oakland, California from 1946 to 1960, Transocean Air Lines DC-4 Skymaster, N9937F. *(Ed Coates)*

glowing with bright lights. On reaching the main runway our speed increased to 50 mph, then 70 mph – the lights on either side of the runway raced towards us. With all four throttles forward, at 90 mph we were airborne. At a height of 400 feet, we banked to starboard to get our last look at Nutts Corner and Ireland before climbing higher. After crossing the Irish coast, the Captain took the aircraft to a height of 6000 feet and increased our speed to 200 mph. At 12 o'clock coffee was served by our charming American air hostess, Miss Baumon. We landed in Iceland (owing to bad weather) at two o'clock (local time). After breakfast we headed for Newfoundland flying at 10,000 feet. At six o'clock I went up to the flight deck. From the pilot's seat I was able to see Greenland far below through a gap in the bed of clouds beneath. Our speed was now 220 mph; height, 10,000 feet. We arrived at Gander, Newfoundland, at eight o'clock (local time). While our aircraft was being refuelled, we again had breakfast, owing to the change of time. We left Gander at ten o'clock and climbed to a height of 7,000 feet; speed, 190 mph. On crossing the coast of Canada, we flew at a height of 5,000 feet. From this height we could see the beautiful country of Canada, full of lakes and forest land.

After a very full description of the Jamboree, Billy wrote of the flight home:

On Sunday morning [at the end of August], thirty-one very sorry boys left Malton Airport for home. We all shall never forget the send-off the Canadian people gave us, and shall always be in their debt. From Malton we flew direct to Gander in Newfoundland, and then back home to Nutts Corner. The trip took 18 hours 20 minutes. We landed on Monday at 10 am. Because of bad weather off the North-West coast of Ireland we came in from the North. We passed over Portstewart and to the starboard we could see Coleraine 4,000 feet below. It was raining as we stepped from the aircraft.

A sister ship of G-AMGX, Handley Page HPR.1 Marathon 1, G-AMEW of Derby Airways, a type which had very limited commercial success. *(Dave Welch Collection)*

At about that time Brian Finch spotted and photographed the DH86B Express, G-ACZP, of the Lancashire Aircraft Corporation, this was the last of this type of 4-engine, pre-war biplane to remain on the UK register.[3] On the same page in his logbook there is an intriguing reference to a rare Handley Page HPR-1 Marathon, G-AMGX, of Balfour Marine Engineering as a 'juke box transport'. Apparently, it had been fitted out with

---

3 The DH86s, along with the smaller DH84s and DH89s had been very significant in the development of sustained scheduled passenger services in Britain in the 1930s, including to Belfast Harbour Airport from 1938.

A BKS Airspeed Ambassador taxying out to line up on Runway 28 at Nutts Corner. *(Ernie Cromie Collection)*

A publicity shot taken for the Northern Ireland Tourist Board of passengers just before they boarded their aircraft. *(Ernie Cromie Collection)*

BAL-AMi juke boxes[4] as a mobile showroom for a sales tour of America which had to be curtailed as it did not have the range to fly as far as Iceland to refuel.

BKS Air Transport provided services to Leeds/Bradford starting on 15th May 1955, Edinburgh in 1956 and Newcastle from 23rd May 1958, to begin with using Dakotas and then also Ambassadors from 1957. In October it was recorded that 18,714 passengers had used Nutts Corner that month making it the third busiest in the UK outside London.

In May 1956 the former King Leopold III of Belgium arrived at Nutts Corner in BEA Viscount, G-AODG, being greeted on the tarmac by Lord Wakehurst, the Governor of Northern Ireland. On that day, Leopold received the Freedom of Enniskillen with all due ceremony, in his role as Colonel-in-Chief of the 5th Royal Inniskilling Dragoon Guards.

Also in 1956, Jersey-Belfast was added to the BEA route structure, using Pionairs. In May 1956, Cambrian Airways began operating from Cardiff and Bristol to Belfast, with 17 passenger 4-engine DH Herons, with Brian Finch logging the first flight by G-AOGU. In 1958 the service was suspended for a time when the company experienced financial difficulties.

Bob Wilson noted two lesser spotted visitors in his log:

Wednesday, 3rd July Percival Prince, G-AMKY – parked in the corner of the apron nearest the control tower at Nutts Corner, this aircraft was operated by the Ministry of Transport and Civil Aviation (MTCA).

Cambrian Airways timetable. *(Guy Warner Collection)*

---

4 BAL-AMi was the biggest British manufacturer and distributor of jukeboxes from the mid-1950s through to the early 1960s.

Sunday, 19th August 1956. Tiger Moth, EI-AHK – based at Weston, Co Dublin, this aircraft appeared over Nutts Corner on a sunny Sunday afternoon and made a low-level left hand circuit around the signals square. After a green Verey light flare was fired from the tower, the pilot landed the aircraft on Runway 22.

Percival P.54 Prince 6B, G-AMKY, spotted by Bob Wilson on 3rd July 1956. *(Chris England)*

By this time, as previously noted, a new visual control room had been erected on the tower. Of octagonal steel and glass construction, it was the first of its kind locally and replaced a smaller structure nearby which had originally been built by the USAAF on top of the control tower at Langford Lodge. Contrary to popular belief, the airport terminal building at Nutts Corner adjacent to the tower was not a converted wartime structure but was purpose-built by the MTCA, albeit in the same general '1940s' style as the buildings nearby but a modest attempt had been made to provide a more modern façade towards the apron where a neat hedge enclosed the visitors' area and the famous fossilised tree trunk. Much use was also made of beds of heather and flowers to give the airport a welcoming atmosphere. The display of QDM boards (Radio navigation code giving magnetic bearing to a station) and the 'C' sign in yellow and black on the white tower complemented the evocative aviation panorama.

Two Viscounts on the apron in the new BEA Red Square livery, introduced by BEA in the late 1950s, with a Dakota in the background. *(John Douglas)*

Taken at about the same time, this photograph shows the terminal entrance and the control tower. Just visible on the right, the little first floor structure with inward-sloping windows was initially constructed by the Americans at Langford Lodge in the latter part of the Second World War to create an additional storey on the control tower there. After the end of the war, it was dismantled and brought to Nutts Corner to be reused. *(John Douglas)*

Towards the end of 1956 the extensive completion work on the aircraft carrier HMCS *Bonaventure* for the Royal Canadian Navy was near to fulfilment. *Bonaventure* had been laid down in Belfast at Harland & Wolff in 1943 as HMS *Powerful*, the construction of which was suspended at the end of the war and not begun again until 1952. A Canadair North Star[5] of the Royal Canadian Air Force delivered the US radar equipment to Nutts Corner for ground transportation to the shipyard.

To quote Bob Wilson again:

> Sunday, 13th January 1957. Boeing Stratocruiser, G-AKGK, *Canopus*, this BOAC aircraft was seen climbing out from Runway 10 after landing earlier from Gander, Newfoundland with an engine problem. Stratocruisers were rare visitors at Nutts Corner, being more usually observed high over Belfast on flights to the USA with Pan American and BOAC.
>
> At their normal altitudes of around 20,000 feet they could be easily confused with WB-50 Superfortresses of the USAF's 53rd Weather Squadron at RAF Burtonwood, which were also commonly seen over Belfast in the late evening, albeit these aircraft were usually going in the opposite direction after weather reconnaissance flights over the Atlantic.
>
> G-AKGK, together with Stratocruisers G-ANUB, *Calypso*, G-ANUM, *Clyde* and G-AKGL, *Cabot*, had brought Royal Canadian Navy seamen to Belfast for the commissioning of HMCS *Bonaventure*[6].
>
> On Thursday 17th January 1957, the one-off Canadair C-5 North Star 17524 (VIP serial 10000) was seen climbing out from Nutts Corner after bringing in more top brass. It was unique among the RCAF North Stars in having radials rather than the usual Merlin in-line engines. About 600 RCN personnel in total were flown to Nutts Corner in connection with the commissioning, by a fleet of aircraft which also included three DC-4 Skymasters of Maritime Central Airways.

HMCS *Bonaventure* of the Royal Canadian Navy, with a Grumman CS2F Tracker anti-submarine aircraft ready for take-off. *(Guy Warner Collection)*

A pair of BOAC Boeing Stratocruisers at Nutts Corner, the Airport Fire Station is to the bottom left, with a Bristol Freighter lurking behind. *(Ernie Cromie Collection)*

---
5 A Canadian-built version of the Douglas DC-4 with Rolls-Royce Merlin Engines.
6 HMCS *Bonaventure* was a *Majestic*-class aircraft carrier, the third and last aircraft carrier in service with Canada's armed forces.

The unique Pratt & Whitney R-2800 Double Wasp-powered Canadair C-5 North Star 17524 (VIP serial 10000). *(RCAF Photo)*

DC-4 Skymaster, CF-MCB, of Maritime Central Airways, which was based in Moncton, New Brunswick. *(RA Scholefield Collection)*

In complete contrast, a Seaboard & Western Airlines Skymaster was noted as taking, 'Eight Jersey cows to America.' These had been delivered from Jersey in an Airwork Ltd Dakota.

Other ships' crews were brought from Stavanger in a KLM DC-4 and a Fred Olsen Dakota, as well as Hunting-Clan Avro York from the Far East. Yet another arrival was a DH Dove of Morton Air Services, which had been chartered by the Donaghadee-based carpet magnate, Cyril Lord[7]. From time to time he would use the extra volume afforded by Silver City's Bristol Freighters for transporting bulk consignments of carpets. Some readers may remember (however much they may have tried to forget) the catchy musical jingle which accompanied adverts on Ulster Television, 'This is luxury you can afford from Cyril Lord!' On a more serious note, a BEA Sikorsky S-55 helicopter, G-AOCF, named *Sir Lionel*, was a rare visitor in 1957, 'based at the airport during a Civil Defence Exercise.' Other significant arrivals recorded in Brian Finch's log include multiple Aer Lingus diversions from Dublin, when that airport was fogbound.

De Havilland DH.104 Dove 1B, G-AMYO, as chartered by Cyril Lord. *(Barry Friend)*

In 1957 the first of the larger Viscount 800 series began operating with BEA from Nutts Corner to Heathrow. This was configured for sixteen first class and forty-two economy passengers and could cruise at 325 mph. By this time the whole London schedule was operated by Viscounts.

Following the Hungarian Uprising against Communist rule in 1956, several hundred refugees made their way to the USA and Canada in 1957 via Nutts Corner, with Slick and the Flying Tiger Line. The

---

7 (1911–1984) The carpet factory at Donaghadee and was largely designed by Billy McAlister, a Belfast architect, and his team, who would go on to design the distinctive terminal at Aldergrove airport.

The BEA Sikorsky S-55 helicopter, G-AOCF, *Sir Lionel*, which visited Nutts Corner for a Civil Defence exercise. *(Dave Welch Collection)*

Aer Lingus DC-3, EI-AFC, at Nutts Corner. *(Bert Magowan Collection)*

most passengers to leave on one flight was on 4th May 1957 when 114 Hungarian refugees left for Toronto on a Super Constellation.

Meanwhile, there had been an increase in Transatlantic 'affiliated charter' business. This scheme was a means whereby a sporting or social club or society could travel at a group discount rate. It was very popular and involved such airlines as Slick Airways of San Francisco, which took a party to Toronto and American International Airways of Burbank, which conveyed the Belfast Tradesmen's Social Club to New York. Freight was brought inbound by Super Constellations of Seaboard & Western, while Irish linen was exported in similar aeroplanes of the Flying Tiger Line. An unusual cargo came in 1957 in a Douglas R6D-1 Liftmaster of the US Navy, clearing customs before flying on to RNAS Eglinton with a radar for the USN base in Londonderry.

L-1049 Super Constellation, N6919C, of the Flying Tiger Line landing at Nutts Corner. *(Ernie Cromie Collection)*

The Canadian Orangemen's Douglas C-54A Skymaster, CF-WAL, of Wheeler Airlines. *(Ian McFarlane)*

Yet another out-of-the-ordinary arrival that year was a DC-4 of Wheeler Airlines bringing a group of Canadian Orangemen to take part in the 'Twelfth'. In August 1957 the *Belfast Telegraph* reported that a DC-6B of Slick Airways had flown from New York to Belfast in a record time of 10 hours and 16 minutes, some six hours faster than the normal time for the journey. Under the command of Captain Hugo Hesson, it took off from New York at 21.33 and landed at Nutts Corner at 07.49 the following day. The flight had no passengers, its purpose was to pick up 44 'Ulster Exiles' returning to Canada from holiday and a similar number from Prestwick. Captain Hesson told the *Telegraph*'s reporter, 'We weren't out to break the record, we flew at 17,000 feet and the strong 100-knot tailwind just blew us across.' The reporter also found out that Hugo Hesson had flown B-17s in the war, delivering quite a number to Nutts Corner.

On the afternoon of 23rd October 1957 BEA Viscount, G-AOJA, on a non-scheduled, positioning flight from London, crashed at Nutts Corner when overshooting following a radar approach in bad weather with the loss of all on board, five crew and two passengers. Those killed were Captain Robert M Stewart, First Officer William G Tomkins DFC, Stewardess JA Medhurst, Steward E Bebington, Steward A Hall, John Galpin (the BEA Sales Superintendent in Northern Ireland) and his wife, Irene. No official cause of the crash could be determined by the subsequent Public Enquiry.

At 16.45 the aircraft was taken over by the Precision Approach Controller for a GCA talk down on Runway 28, in weather conditions which the captain thought would allow him to become visual at or above his critical height of 500 feet. Soon after, 'three-quarters of a mile from touchdown', the aircraft was to the right of the centreline and shortly afterwards was, 'well right of centreline'. Just after, 'half a mile from touchdown', the Precision Approach Controller said, 'if you're overshooting turn left 5° on overshoot, over', to which the reply came '… overshooting'. At about this time a number of witnesses heard the aircraft 'rev-up'. Shortly thereafter (at 16.51 hours) the aircraft crashed within the boundary of the airport approximately 1000 feet to the south of the western end of Runway 28. There was some evidence to suggest that the airport's approach lighting may have been switched off at the time of the Viscount's landing attempt but this could not be proven. A bent screwdriver was found in the wreckage but was removed before its position in the wreckage could be determined and the likelihood of it jamming the flight controls could not be assessed.

Once more, Bob Wilson describes an unusual arrival:

Seen again in Glengall Street, a Leyland PS2/10 semi-decker, with bodywork built by UTA; the large luggage compartment being particularly useful for the airport service. *(Guy Warner Collection)*

> Saturday, 21st December 1957. Blackburn Beverley, at 11.40 on a bright, clear morning, the tranquillity was shattered as the huge behemoth thundered over the Cregagh

Blackburn Beverley C.1, XB269, of 47 Squadron at Aldergrove in the late 1950s. *(Ernie Cromie Collection)*

Hills at 2,000 feet, tracking from the Portaferry fan marker towards the Nutts Corner Runway 28 final approach at the former Standard Beam Approach (SBA) outer marker alongside Ballyutoag Road near Squires Hill – a popular routeing which ensured constant sighting opportunities over Belfast. The huge RAF freighter was operating a charter for BEA carrying a back-log of three tons of Royal Mail. This was also the first visit of the type locally and the aircraft was seen again at 15.25, climbing out from Runway 28 towards the south-east.

And in the following year:

Sunday, 12th January 1958. Douglas DC-7C, I-DUVA, belonging to Alitalia; this aircraft was bringing in the Italian football team for an international match in Belfast and was seen over the city at 14.25 hours on left-base for Runway 28. This was in the heyday of the big piston airliners and many could be seen but mostly heard high above on Airway Red 3, heading for Tory Island Non-Directional Beacon (NDB) off the coast of Donegal. As the most westerly UK airport, Nutts Corner often handled aircraft on diversions due to weather or visits for fuel, including Super Constellation VT-DHN of Air India on Friday 10th January, Curtiss C-46, N10427, of Seaboard and Western on Wednesday 15th, Douglas R6D, 131581, of the United States Navy on Monday 20th and C-46, LX-LAA, of Luxair on the 28th.

In this case seen at London Heathrow, the Alitalia Douglas DC-7C, I-DUVA, which brought in the Italian football team for a match in Belfast. *(Robin A Walker)*

Sunday, 30th March 1958. Avro York, G-AGNO, seen on the approach to Runway 28, the aircraft was a passenger and freight derivative of the wartime Lancaster and had a square fuselage section long before the Shorts 'shoebox' designs were thought of. This York belonged to the independent airline Skyways of London, the main operator of the type at the time. Another visitor to the airport in early 1958 was Liverpool-based Starways, with DC-4, G-APEZ, being seen on Wednesday 21st May.

A new schedule was introduced a few months later by Silver City Airways from Blackpool, using DH Herons, DC-3s and Bristol Freighters; which was reported in *Flight*:

Silver City are to operate a new service between Blackpool and Nutts Corner,

Silver City DH Heron, G-AOZN, which was used on the schedule to Blackpool. *(Richard Riding Collection)*

Belfast, from 17th May 1958. This will follow the transfer, on 15th April, of the airline's Northern Ireland headquarters from Newtownards. Fares on the new service range between £6 18s return on Fridays and Sundays and £7 18s on Saturdays.'

Silver City had also used the capacious Bristol from 1955 to 1957 on a car ferry service between Castle Kennedy (near Stranraer) and Newtownards (also flying from the Harbour Airport for a few months in 1956 while the runway at Ards was extended). Flights to RAF Woodvale and the Isle of Man were also offered from Ards briefly during 1955-6. On occasion these would land at Nutts Corner instead if diverted due to adverse weather conditions.

During 1958, the Ulster Aeroplane Group carried out night flying at Nutts Corner in their newly-acquired Percival P.31 Proctor 4, G-ANYS, which must have been a first for local private fliers. At night, the airfield was very colourful, all lighting being clearly visible from the car parking area in front of the tower, with blue and amber taxiway lighting and white and red runway and approach lights. The airport was distinguished from nearby RAF Aldergrove by a green/white rotating beacon on a lattice tower and a huge neon beacon continually flashing a red 'AG' in morse from a prominent position on top of the water tower at the main camp. Runway 28 at Nutts Corner had Calvert type approach lighting and Visual Glide Path Indicator lights while Runway 10 had high intensity approach lighting and was equipped with the first ILS to be installed locally.

As has been noted, teenager Joe Brown recorded his impressions of Nutts Corner as it was in the late 1950s (with a few later comments in brackets). He was born in 1942 and lived nearby:

> Part of our farm was requisitioned for accommodation blocks for the RAF. All

A Jaguar D-Type sports car drives off the Silver City Bristol Freighter, G-AGVC, at Ards. *(Tommy Maddock)*

regular travellers are familiar with the single storey passenger terminal with telephone kiosks and toilets in the entrance hall and, beyond this, the main lounge has three reception desks belonging to BEA, BKS and Silver City. These also provide facilities for other airlines. Those travellers who have checked in their baggage in Belfast in the Glengall Street Air Terminal 55 minutes before aircraft departure time, on arriving by UTA bus (one for each flight) at Nutts Corner can alight and go straight into the passenger terminal. Others, going independently to the airport, have their baggage weighed at the airline reception desks on large scales and watch the big hand anxiously as it moves clockwise round the dial – up to or beyond the BEA free limit of 15 kilogrammes (33 lbs). Excess to London is one shilling and 11 pence per kilo (about 10 pence). Arriving passengers claim their baggage as it is unloaded from the baggage trucks at the side or front of the terminal. Around the lounge are the Coats of Arms of the counties of Northern Ireland and, near the exit to departure, a machine to purchase flight insurance. To the left, opening from the lounge, is the restaurant and passenger buffet. Beyond the main lounge is the waiting room and the three departure areas – two for domestic passengers and the third reached by passing through Customs and Immigration. Passengers are directed to these lounges following routes marked by lights, red, green and blue. (I recall at least some of the lounges had very comfortable leather settees and there were a few typewriters for passenger use.)

The airline receptionist then leads the passengers to the aircraft where they are shown to their seat by the steward or stewardess. When the marshaller has guided the aircraft off the apron using his batons, the aircraft taxies towards one of two runways and, if piston-engined like the DC-3, will run-up the engines one by one for a few minutes until the captain is satisfied it is ready for take-off. Turboprops like the Viscount are ready for take-off more quickly. Interest is also caused by the circus of vehicles painted in orange and white squares that are sited near the end of the active runway. These contain the GCA – Ground Controlled Approach equipment and controllers can be seen moving from one runway to another as determined by wind direction. (I do not think the apron had marked stands – the marshaller had to plan where to position the aircraft. Moreover, I recall that in foggy conditions in addition to approach and runway lights, the 'goosenecks' were positioned at frequent intervals down both sides of the runway. Positioned manually, they were paraffin cylinders which gave off both light and heat to help dispel the fog – they were smelly too!

A signpost shows the way to Nutts Corner. *(Joe Brown)*

Ah! Those were the days, it was sunny for a start, all that separated the spectators from the apron and the aircraft was what looks like a hedge and you could have sat all afternoon with your picnic and flask. Or you could have ventured into the snack bar and had a cuppa and a Lyons chocolate mini roll and still have had change from 6d.).

The fire station beside the apron has the latest emergency equipment and vehicles that unfortunately have had to be used for aircraft crashes occasionally; however, the airport fire service received commendation for their efficient response to emergencies. Nearby, the free spectators' enclosure is within 40 yards of the nearest aircraft. On display in its centre is the trunk of a tree excavated from Lough Neagh and thought to be more than a million years old – so hard it could be mistaken for a rock (where is this now – does anyone know?). Relatives and friends can shake hands or give their departing friends a final kiss goodbye over the low hedge as they pass by the enclosure. It is also a favourite haunt for families, especially at weekends when they 'take a run up to Nutts Corner to see the planes', and purchase ice cream of course. Car parking was free at one stage but now only for 30 minutes and thereafter one shilling for up to six hours and two shillings for 24 hours. The main road to Crumlin is just over the hedge from the main runway 28/10 and is also a popular vantage point. An additional attraction was watching the groups of hares playing, oblivious of the activity around them.

Many years later Joe added:

> When Belfast Nutts Corner Airport was in its heyday it was very much the centre of a happy community. Many of the employees were local people, often more than one generation of the same family in the various operations. I recall the Ministry of Transport & Civil Aviation (MTCA) and later MoA, Air Traffic Control, Fire Service, British European Airways, BKS, and other airlines. The Ulster Transport Authority operated a dedicated bus service for each flight from the BEA Air Terminal check-in at Glengall Street, Belfast. A building was provided to park bicycles, regularly including mine, and perhaps because I knew the locals it seemed I could almost wander around at will. I have fond memories of going to the departure lounges, mingling with departing travellers and to get the opportunity for autographs of celebrities such as Bill Haley, Tommy Steele, Diana Dors and Derek Ibbotson (the first athlete to run a mile in exactly four minutes). And sometimes the celebrities did engage me in conversation perhaps out of curiosity when they heard my country accent. You really could rub shoulders with politicians and VIPs, especially arriving off BEA's First Class *Ulster Flyer* from Heathrow. I think it arrived about 21.00 hours and in the still of the evening there was the beautiful distinctive sound of the high-wing Elizabethan (Airspeed Ambassador, the type of the ill-fated Manchester United Munich disaster) on the 28-approach and throttling back on touchdown. Then there was the airport 'Club' – a separate licensed premises which was certainly not approved of by some in the farming community but a welcome social addition to others.

An interior view of the terminal building at Nutts Corner. *(Ernie Cromie Collection)*

By the end of the 1950s the comparatively steep approach necessary for aircraft flying to Nutts Corner was deemed unsuitable. This was due to the location of the airport, close to the Belfast mountains and the obstacles located there, particularly transmitters and aerials.

Another factor was the fact that of Nutts Corner's three runways, only one was of sufficient length for modern aircraft. Aldergrove's two perpendicular runways made operations possible there even if conditions (particularly wind) changed dramatically.

An article appeared in the *Belfast Telegraph* on 9th December 1958 headed 'Doubts on Airport'. Earlier that year, the Ministry of Civil Aviation had decided to retain Nutts Corner as the civil airport, however the *Telegraph* was moved to comment,

> If Nutts Corner is not the best possible site, it is as well that the issue should be thrashed out before the £500,000 improvement scheme is far advanced. The local Aviation Advisory Council backed by British European Airways is pressing for reconsideration of the plan. It believes, apparently, that Aldergrove is the best site and that the provision of new buildings and other facilities at Nutts Corner is not putting first things first, since the runways there will not be adequate for the big jets of the future.

The chief executive officer of BEA, Anthony Milward, gave his views at a press conference following a Council meeting:

> Nutts Corner can never be an international airport. It can never be made big enough for the big jets and the Advisory Council feels that Northern Ireland should have an international airport. Only one site would be a suitable alternative airport – Aldergrove.

A few months later, in April 1959, the Chairman of Short Brothers, Rear Admiral Sir Matthew Slattery, entered the debate. He recommended strongly that Aldergrove should be developed for joint military and civilian use, with the proviso that Sydenham should be enhanced to act as a potential diversion airfield.

Other options considered were Belfast Harbour Airport at Sydenham and the wartime airfields at Ballyhalbert, Bishops Court, Long Kesh and Langford Lodge.

Meanwhile, the 57 passengers and five crew on board Viscount G-AOHN were fortunate, all escaping serious injury. Captain David Gray, on the early afternoon flight from London on 13th April 1959 made good landing on a wet Runway 28 in a cross-wind of 25-30 knots when, due to a sudden gust, the aircraft ran off the side on to soft ground and the nose-wheel collapsed. Joe Brown witnessed this from the Terminal:

> It was Easter school holidays. The Fire Service was on its way before the Viscount came to a standstill, swiftly laying a carpet of foam. The passengers exited via a canvas escape slide, save for one lady who objected to jumping and sliding onto the muddy verge. The damage to the engines was extensive; and for what seemed for weeks later the repaired engines were being run-up at night after the last BEA flight had been put to bed. This was not popular with the airport's neighbours!

BEA V.802 Viscount, G-AOHN, *Alexander Gordon Laing*, at Nutts Corner on 13th April 1959. *(via Joe Brown)*

The Viscount was repaired and took off again from Nutts Corner on 12th June.

A decision on Nutts Corner's future was made on 29th July 1959, when it was announced at Westminster that Aldergrove had been selected as the site of the new civil airport for Northern Ireland. The local reaction was generally favourable, with the only doubts being raised regarding the feasibility of sharing the site and particularly Air Traffic Control with the military. Interestingly, the civilian controllers at Nutts Corner had in fact been in charge of all traffic using Aldergrove except for those on finals, just taking off or in the circuit. The military controllers' local expertise and experience was therefore much more restricted.

Chapter 18

Nutts Corner in the 1960s

Bob Wilson noted another unusual arrival in the summer of 1960:

> Monday, 15th August, Thruxton Jackaroo G-APHZ – seen landing on Runway 28, this aircraft was a four-seat cabin conversion of the DH Tiger Moth and it had been operating joy-rides out of a field at Carnalridge south of Portrush. It was in a grey scheme with rather grand 'AIR ULSTER' titles on the fuselage and when seen at Portrush was doing a roaring trade flying round Ramore Head and back to the field, long before private strips became the norm locally.

By the end of 1960 Nutts Corner was nearing the end of its days as Northern Ireland's main civil airport; BEA, with its Viscounts held sway on the main trunk routes to London Heathrow, Manchester, Birmingham and Glasgow, whilst also offering flights to the Isle of Man, Liverpool and summer service to Jersey. It also brought the end of the all first class *Ulster Flyer*. In October the Pionairs had been retired from the Irish Sea routes linking Liverpool, Belfast and the Isle of Man. Cambrian Airways provided flights to Cardiff and Bristol, using the smaller Vickers Viscount 700 series, but also still operating DC-3s. BKS Air Transport flew to Leeds/Bradford, Newcastle, Dublin and Edinburgh, using Airspeed Ambassadors and DC-3s. Silver City Airways flew DC-3s to Blackpool and the Isle of Man.

A Cambrian Airways Vickers Viscount – taken from the Dundrod Road. *(Ernie Cromie Collection)*

Silver City Airways DC-3, G-AMWV, which flew services to Blackpool and the Isle of Man. *(Ernie Cromie Collection)*

Cambrian Airways Dakota 3, G-AMFV, at Nutts Corner in 1961. *(Ernie Cromie Collection)*

Aer Lingus was the first airline to operate the Fokker F27 Friendship, shown here is EI-AKE, St Felim. *(J Patience)*

For Christmas 1960, Aer Lingus introduced a series of Dublin-Belfast flights which was geared towards providing connections to the transatlantic service from Dublin. These flights operated on December 19th, 22nd, 23rd and 24th, and they were sufficiently successful to enable a service to be introduced in the following year. On 30th April 1961 Aer Lingus resumed scheduled Dublin to Belfast flights with Fokker F.27 Friendships, the first being EI-AKA. In order to minimise costs, Belfast was an en-route stop between Glasgow and Dublin.

1961 brought the first BEA Vickers Vanguard service from Nutts Corner to Heathrow. The 'double bubble' fuselage Vanguard had a capacity for 139 passengers and three tons of cargo. It was powered by four Rolls Royce Tyne turboprops and cruised at 400 mph. This was a type that was well-loved and admired by aircrew, ground staff, engineers and passengers alike and served the route to London for the next 12 years. The BEA timetable for March 1962 shows that the off peak 23.35 departure from London Heathrow had a Standby fare of £3 3s (compared to First Class £9 and Tourist Monday to Friday £5 9s. Saturday £4 3s) and was extremely popular. It also carried Royal

Two Viscounts and a Vanguard at Nutts Corner, all in the 'Red Square' BEA livery, introduced in the late 1950s. The bus in the foreground is a UTA Leyland PD3/4, one of a batch of four which had specially enlarged luggage boots for use on the airport service. *(Ernie Cromie Collection)*

An aerial view of the terminal area at Nutts Corner in 1961. *(Author's Collection)*

Mail (the carriage of which determined the times of the off-peak flights) and other freight in its capacious lower deck hold.

The eagle eye of Bob Wilson missed little:

Monday, 10th July 1961. Viking, G-AHOW; British European Airways had retired their Viking fleet at the end of 1954 but this one returned to Nutts Corner in the colours of independent airline Air Safaris, operating holiday flights to Mediterranean resorts. Once as common a sight as Dakotas at Nutts Corner, the last one seen was on Thursday 13th June 1963 in Eros Airlines colours.

Monday, 7th August 1961. Handley Page Hermes 4, G-ALDL. Seen from a vantage point on the Dundrod Road, the big airliner trundled down from the apron with all four Hercules radials emitting wisps of blue smoke in the sultry heat. Wearing the green and grey scheme of Air Safaris, it was one of several ex-BOAC examples used by independent operators such as Airwork, Falcon Airways, Skyways and Silver City on trooping and holiday flights. Turning on to the threshold of Runway 28, the crew spent some time checking power and then with a heavy roar from the engines, the Hermes accelerated along the runway and sedately lifted off in a gentle left turn bound for some sunny new Spanish resort.

Thursday, 10th August 1961. Douglas DC-4M-2 Argonaut, G-ALHY, in the white, red and silver scheme of Overseas Aviation, the aircraft made a long, low approach to Runway 28, with the four Merlins sounding their heavy beat and

The Handley Page Hermes 4, G-ALDL, which impressed Bob Wilson, 'with all four Bristol Hercules radials emitting wisps of blue smoke in the sultry heat.' *(Barry Friend Collection)*

popping and firing as they were throttled back on landing. Overseas also had some ex-TCA examples which retained their Canadian registrations. Argonaut was the BOAC name for this Canadair built version of the DC-4 while Trans Canada called theirs the North Star.

As a supplement to Bob's notes, some measure of life in Northern Ireland may be gained from these two letters to *The Times*. The first was headed 'They do things Better Abroad' and was written from the Travellers' Club, Pall Mall by Robin McDouall, who was less than happy:

> Sir, Let anyone who doubts it spend a Sunday evening, waiting for an aircraft at Belfast Airport, the restaurant, the bar and even the bookstall shut. Aptly it is named Nutts Corner.

The Aerodrome Commandant, John Selway[1], replied in typically robust fashion:

> Sir, Certain criticisms of the facilities provided at this airport were made in a letter which appeared in *The Times* on August 31st. You may not be aware that under Northern Ireland legislation it is still impossible to provide alcoholic refreshment on Sundays at this airport. A restaurant or buffet service is, however, always available to passengers up to the time of departure of the last flight. I regret that your correspondent did not find all the facilities he required at the airport, but I can assure him that all possible steps are taken to provide for the comfort of passengers, even during the delays which are unfortunately inevitable at all airports on occasions.

The poor economics of operating second-hand aircraft on new holiday routes finally defeated both Overseas Aviation and Air Safaris, both of which had gone before the end of the year. Meanwhile, the heavily-subsidised BEA appeared to rub salt in by operating the new DH Comet 4B, G-APMC, on the Heathrow route on Wednesday, 2nd August 1961 – the first jet airliner to visit the airport.

In April 1962 Derby Airways, which used DC-3s, commenced flying to Nutts Corner from the old Derby Airport at Burnaston. In the same year Silver City Airways was

Dakota, G-AMSX, of Derby Airlines, which began flying to Nutts Corner from Burnaston in 1962. *(Barry Friend Collection)*

---

1 Wing Commander John Selway OBE, DFC (1914-1998) flew the Bristol Blenheim, Bristol Beaufighter and DH Mosquito operationally, returning to the Ministry of Civil Aviation in 1946. He had become Airport Commandant in July 1957, taking over from HP Finch, who had served in that capacity since 1948.

Above: A postcard of BEA Viscount, G-AODG, purchased at Nutts Corner, sent from London to Jordanstown Road, Newtownabbey in February 1962. It must have been old stock, as the Viscount is in the BEA livery of the 1950s. *(Ernie Cromie Collection)*

Far left: BEA also introduced the Herald at the airport in 1962, in this case, G-APWD. *(Guy Warner Collection)*

absorbed by the British United Airways group and from that time BU(CI) Airways and BU (Manx) Airways provided services to Blackpool, Exeter, Bournemouth and the Isle of Man respectively, using DC-3s and Handley Page Dart Heralds. Cambrian Airways took over the flights to the Isle of Man and Liverpool from BEA in the spring of 1963, using Viscounts purchased from BEA. The Herald also made its first appearance in BEA service at Nutts Corner on 29th March 1963 when G-APWB replaced the normal Viscount on the run from Glasgow.

Bob Wilson was kept busy:

Friday, 18th May 1962. Bristol Freighter, G-AMLJ, seen over Belfast heading for Nutts Corner, this aircraft operated by BKS was a frequent visitor at this time, on contract to Vauxhall Motors transporting cars for the local market. A black T2 hangar near the threshold of Runway 04 was used for storage and had the Vauxhall name in large red and yellow letters painted across the doors facing the airfield. Previous occupants of this hangar had been the Seafires of Royal Navy 879 and 883 Squadrons which disbanded there and at Machrihanish, respectively, in 1946.

Thursday, 28th June 1962. Vickers Vanguard, G-APET, BEA had introduced the Vanguard on most Heathrow schedules by this time and Viscounts had replaced Dakotas on the other routes. G-APET had landed on Runway 28 at 20.32 hours and during the previous hour, four BEA Viscounts had departed, V701s G-AMOG, G-AMOL and G-AMOC plus V802 G-AOHW.

N9720C, a Lockheed Super Constellation of Capitol Airlines

A BEA Vanguard, G-APEN and Viscount, G-AMON, at Nutts Corner, with a Silver City Dakota in the background. *(Joe Brown)*

Another Britannia arrived the next month, CF-CZX, of Canadian Pacific Airlines. *(Dave Welch Collection)*

had also departed and Bristol Britannia 312, G-AOVM, of BOAC had arrived – illustrating a typical summer evening at Nutts Corner in the early 'sixties.

Wednesday, 4th July 1962. Britannia 314, CF-CZX, belonging to Canadian Pacific Airlines, shared the apron with Dakota, PH-MAA, of Martin's Air Charter in the early afternoon. Britannias were now being replaced by the big jets on long-haul routes and CF-CZX was operating a holiday charter. It was the only 314 not built in Belfast and had joined the other five in 1958 when Canadian Pacific had used them extensively on their 4,800 mile routes from Vancouver to Tokyo and Amsterdam. The big piston airliners were also still holding their own at Nutts Corner in what was the last full year of airline operations and during July some examples were Super Constellation N6932C of Flying Tiger on Saturday 7th, DC-7F, N8217H, of Riddle Airlines on Saturday 21st and DC-6B, N90770, of Saturn Airways on Tuesday 31st.

Sunday, 5th August 1962. DC-6B, N738PA, belonging to Pan American, took off from Runway 28 at 0935. It was unusual for Pan Am to visit Nutts Corner, from and to which most of the transatlantic charters were operated by lesser carriers. Various freight operations, transfer of foreign crews to ships at Belfast docks and European refugee flights brought a variety of aircraft to Nutts Corner, including DC-6Bs had visited from President Airlines. On this particular Sunday morning, the scheduled aircraft included Dakota G-AIWB and Ambassador G-ALZW operating with BKS, Dakota G-AMNV, with Tyne-Tees Airways markings and Aer Lingus F27 EI-AKB. Regulars from BEA were Vanguard G-APET and Viscounts G-APEX, G-ALWF and G-AMOC.

Spotted by Bob Wilson on 5th August 1962, Dakota G-AMNV of Tyne-Tees Airways. *(Ralf Manteufel)*

An interesting arrival, which escaped Bob's attention, was that of former US president, Dwight D Eisenhower, who landed at the airport, accompanied by his wife and grandchildren, in a Douglas C-118 Liftmaster of the USAF, on 21st August, as part of a four-day tour of Ireland. He was greeted on the tarmac by the Governor, Lord Wakehurst and the Prime Minister, Lord Brookeborough.

A very rare colour image of the control tower at Nutts Corner. *(Ernie Cromie Collection)*

Joe Brown writes, 'Nutts Corner was a very user-friendly airport for staff, traveller, and spectator alike. I took this photo of USA Ex-President Dwight D Eisenhower (the 34th President only seven months out of office) and Lord Brookeborough Prime Minister of Northern Ireland on a simple no zoom camera, almost at arm's length.'

Bob continues:

Sunday, 26th August 1962. While I was on a visit to the tower at Nutts Corner, the radar was on weekly maintenance when a conflict occurred as two aircraft approached the 'BEL' Non-Directional Beacon (NDB) with Estimated Times of Arrival (ETA) at exactly the same time. One was an RAF Avro Shackleton at 5000 feet heading south east for Airway Red 3 through the Belfast Control Zone and the other was a new BEA Handley Page Herald, G-APWC, operating the Glasgow service, heading south west from the Kintyre NDB on Airway Blue 2 at 8000 feet. With no radar available, the separation had to be procedural and the two aircraft were duly observed visually from the tower crossing over the 'BEL' which, in those days, transmitted from a site north of the Runway 10 threshold on the other side of the Nutts Corner to Crumlin road.

With separation confirmed, the crew of the Herald then took the opportunity to conduct a full procedural NDB let-down for an Instrument Landing System (ILS) approach to Runway 10. After Piper Commanche, G-ARIE, had taken off for Denham, climbing overhead to pick up the Airway centreline, the radar came back into service and, shortly afterwards, 'Speedbird Double India' coming in from New York via Prestwick requested a (GCA) talk-down for Runway 28, as the cloud cover had increased. The radar controller left the tower and departed in the yellow and black Hillman Husky for the GCA radar caravans parked on a disused taxiway on the left of 28 towards the upwind end. The red and white vertical pillar of the search radar began to revolve and the full talk-down was heard on speakers in the tower. When the pilot reported encountering turbulence, the controller responded that this was due to the aircraft being over the hills on the approach. In due course, the DC-7F, G-AOII, in BOAC cargo colours taxied up to the apron and parked in the Customs Area marked out on the northern edge of the tarmac. No sooner had the radar controller left the GCA caravan when an RAF Handley Page Hastings of 202 Squadron returning from a weather sortie called up and requested a GCA talkdown for continuation training. The tower controller called the Husky but there was no immediate response and the Aldis lamp was flashed towards the vehicle, alerting the radar controller to call on the vehicle radio. He returned to the GCA caravan and talked-down the Hastings which went around off Runway 28 for a landing at Aldergrove.

A Hastings Met 1 of 202 Squadron, on static display at the RAF Aldergrove 'At Home' Day in 1960. They often practised with ATC at Nutts Corner. Note the formation of Gloster Javelins above and behind. *(Tommy Maddock)*

Nutts Corner appeared to welcome all-comers and the smallest aircraft seen was the single-seat ultra-light, Druine D.31 Turbulent, G-APCM, parked on the apron alongside the airliners, on Wednesday, 5th September 1962. These included, DC-4M-2 Argonaut, OY-AAH, operated by the Danish airline Flying Enterprise, was seen parked on the south side of the apron. This was another of the ex-BOAC machines and is representative of the European flights which visited Nutts Corner at all hours including DC-6A, PH-DFA, and Convair 240, PH-CGH, both KLM, as well as DH Doves and DC-3 Dakotas of Martin's Air Charter.

At the height of the severe winter of 1963 all flights in and out of Nutts Corner were suspended for a short period. A party of 40 staff were also cut off – though their circumstances were perhaps more comfortable – their location being the Templeton Arms public house, not far from from the airport. The BEA Superintendent, Ralph Thurley, was able to send out a message by telephone, 'The food situation is desperate – although we have plenty to drink.' Food was brought to them by the Airport Commandant, John Selway, who put on his skis to make the journey from Nutts Corner to the pub with provisions.

Douglas DC-4M-2 Argonaut, OY-AAH, owned by Danish airline, Flying Enterprise. *(Iain MacKay)*

At Nutts Corner, Noel Gordon, a BEA engineer, had been stranded at the airport for several days in early February. He continued working on servicing three Vickers Viscounts in a hangar, which was a quarter of a mile from the main maintenance complex. He trudged through the wind and snow to work in freezing cold temperatures. That morning while completing a job on the upper part of one of the aircraft, he fell from the staging and sustained a badly fractured knee cap. For 30 minutes he was all alone and in great pain. Luckily a colleague found him, he was taken to the sick bay and a military helicopter from

Aldergrove was requested. It soon arrived but so great was the velocity of the gusting wind that it tore the door off it hinges, so rendering the aircraft inoperable. Another helicopter was summoned but so intense was the demand to deal with other emergencies across the country, it was to be another six hours before it arrived. This one was flown by Lieutenant Martin Tweed of 2 Reconnaissance Flight, Royal Armoured Corps in Saunders Roe Skeeter, XN339, who had already ferried an expectant mother, Mrs Margaret McKee, to the Lagan Valley hospital earlier that day. Noel Gordon had to bend his leg to sit in the tiny cockpit – the agony was excruciating. In very marginal weather and at low level the helicopter followed the roads and railway lines from Nutts Corner to Carrickfergus Hospital. Noel Gordon was very grateful to the pilot but was very relieved when they arrived at hospital.

Noel wrote to the author with a few personal reminiscences:

This Skeeter, XM561, has landed at RUC Headquarters, Knock. (RUC Foundation)

> The following memories and incidents are recorded as isolated incidents spread over a number of years and not every day occurrences! First of all, we used to have a BEA Captain called John Welford, known to everyone as Daddy Welford[2]. He was an enormous man stood some six feet high and as broad, with a large white beard, something like a Santa Claus figure. He was a well known figure in and around Nutts Corner, as he used to visit Lough Neagh on his days off to fish and he was known very well for his practical jokes. One of his favourites was to sing to his passengers on the terminal building Tannoy system before departure and on one occasion that we know of was said to have boarded his aircraft wearing a rain coat over his uniform, sit at the back of the cabin complaining about being late, then saying to the passengers, 'If no one else was going to fly this aircraft I will.' He would then make his way to the cockpit, much to the dismay of the passengers, only revealing his identity at the last minute. Funny enough this used to raise quite a laugh from his passengers.
>
> BKS operated a Bristol Freighter out of Nutts Corner, it used to do a round-the-houses freight run at night and then lie up on the tarmac during the day. On one occasion I remember the aircraft being parked right outside our office and during the day a very stiff wind blew up 50/60 kts. The aeroplane was taking quite a buffeting, so much so that we noticed the chocks were slowly being displaced. We rang BKS and told them but before any one could get there, the aircraft slowly moved off (the Bristol Freighter had the old bag-type air brakes which used to leak after a period

---

2 He has another claim to fame, as the pilot of a Hawker Siddeley Trident 1c, which made the fastest chock to chock time between London and Aldergrove of only 39 minutes.

of time, leaving the aircraft with next to no braking system). The tarmac at Nutts Corner was on a gradient so the aircraft just taxied off on its own and ended up on the grass beside the taxiway. We ended up giving the BKS boys a hand to drag it out. Obviously steps were taken very quickly to ensure this incident didn't happen again.

John Selway during his RAF service. *(Battle of Britain Archive)*

In late 1962 a working party under the chairmanship of John Selway was established to manage the move from Nutts Corner to Aldergrove.

The planned opening date was 1st May 1963 but the onset of a prolonged spell of very severe weather after Christmas 1962 was a contributing factor to delays in the building work on the terminal, aircraft apron, control tower, instrument landing system (ILS) and airfield lighting which caused an initial postponement to an unspecified date in June. The hard and persistent frost had made concreting all but impossible. The three major airline customers, BEA, BKS and BUA, were consulted about altering the date. BEA advised that it would need a month's notice of any move and, additionally, would require the completion of a freight shed, catering facilities for 40–60 staff and provision for aircraft refuelling. The consensus of opinion was that if the move could not be made in June, then it would be best to wait until September, after the peak summer period. Therefore, in March it was decided that the date would be fixed as 26th September.

Meanwhile the RAF had raised objections concerning the name of the airport and argued that as it still owned the airfield, all road signs should refer not to 'Belfast Airport' or 'Civil Airport' but instead to 'Belfast Civil Air Terminal' or 'Civil Air Terminal'. The Ministry of Aviation did not agree and ignored the RAF's hair splitting. Another problem arose regarding the security of the site between the end of June when most of the contractors had finished work and September; in effect two or three months of the site lying fallow. The RAF stated very firmly that it would not assume policing responsibility. This problem was passed over to Sergeant Best, the senior police officer at Nutts Corner, who advised that he would consult the Royal Ulster Constabulary, and there the matter rested. By the middle of July, the ILS had been calibrated and the approach lighting on runway 08/26 had been installed. The control tower became operational in August.

Many of those who worked there have fond memories of Nutts Corner, it was by no means imposing or impressive but the homely collection of red-roofed, whitewashed buildings was welcoming and friendly. Staff relationships were excellent across the board, there was a great feeling of belonging and teamwork. The canteen was the hub of conversation and news, where airport, airline and air traffic personnel mixed. Noel Russell started work there as an apprentice fitter in 1959 and by the time he retired as Belfast International Airport's Operations Director in 1998, he had become the longest serving employee. To his 39 years could be added another 31 from his father, who had been at Nutts Corner since 1946. He remembers a time when fewer people had cars. Staff and crew buses operated from outlying districts every day, while passengers who had their own vehicles were met by porters who parked or garaged these to await their return. It was a much more deferential age, as another well-known figure on the Ulster travel scene, Maggie Gordon remembers, 'We didn't address a Captain or First Officer; we practically curtsied in their presence.' Maggie had regularly visited her uncle at Nutts Corner, who managed BKS, before starting in check-in and reservations at the age of 19, two years after the Aldergrove move.

Noel continued:

> Technology was much more rudimentary, de-icing the runway was simply a question of shovelling sand off the back of a lorry, the radar equipment was housed in a mobile unit and poor visibility landings were aided by paraffin fuelled Gooseneck flares. These were lit by hand and placed in rows either side of the runway to act as a flarepath. The operation was not without hazard, as on the occasion when an over-enthusiastic member of the ops team set the lorry carrying the flares on fire. Many of the staff came from the local area and supplemented farming incomes with airport work. Farming skills came into their own in the move to Aldergrove; specialist vehicle driving was a natural step from farm equipment. Workers were jacks of all trades, checking in, loading and portering.

Avro Anson G-APHV, belonging to BKS Air Survey Ltd. *(Dave Welch Collection)*

Bob Wilson made some more entries in his log:

> Thursday, 13th June 1963. Avro Anson G-APHV, belonging to BKS Air Survey Ltd, the aircraft was seen resting on the apron after completing a recent extensive local aerial survey programme.
>
> Wednesday, 19th June 1963. Herald G-APWF, operating a scheduled service from Bournemouth with British United Airways, landed at 12.22 hours on Runway 28. By this time, many new liveries were appearing on scheduled airliners. Other arrivals were Cambrian Airways Viscount, G-AMON, from Liverpool and Dakota, G-AHCZ, from Cardiff, Derby Airways Dakota, G-AMSX, from Derby via Carlisle, Aer Lingus F.27 Friendship, EI-AKC, from Dublin to Glasgow, BKS Ambassador, G-ALZW, from Newcastle to Dublin and that airline's new Avro 748,

Cambrian Airways Viscount, G-AMON. *(Barry Friend Collection)*

This HS-748 Srs.1101, G-ARMW, of BKS was new arrival at Nutts Corner in 1963. *(Dave Welch)*

Loading mail from a Morris Commercial LC5 onto a BEA Viscount at Nutts Corner in 1961. *(North of Ireland Philatelic Society)*

Dakota G-AJRY, operated by Standard Telephones. *(Ralf Manteufel)*

Swedish Air Force DHC-4 Caribou, 5501, of 7 Wing, taken at Le Bourget in 1963. *(Robin A Walker)*

G-ARMW, from Leeds. BEA Vanguards were G-APEH, G-APEI and G-APEK from both Glasgow and Heathrow.

Friday, 21st June 1963. Dakota G-AJRY, operated by Standard Telephones, in a pale blue scheme, landed on Runway 28 at 12.19 hours. The company had a factory at Monkstown in Newtownabbey and also serviced Beam Approach systems at airfields although the SBA was now being replaced by ILS.

Tuesday, 16th July 1963. DHC-4 Caribou, 5501, seen climbing out from Runway 10, the aircraft headed south east over Belfast towards Portaferry. Operated by the Swedish Air Force, this light transport aircraft had visited both Nutts Corner and Sydenham during the previous year along with other unusual types such as Piaggio P166, G-ARUJ and Beech 18, F-BHMM.

Sunday, 15th September 1963. Douglas

Piaggio P166, G-ARUJ; the co-author, who was 10 years old, spotted this aircraft when standing on the open-air observation platform at Aldergrove a year or two later, and, with the aid of The Observer's Book of Aircraft, was delighted to identify it. *(Peter Fitzmaurice)*

Globemaster 1, HP-367, operated by Aeronaves de Panama, this aircraft was one of the strangest ever to visit Nutts Corner. Parked in the customs area facing south, it was in a drab red and silver scheme and looked every bit the hard-pressed freighter. One of 13 production C-74As built in 1946 for the USAF, it had separate side-by-side cockpits and had originally been 42-65408. HP-367 was one of three operated by Aeronaves de Panama which were based at Copenhagen from early 1963 for freight charter work. When Aeronaves went out of business in 1968, the aircraft was abandoned at Milan-Malpensa and was eventually broken up there in 1972.

Wednesday, 25th September 1963. Dakota G-AMSX, on the last day of airline operations at Belfast (Nutts Corner) Airport, the aircraft taxied away from the apron at 17.45 hours using the parallel taxiway to the threshold of Runway 22 and almost disappeared from sight behind the pronounced hump at that end, which was the only blemish on an otherwise very picturesque airfield. Operated by Derby Airways, forerunner of British Midland, the Dakota lined up on the 4,500 Runway 22 and came roaring up over the hump to become possibly the last aircraft ever to take off from that runway. Interestingly, the apron and the parallel taxiways which had enhanced airline operations from 1946 were the result of upgrading in 1943 to bring the airfield up to USAAF Air Transport Command specification. Nutts Corner was one of only four airfields in the United Kingdom to receive this upgrade, the others being Prestwick, Valley and St Mawgan.

The largest aircraft to land at Nutts Corner was this C-74 Douglas Globemaster in 1963. *(Ernie Cromie)*

Chapter 19

End of an Era

A VALEDICTORY ARTICLE APPEARED in the October 1963 issue of BEA Magazine, written by 'M':

It didn't seem possible but there it was in black and white, 'From Thursday (26th September) all BEA flights serving Belfast will operate from the new civil airport at Aldergrove, sixteen miles west of the city. The newly designed civil airport and terminal will replace that at Nutts Corner which BEA has used since February 1947. So, Nutts Corner was to become a part of the past? Not that this should have been such startling news, for construction at Aldergrove had been underway for some time, but the announcement of the cessation of operations at Nutts Corner made one realise that a part of BEA was about to become just a name in our history book, so it was an occasion deserving of a tribute and, to produce that I crossed to Belfast to be at Nutts Corner for the last twenty-four hours of its life.

It was a sentimental journey in more ways than one, for, almost twenty years earlier I had a far less comfortable crossing for a period of RAF service and it was inevitable that, as Northern Ireland drew near, my thoughts should return to what had been for me a fairly depressing time. One of the less depressing features of my previous trip to Ireland had been the countryside and as the Vanguard crossed the coastline, there once again were the fields, greener even than I'd remembered, the little whitewashed cottages and the hills of County Antrim. So much for the past, for the plane was already taxying across the tarmac and there were the buildings of Nutts Corner.

Now, here it was with little over twenty-four hours' operational life ahead for Nutts Corner. For the staff, the majority of whom have been there from the beginning, the day ahead was obviously to be one tinged with sadness, for one can't work for so many years at one place without developing some affection for it and it was obvious from subsequent conversations with the staff that the following day, hectic though it promised to be, and despite the bright future at Aldergrove, would indeed be something of a sad one.

Already preparations for the move were in hand. Desks were being emptied, wastepaper baskets were full, numerous documents were produced and the general question was, 'Do you remember this …?'

A man with much to remember, and for whom the transfer to Aldergrove signals the end of an era is Robert Carter, BEA's Manager, Northern Ireland, until his retirement at the end of August 1963. Robert, 'Nick' to his friends, has been associated with aviation all his working life, firstly as a Sopwith Camel pilot in the RFC, followed by stints with Imperial Airways, the Aviation Division of the Ford Motor Company, Olley Air Services, Isle of Man Air Services and, from 1947, BEA. He was appointed BEA Manager, Northern Ireland in 1951. When asked how he felt, he replied, 'Well, mixed feelings, really. Of course, I'm sorry to see the end of Nutts Corner in a way. but we've grown out of it. I've been connected with Aldergrove since it first became obvious we'd have to move, so for me it's the realisation come true of what was once only a few notes on a piece of paper. It will seem strange at first, but then so do the first few days anywhere – besides, it's going to be so much easier for the passengers, staff, in fact everybody.' He looked at his watch as he made his way home. The hour was 10.15 pm, 'Tomorrow at this time,' he said, 'we'll be getting ready to see the last flight off.' As it turned out – he was wrong.

Robert Carter, John Kennedy and Ralph Thurley with the model of Aldergrove on display at Nutts Corner. *(WS Crawford and BA Archive)*

The following day dawned a bright one, thankfully, and the transfer began. Van load after van load operating a shuttle service from Nutts Corner to Aldergrove. Desks, chairs, lockers, equipment both light and heavy, all were carefully stacked and dispatched, and by lunch time many of the offices had already acquired a forlorn and deserted look. Business, however, continued as usual and looking at the number of people in the restaurant and waiting rooms I wondered how many, if indeed any, could sense the air of something special which to me seemed so very prevalent.

I viewed all this activity from a distance, feeling the moment not quite opportune to interrupt the operation, and this continued non-stop throughout the morning. At the centre of it all was BEA Station Superintendent Ralph Thurley, of whom someone said to me, 'He is Nutts Corner.' It was mid-afternoon before I was able to talk to him about it. His office was, with the exception of a small table, an upright chair and an assortment of stick-on-labels, empty, and, as he talked to me, he stood by the window looking out over the airfield, a view he has seen almost daily since December 1946.

Going to Aldergrove will, for him, be a case of 'this is where I came in' for it was at Aldergrove that he began his civil aviation career in 1934 with Railway Air Services. He was the first Station Superintendent at Nutts Corner when services were transferred there in December 1946, and he has the distinction of having been the only Station Superintendent throughout the entire period of operations. His feelings on the move were practical. 'You can't regret an improvement,' he said, 'and that's exactly what this is. Nutts Corner has done its job, and done a good job. Tomorrow it's the turn of Aldergrove.'

By this time the early morning blue sky had clouded over, the wind had dropped and there was a steady drizzle of rain. Almost within seconds it had developed into a heavy downpour. I ventured to suggest it might not last very long but Ralph, who obviously knows his Nutts Corner weather, as was indeed proved, thought otherwise, adding, 'This is all we needed.' He left me to see just how much this turn in the weather might affect the rest of the move, for there was still much to go to Aldergrove. Much of the equipment could not be moved until after the departure of the last flight out at 10.45 pm, and heavy rain combined with winding country lanes in darkness was, as Ralph so aptly put it, 'all we needed'. Raincoats were donned, tarpaulins produced and the work went on.

One closely connected with the move, and responsible for the organisation of it, is John R Kennedy, Station Engineer, and another Nutts Corner resident since 1946. For the past two years he has played a dual role – for in addition to his routine duties he was co-opted as 'clerk-of-works' for Property Branch, with which, in connection with the new airport there has been very close liaison. A partner in this liaison was Dennis A Cook, Senior Assistant Architect, who arrived on the afternoon flight from London, and was delighted to learn from John that, apart from the rain, all was going according to plan.

A further van load was dispatched en-route for Aldergrove, and John was able to relax a little, and talk about the staff. He agreed that Nutts Corner probably had more long serving staff than any other station. Duty Officers, Assistant Foremen. Fitters, Aircraft Cleaner, Storekeeper – all have been there since the early days, and all were moving to Aldergrove. One interesting point made by John was that in 1946 there were only two licensed engineers, whereas there were now twenty, all of them fully trained within BEA. The one piece of bad planning, so far as John was concerned, was that he would be unable to see his son Jack playing in goal for Distillery that evening against Benfica![1]

As another empty van returned for a further load John introduced me to William Cummings, Cargo Officer, and another of the long-distance-runner brigade. Bill clearly remembers the days of 1947 when the average monthly export cargo was 4000 kilos – compared with today's monthly 180,000 kilos! Cargo recently had the heaviest item brought into Northern Ireland by air – two generators from Copenhagen, each weighing 8½ tons. Bill can also recall taking coals to Newcastle! This happened about 1949 and although it's true, these were only coal samples it was too good a line to miss.

---

1 The match was a remarkable 3-3 draw.

The model of the new Belfast Airport which was on display at Nutts Corner in 1962. *(Author's Collection)*

The rain by now was little short of torrential, adding to the general air of desertion outside. In the waiting room, however, there was plenty of activity, and already passengers had arrived to check in for the last flight out. Not only passengers, for there were quite a few of the staff, whose duty had finished, waiting about, and staff had also come out from the city office to send off the last aircraft from Nutts Corner. One of these spectators was Jean Stanley, whose first association with Nutts Corner was in 1947, when she was secretary to Ralph Thurley, leaving him in 1950 to become secretary to the Manager, Northern Ireland. She was with Nick Carter throughout his entire period of office, and is already proving herself to be a pillar of strength to new 'boss', John Swann. I asked Jean if she could explain this feeling most of the staff had for Nutts Corner, but for her, as with all the others with whom I had spoken, it was 'just one of those things, I can't explain it – it's just that after so long… well, I suppose people will feel the same about Aldergrove ten years from now.'

Yes, I suppose they will. I'm also equally sure they'll still remember with great affection the days at Nutts Corner, whose very last day was now almost over. In the distance could be heard the Vanguard from London, the aircraft to be, or so we thought, the last one out from Nutts Corner. Suddenly, instead of the engine noise increasing, it began to fade, and within a few seconds came the announcement over the Tannoy that, due to the notorious crosswinds, the aircraft had been diverted to Aldergrove.[2] There was after all to be no sentimental farewell, the last one to leave

---

2   This was G-APEF, the 9.40pm BE6062 service from London to which reference is made in the signal below.

G-APEF, the first BEA Vanguard to land at Aldergrove on 25th September 1963 – a diversion from Nutts Corner because of bad weather. *(Joe Brown)*

had already gone without ceremony, the reign of Nutts Corner was over.

Now the final stages of the move could be made and equipment held back for the last flight was already being loaded on vans within a few minutes of the diversion announcement.[3] Passengers were transferred over to Aldergrove, where disembarkation of the first aircraft several hours before any arrival was expected had gone very smoothly. Extremely pleased with the operation was Senior Traffic Officer Thomas F Browne – yet another of the early Nutts Corner fraternity. 'You see,' said Tom, 'we have always been one happy family. And I'm sure we're going to be just as happy in our new home.'

Proud new parent of this family is Scotsman John Swann, who has succeeded Nick Carter as Manager, Northern Ireland. It seemed right that he was at Aldergrove to see the first one in – a new Airport and a new Manager. Like his predecessor, Mr Swann has many years experience in civil aviation behind him – 27 years in fact, having begun his career as Traffic Officer with Northern and Scottish Airways at Renfrew, Glasgow. John, who served with the Fleet Air Arm during the war as a Flying Control Officer, saw service at home, overseas and afloat – on escort carriers. On the formation of BEA in January 1946 he was appointed Traffic Superintendent of the Scottish Division, a post he held until transferring to Bealine in 1956 as Passenger Services Manager. During the last few minutes prior to embarkation, I talked to John about Aldergrove, specifically designed for handling heavy domestic air traffic demanding quick 'turn-rounds' and high density airliners. Like the new proud parent he is, John was full of enthusiasm. 'The new airport terminal building at Aldergrove is functionally the best in Europe, if not the world, for coping with the existing and developing traffic pattern.'

He read out a signal from Anthony Milward, the Chief Executive of BEA:
MY BEST WISHES TO YOU AND ALL YOUR STAFF ON THE MOVE TO ALDERGROVE THURSDAY stop YOU HAVE ALL ACHIEVED MIRACLES DURING THESE DIFFICULT YEARS AT NUTTS CORNER AND I KNOW HOW PLEASED YOU WILL BE TO HAVE A NEW AIRPORT WITH WHICH TO WORK.

A reply was sent in the early hours of 26th September, after the arrival of the first scheduled flight:

---

3 Jim Logan, then a young traffic clerk but later to become the BA Regional Manager, particularly remembers the long trains of baggage trucks being pulled along the winding country road between the two airports.

YOUR SIGNAL AND GOOD WISHES MUCH APPRECIATED BY US ALL stop NOW AT ALDERGROVE AND TRANSFER COMPLETED stop BE6062 DIVERTED HERE DUE WEATHER NUTTS CORNER stop ALL STAFF HAVE DONE A SPLENDID JOB stop VISCOUNT FROM MANCHESTER LANDED AT 00.16 HOURS AND VANGUARD FROM LONDON HAS JUST LANDED.

It was time for 'M' to return by Vanguard to London, not on the last flight out of Nutts Corner as planned but instead, the first departure from Aldergrove:

> The engines were revving up and through the curtain of rain I could see the sizeable crowd waiting to see us off and within a matter of seconds we were underway. The lights from Aldergrove quickly faded from view and we were soon out of the bad weather and cruising smoothly through the night. The pilot of the aircraft, Captain AJB Macreth was to provide the last coincidence of the trip. It seemed only fair that he should take the first aircraft out of Aldergrove, where, in 1931, he trained with the RAF as a Navigator/Air Gunner.'

So, on 26th September 1963, operations transferred to Aldergrove, which therefore became the civil airport for Northern Ireland, while remaining a major RAF station. The first commercial flight that day was an incoming BEA Viscount from Manchester, which arrived on stand at 00.23, followed by a Vanguard, G-APEH, from London. The previous evening, the last flight due to land at Nutts Corner, G-APEF, a Vanguard from London, had been diverted to Aldergrove owing to the weather.

Some of the first travellers commented to a reporter, Mr Leslie Mackie said:

> I am inclined to believe that it has not been built sufficiently large to cope with expanding traffic. [He would be proved right within a very short space of time.]

Miss Rosemary Wheeler added:

> I feel rather sad at the change. Somehow Nutts Corner had come to mean home to me but I suppose we really needed something bigger than the huts.

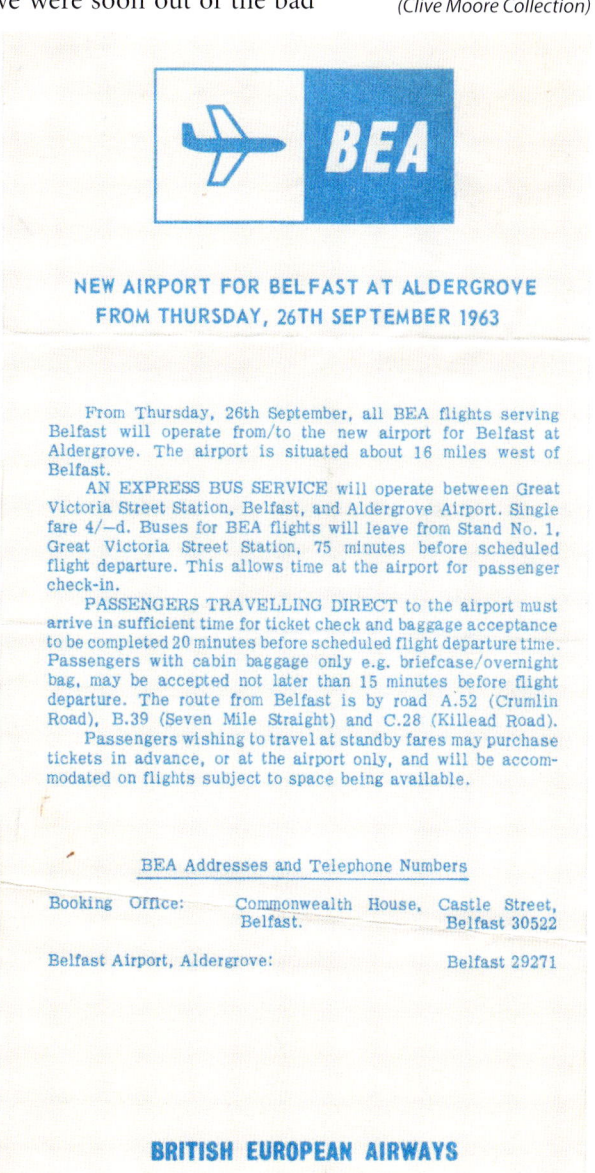

An announcement from BEA in 1963. *(Clive Moore Collection)*

According to Mr Thomas McClinton:

> The two biggest improvements from my point of view are the finger arrangement which means we don't have to run three or four hundred yards through the rain and the fact that luggage is collected under cover.

Other long-standing Nutts Corner residents, by all accounts, decided to move as well as the airport and airline staff. Over the years, hares on the airfield had been a very familiar sight and frequently played 'dare' with landing aircraft. Within a month of the move to Aldergrove, hares appeared there too. The RAF swore there were no hares before the airliners arrived and more than one flight crew over the succeeding decades has experienced a 'hare miss' while taxying.

An explanation can be given for the apparently peculiar name for an airport, Nutts Corner, reportedly the butt of some jokes by visiting cockpit personnel! The Ordnance Survey Historical map 1st Edition of 1832 had no mention of Nutts Corner but by the 3rd Edition in 1900 there it was, Nutts Corner together with its post office at the crossroads. There were ten members of the Nutt[4] families recorded in the 1851 census. Also, the Killultagh Old Rock & Chichester Fox Hunt were recorded in an exhibition in Lisburn Museum as meeting at Nutts Corner.

William and Martha Nutt on the runway at Nutts Corner. *(Joe Brown Collection)*

---

4 The surname Nutt is of English origin, and may possibly refer to someone who lived by a nut-tree. Alternatively, it may be derived from an individual with a round head or a brown complexion (Old English *hnutu*). Nutts are common in Co Antrim, Londonderry and Down, and it is said locally that Nutts Corner is named after an individual named Isaac Nutt, said to have been hanged there in 1798. The practice of naming road junctions after a prominent nearby farming family is not uncommon, see, for example Coleman's Corner and Houston's Corner on the A8 Belfast to Larne road.

A photograph appeared in the *Daily Mail* on 27th September 1963 (the day after the airport officially closed) of 70-year-old William and wife Martha Nutt walking on the main runway-28. William, a farmer, was reported as saying, 'I took rather a pride in the family name being so well known.' The Nutt family connection still exists in the early 2020s as their daughter Elizabeth Nutt (great-granddaughter of Thomas of the 1851 census) now lives in Antrim. She worked at Nutts Corner and subsequently Aldergrove. Elizabeth was on first name terms with all ranks from her catering job and Eason's shop.[5]

Two months later, in November, the *Belfast Telegraph* noted that the perimeter and the silent, empty buildings were still being patrolled by Constable Sydney Crawford and three other Ministry of Aviation policemen, to guard against vandalism while it was decided what should be done with the site and to protect residual items of equipment that remained to be moved.

A collection of BEA baggage labels from Nutts Corner late 1950s/early 1960s, preserved by Joe Brown.

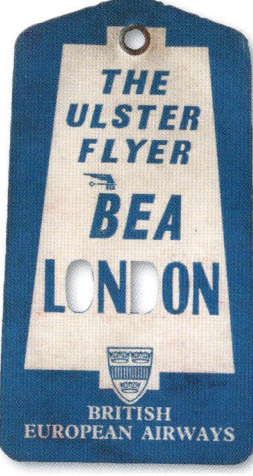

---

5 In 1851 there were two farms in the townland belonging to different branches of the Nutt family. Thomas Nutt had been born in 1815, his son, Hugh was three years old at the time of the census. The 1901 census records that he had two sons, John and William, the latter being the father of Elizabeth.

Chapter 20

Not Quite the End

There was, however, a swansong, faithfully recorded by Bob Wilson:

Friday, 23rd April 1965. Beverley, XB287 'T'. Nutts Corner had been closed for more than a year and a half when, in mid-morning, this aircraft made an intentional and fully controlled landing on the still-intact 6,000 feet Runway 10. Even more bizarrely, it was followed in quick succession by Hastings, TG556, and Armstrong Whitworth Argosy, XR143. All three RAF machines taxied up to the apron, where military equipment and vehicles were unloaded by Army personnel. Patrols by Army units appeared along surrounding roads and a radio installation was observed at the Runway 28 threshold. The Beverley, resplendent in Transport Command grey and white with the green diamond of No 47 Squadron on its fins, took off from Runway 10 and headed off to the south east while the Argosy set up a shuttle service to and from Aldergrove, taking off from 10 landing on 26, taking off from 17 and, with an immediate low-level left turn, landing on 10 at Nutts Corner again. Very short turn-arounds provided constant exercise in loading and unloading as more Hastings aircraft arrived at Aldergrove from Great Britain. This large-scale airhead exercise, which was somehow an appropriate end to the military flying career of Nutts Corner airfield, continued through the weekend, finishing on Monday, 26th April. Once again, the runways had echoed to the sound of military piston engines which had resonated from 1941 with based B-24 Liberators, B-17 Fortresses, Wellingtons, Stirlings and Yorks, arguably the most famous individual being the 5,000th B-17 built, 43-37716 '5 GRAND' which transited on delivery in May 1944, completely covered with Boeing workers' signatures.

And finally, a young Belfast mechanical engineer, WH 'Bill' Ekin had built a Bensen Gyrocopter which, in 1968, he flew at Nutts Corner, close to Crumlin Woollen Mill which became his base. Enthused, he purchased a gyroplane, G-ATXW, from the engineer, Rex McCandless, and secured the rights to build the McCandless machines. In 1969 and 1970, he formed two companies to build and market, respectively, McCandless-type gyroplanes. After many essential changes to the McCandless design and with the help of the retired Squadron Leader Desmond Mock as test pilot, the outcome was the WHE 'Airbuggy'.

All that remains of Nutts Corner. *(Ernie Cromie Collection)*

Despite many setbacks, including the collapse of the mill roof on top of two machines and several crashes, by the 1980s Bill had succeeded in building and selling six Airbuggys.

On which fitting note, the story of Nutts Corner airfield closes. Today the site is occupied by the Transport Training Board for Northern Ireland, a kart and motorcycle racing circuit, a venue for flying model aircraft enthusiasts, a farm implement dealership, a Sunday market, LIDL warehouse and a major road roundabout – Runway 22/04 becoming the A26 towards Moira.

The McCandless WHE Airbuggy autogyro, G-ATXW, purchased by Bill Ekin, at Ards. In the background is a DH Tiger Moth. *(Ernie Cromie Collection)*

Appendix
Passenger and cargo figures 1944–1963

Year	Passengers	% Change	Intnl. Pax	Tonnes	Comments
1944	16831				Belfast Harbour (BHD)
1945	27851	38.3			BHD
1946	48114	41.2	n/k	n/k	BHD
1947	78502	63.2	n/k	n/k	Nutts Corner from December 1946
1948	81865	4.3	n/k	n/k	
1949	109298	33.5	n/k	n/k	
1950	117165	7.2	n/k	n/k	
1951	129621	10.6	n/k	n/k	
1952	144790	11.7	n/k	n/k	
1953	164685	13.7	n/k	n/k	
1954	185851	12.9	n/k	n/k	
1955	227000	22.1	n/k	3900	
1956	217990	17.3	n/k	n/k	
1957	284099	30.3	n/k	3678	
1958	269566	-5.1	n/k	4058	
1959	323755	20.1	n/k	5676	
1960	428533	32.4	n/k	8584	
1961	515704	20.3	n/k	6450	
1962	585239	13.5	n/k	7736	
1963	661834	13.1	n/k	9264	Aldergrove from 27th September 1963

Bibliography

Bardon, Jonathan, *A History of Ulster* (Belfast 1996)

Bowyer, Chaz, *Coastal Command at War* (London 1979)

Butler, PH, *An Illustrated History of Liverpool Airport* (Liverpool 1983)

Byrne, Liam, *History of Aviation in Ireland* (Dublin 1980)

Cameron, Dugald, *Glasgow's Airport* (Glasgow 1990)

Corlett, John, *Aviation in Ulster* (Belfast 1981)

Cromie, Ernie, *Overhead and Over Here* (Belfast 2015)

Day, Angelique, McWilliams, Patrick and English, Lisa (editors), *Ordnance Survey Memoirs of Ireland 1833–38 Vol. 35 Parishes of County Antrim XIII* (Belfast 1996)

Gilbert, Martin, *The Boys* (London 1996)

Jefford, Wing Commander CG *RAF Squadrons* (Shrewsbury 1998)

Lo Bao, Phil, *An Illustrated History of British European Airways* (Feltham 1989)

Merton Jones, AC *British Independent Airlines Since 1946* (Liverpool 1977)

Moore, Clive, *The American Red Cross in Northern Ireland* (Belfast 2023)

Ponsford, Rob, *80th Anniversary of the formation of the Glider Pilot Regiment 1942–1957* (2022)

Price, Dr Alfred, *Aircraft versus Submarine* (London 1980)

Scholefield, RA *Manchester Airport* (Stroud 1998)

Scott Cairns, DA *Report of the Court Investigation on the Accident to Viking G-AJDL* (London 1953)

Share, Bernard, *The Flight of the Iolar* (Dublin 1986)

Skaarup, Harold A, *Canadian Warplanes 9: General Aircraft Hotspur Glider*

Smith, David J, *Action Stations 7. Military Airfields of the North East and Northern Ireland* (Yeovil 1983)

Staddon, TG, *History of Cambrian Airways* (London 1979)

Stroud, John, *Railway Air Services* (London 1987)

Sturtivant, Ray and Balance, Theo, *The Squadrons of the Fleet Air Arm* (Tonbridge 1994)

Sturtivant, Ray with Hamlin, John, *RAF Flying Training and Support Units since 1912* (Tonbridge 1997)

Swann, John, *40 Years of Air Transport in Northern Ireland* (Belfast 1971)

Warner, Guy and Woods, Jack, *In the Heart of the City* (Belfast 1998)

Warner, Guy and Woods, Jack, *Belfast International Airport – Aviation at Aldergrove since 1918* (Newtownards 2001)

Warner, Guy, *Flying from Derry – Eglinton and the story of Naval Aviation in Northern Ireland* (Belfast 2007)

Warner, Guy and Cromie, Ernie, *Military Aviation in Northern Ireland – An Illustrated History 1913 to the Present Day* (Newtownards 2012)

Warner, Guy and Cromie, Ernie, *Civil Aviation in Northern Ireland – An Illustrated History 1909 to the Present Day* (Newtownards 2013)

Woodley, Charles, *Golden Age British Civil Aviation 1945–1965* (Shrewsbury 1992)

Wight, PG and Rennison SP, *No 120 Squadron Royal Air Force 1918–1998* (1998)

Acknowledgements

Grateful thanks are due to: Peter Amos, Ron Bishop, Joe Brown, Dennis Burke, Chalmers Butterfield, Mike Charlton, Allen Clarke, Ed Coates, Wing Commander Colin Cummings, Jim Davies, deepseatrawlers.co.uk, Peter Devitt, Richard Doherty, John Douglas, Dr Dan Ellin, L Engelen, Chris England, Stephen Finney, Peter Fitzmaurice, Barry Friend, Tony Hancke, Gordon Harper, Keith Hayward, Wing Commander Dave Higgins, Darrell Hillier, Bert Hutchinson, Peter Jones, Dr Frances Kane, Seamus Leheny, John Levesley, Dr Keith Lilley, Iain MacKay, Tommy Maddock, Bert Magowan, Ralf Manteufel, Keith McCloskey, Ian McFarlane, Clive Moore, Peter Myers, Dr James O'Neill, Major Fred Paradie RCAF, J Patience, Rob Ponsford, Jim Rankin, Richard Riding, Mrs Mavis Riley, Stephen Riley, Ray Rimell, RA Scholefield, RJ Spencer, Nick Stroud, Alan Thomas, Daz Tindall, Fedor van der Pol, Robin A Walker, Dave Welch, Alan Wilson and Bob Wilson for their invaluable help; some of whom are, sadly, no longer with us. The creative input and expertise of Malcolm Johnston and the team at Colourpoint Books is, as always, greatly appreciated.

Four front pages from the timetables of Railway Air Services, Silver City, BKS and BEA, trace the history of Nutts Corner from the 1940s to the 1960s. *(Guy Warner Collection)*

Index

Places

Aberdeen 122
Agnew's Hill 34
Ailsa Craig 94
Aldergrove
    Civil Airport 174-80
Algeria 53
    Oran Tafraoui Airport 53
Alloa 33
Alva 33
Amsterdam 166
Antrim 60
    Clotworthy House 60
    Massereene Hotel 120
    Six Mile Water 60
Ards Peninsula 101, 129
Armagh 86
ATC Station 1009 75
Aughnamullan 9
Aughrim Hill 98
Auschwitz 100
BAD 1 Burtonwood 64
BAD 2 Warton 64
BAD 3 Langford Lodge 9, 64, 72, 76, 79, 80, 90, 148
Ballintrillick 73
Ballykinler 44
Ballymena 46
Ballymoney 57, 67
Bangor 22, 86, 134
Bay of Biscay 33, 37, 39
Belfast 16, 22, 65, 86, 94, 108, 109, 111, 149
    Ardoyne 138
    Ben Madigan Park 85
    Carlton Ballroom 118
    City Hall 118
    Cliftonville Circus 94
    Donegall Place 118
    Donegall Quay 126
    Donegall Square East 115, 123
    Four Hundred Club 94
    Glengall Street 123, 156, 158
    Grand Central Hotel 27, 94
    Great Northern Station 130
    Harbour 43, 44
    Harbour Airport 108-109, 111, 113-14, 118-19, 155, 159, 172
    Imperial House 115, 122
    Musgrave Park 66
    Parliament Buildings 44
    Queen's University 140
    Stormont 44
    Sydenham 39
    Woodvale Presbyterian 133
Belfast Lough 85
    Mew Island 119
Bellaghy 53
Belleek 90
Biarritz 33
Birmingham Airport
    Elmdon 125, 131, 161
Blackpool Airport
    Squire's Gate 117, 122, 125, 127, 154, 161, 165
Bordeaux 38
Bournemouth Airport
    Hurn 125, 165, 171
Bristol Airport
    Whitchurch 125, 147
    Lulsgate 161
Bryansford 58
Burbank 151
Burnaston
    Derby Airport 164, 171
Caithness 34
California 140
Cape Finisterre 37
Cardiff Airport

Rhoose 125, 147, 161, 171
Carlisle Airport
    Crosby 47, 112, 113, 171
Carrickfergus
    Eden 74
    Hospital 169
Castle Kennedy 155
Castlereagh Hills 85
Cave Hill 85
Coagh 57
Coleraine 90, 145-46
Copenhagen 173, 176
Cork 28
Cregagh Hills 153
Croydon
    Greyhound Inn 139
Crumlin 86, 158
    Belfast Road 38
    Boltnaconnell Road 23
    Glenavy 41
    Railway Station 23
    St Joseph's Churchyard 41
    Woollen Mill 181
Crumlin River 62
Cushendall 90-91, 98
Cushleake Mountain 85
Czechoslovakia
    Prague 100
    Ruzyně Airport 101
Daventry 142
Denham Airfield 167
Derbyshire 47
Divis Mountain 27, 40, 58, 66
Donaghadee 49, 101, 150
Donegal 154
Dromore 16
Dublin 115, 119, 123, 150, 161, 162, 171
Dumfries 47
Dundesert 9, 60
Dundrod 22, 26, 135, 137
Dunseverick 99
Edinburgh Airport
    Turnhouse 147, 161
Enniskillen 73, 147

Exeter Airport 165
Falkirk 50
Ferrol 38
Gander Airport 140, 146, 149,
Giant's Causeway 86
Glasgow Airport
    Renfrew 103, 109, 112, 116, 119, 125, 126,
        131, 143, 161, 162, 165, 171, 172, 178
Gourock 50
Graan 73
Greenland 64
    Bluie West-1 (Narsarsuaq Air Base) 64
Heysham 139
Hillsborough 44
    Government House 44
Holywood 85
Hungary 100
Iceland 39, 147
    Meeks Field (Naval Air Station Keflavik)
        64, 66, 82
    Reykjavik 34
Isle of Man 55, 109
    Calf of Man 50
    Ronaldsway Airport 108, 112, 113, 120,
        122, 129, 155, 161, 165
    Onchan 50
Japan 38
    Tokyo 166
Jersey 147, 150, 161
Johnstown 74
Kilkenny 74
Killead 9
Kintyre 167
La Pallice 38
La Rochelle 38
Lagan Valley 129
    Hospital 169
Langford Lodge 90, 159
Larne 23, 46
Leeds/Bradford Airport
    Yeadon 122, 125, 147, 161, 172
    Lewis 59
    Uig Bay 59
Lewisburg 86

Lisburn 108
Lisnabreeny American Military Cemetery 85
Liverpool 15, 36
    Speke Airport 108, 109, 111, 112, 115, 116, 119, 120, 125, 126, 154, 161, 165, 171
London
    Buckingham Palace 32
    Croydon Airport 108, 109, 111-13, 117, 125
    Heathrow/London Airport 124, 125, 140-42, 150, 152, 158, 161-62, 164-65, 172, 176-77, 179
    Northolt Airport 109, 112, 119, 124-25, 131, 136, 142
Londonderry 86, 129, 145
    City Hotel 139
    Naval Base 33, 34, 76, 79
Lough Neagh 9, 24, 29, 57, 76, 80-82, 90, 114, 129, 132-33, 158, 169
    Ardmore Boatyard 79
    Bombing and Gunnery Ranges 29, 36, 51, 55, 80
    Camp Ben Neagh 78-79
    Ram's Island 76
    Sandy Bay 76-82
Lyle's Hill 85
McGowan's Hill 58
Magherafelt 28
Manchester
    Ringway Airport 108, 109, 112, 116, 119, 127, 131, 132, 161, 179
Mallusk 32
Milan-Malpensa 173
Millisle 101
    Ballyrolly House 101
Moira 44
Monkstown 172
Montreal 140
Moray Firth 94
Morocco 77, 80
    Port Lyautey 77, 80
Mossley 85
Mourne Mountains 54, 129
Munich 158
Newferry 53

New York 66, 76, 78, 80, 82, 140, 151-52, 167
    Marine Air Terminal 81
Newcastle, Co Down 86
Newcastle upon Tyne Airport
    Woolsington 112-13, 142-43, 147, 161, 171, 176
Newfoundland
    Botwood 76, 77, 80
Newtownards 47
    Airport 122, 155
Niagara-on-the-Lake 144
North Channel 23
North Sea 32
Norway 40, 59
    North Cape 40
Oban 34
Ochil Hills 33
Oldham 127
Paris
    Le Bourget 125-26
Polmont 50
Portaferry 154, 172
Portpatrick 47
Portrush 86, 99, 161
    Ramore Head 161
Portstewart 146
Prestwick 20, 108, 113, 125, 131, 140, 152, 167, 173
Prince Edward Island 81
    Shediac 81
Rhodesia 23
River Bann 52-53
Rostrevor 44
RAF Aldergrove 9, 15, 17, 23, 34-35, 51-52, 59-60, 74, 76-77, 159-60, 168-70, 181
RAF Andreas 50, 55
RAF Ballyhalbert 43, 55, 74, 159
RAF Ballykelly 36, 46, 50
RAF Beaulieu 51
RAF Belfast 74
RAF Bishops Court 159
RAF Brackla 94
RAF Bramcote 57
RAF Burtonwood 149

RAF Clifton 55
RAF Cluntoe 72, 74
RAF Cranwell 131
RAF Dunkeswell 63
RAF Dyce 33
RAF Gloucester 90
RAF Hendon 68
RAF Kimbolton 68
RAF Limavady 18, 26, 28
RAF Long Kesh 47-48, 52, 54, 68, 89, 108, 159
RAF Longtown 92
RAF Lyneham 41
RAF Macrahanish 165
RAF Maghaberry 44, 52, 54, 64
RAF Mullaghmore 57, 90-91, 97
RAF Netheravon 47, 49-50, 75
RAF Newtownards 54
RAF Polebrook 35
RAF Predannack 41
RAF Prestwick 27-30, 61, 64, 67-68, 74, 77, 90, 94
RAF Ramsbury 51
RAF Reykjavík 21, 63
RAF Riccall 95
RAF Ringway 47
RAF Ronaldsway 50
RAF St Angelo 27, 73-74
RAF St Eval 33, 37
RAF St Mawgan 62-63, 66, 173
RAF Shipdham 64
RAF Shobdon 47
RAF Stoney Cross 93
RAF Stornoway 41, 69-70, 89
RAF Stranraer 28
RAF Thorney Island 25
RAF Tiree 29, 41
RAF Toome 57, 72
RAF Valley 62, 84, 173
RAF Waddington 41
RAF West Freugh 55
RAF West Malling 16
RAF Wick 34
RAF Woodvale 155
RCAF Gander 63, 67, 82, 84

RCAF Goose Bay 64, 68-69, 73-75, 82
RN Shore Establishments
    HMS Gadwall 100-101
    HMS Pintail 96
    RNAS Eglinton 68, 151
    RNAS Maydown 72
Ruthenia 100
Saddleworth Moor 127
    Wimberry Stones 127
San Francisco 151
Sierra Leone 42
    Freetown 42
Shannon Airport 140
Slieveanorra Mountain 67
Slievenanee Mountain 98
Sligo 73
Sperrin Mountains 54
Squires Hill 154
Strangford Lough 129
Stavanger 150
Stornoway 59
Stranraer 23, 155
Sweden 40
    Falun 40
Templepatrick 168
    Templeton Arms 168
The Minches 34
Tipperary 41
Tokyo 166
Toronto 84, 151
    Malton Airport 146
Tory Island 154
Truskmore Mountain 73
Tyrone 129
USNOB Londonderry 76, 78-79
USN Communications Station 144, 151
Vancouver Airport 126, 166
Welsh Mountains 39
Weston Airfield 148
Weston-Super-Mare 125
Wrexham 47

People

Abrahamson, Captain O 81
Absolom, AH 118
Adams, Bob 128
Allgood, Flight Sergeant EA 40
Anderson, Corporal D 22
Andrews, JM 43
Appleby, Flight Lieutenant A 100
Attenborough, Lord 84
Baker, Flight Lieutenant D 100
Baker, Roy 94
Ball, Flying Officer PA 42, 43
Bannister, Flying Officer BS 21, 25, 29, 39
Barclay, Wing Commander RAC 96
Barlow, Flight Lieutenant TPE 42
Barratt, Air Marshal Sir Arthur 48
Baxter, Raymond 142
Bebington, E 152
Berry, Homer G 21, 26
Best, Sergeant 170
Bilsland, Sir Stephen 108
Bira, Prince of Siam 135
Blackett, Professor Patrick 36
Booker, Sergeant EJ 40
Borchert, 2nd Lieutenant M 72
Boyle, James 9
Brooke, Sir Basil 81, 82, 166
Brooks, Flight Officer L 84, 85
Brown, Andy 23
Brown, Joe 23, 136, 155, 158, 159
Brown, Air Commodore V 120
Browne, Thomas F 178
Bruce, William 117
Bulloch, Flight Lieutenant TM 21, 22, 27-33
Butler, Corporal 50
Cable, Charlie 128
Caesar-Gordon, Captain A 142
Cairns, Sir David 138
Carson, 2nd Lieutenant C 68, 72
Carter, Robert 175, 177-78
Chapman, Sergeant 16
Chasty, Bill 138
Cheek, WOp/AG E 23, 34-35
Clark, Technical Sergeant FS 65
Claydon, Flying Officer 39
Cole-Hamilton, Air Vice Marshal JB 43
Colyer, Air Vice Marshal D 44
Connor, Billy 145-46
Cook, Dennis A 176
Cooper, Wing Commander TB 48
Corkran, Sergeant TJ 23, 40
Crawford, Bertie 138
Crawford, Constable Sydney 181
Cree, Mr & Mrs 94
Culnane, Flight Sergeant J 40
Cundy, Flying Officer PJ 25, 37-38
Cumming, Wing Commander WN 21, 26-28
Cummings, William 176
Cunningham, George 9
Cupples, Miss ME 116
Dainty, Warrant Officer E 42
Dann, Wing Commander CL 29
Davis, Miss Carol Lee 86
Davis, Mrs Jean 26
Dempster, Corporal E 49
Dennison, Lieutenant M 48-49
Densham, Pilot Officer WM 39
Dew, Flying Officer A 52
D'Erlanger, G 123-24
Dooley, John 118
Dors, Diana 158
Doxsey, Warrant Officer JA 92
Dundon, Staff Sergeant LE 84
Durst, Captain AD 77
Eames, Bill 119
Edmenson, WA 123
Eisenhower, Dwight D 166
Ekin, WH 182
Engelen, L 129
Esler, Flying Officer SE 22
Evans, Flight Lieutenant D 25
Evans, Flight Lieutenant DE 60
Fabel, Flying Officer 38
Finch, Brian 126, 135, 142, 146, 147
Finch, HP 126
Fletcher, Flight Sergeant MJ 58
Freydig, Major Paul E 62

INDEX

Galpin, John 152
Galpin, Irene 152
Gamble, Flight Sergeant G 34
Gamble, W 109, 115, 117, 122, 128
Gash, Sergeant 16
Gates, Squadron Leader RTF 32, 34, 36
Geiger, 2nd Lieutenant TE 74
George, Captain GC 80
Gibson, Corporal A 22
Gilbert, Aircraftman 39
Gooder, Sergeant J 40
Gordon, Maggie 170
Gordon, Noel 168-69
Granville, 4th Earl 43-44, 115, 123
Granville, Countess 43-44
Gray, Captain David 159
Greenberg, Victor 100
Griffith, 2nd Lieutenant R C 64
Grim, 2nd Lieutenant M 73
Haley, Bill 158
Hall, A 152
Hallam, Wing Commander M 56
Harper, Gordon 139
Harper, T 78
Harrison, Ms Elizabeth 86
Harrison, Flight Lieutenant SJ 21-22, 27-28, 46
Hartley, Captain Gordon 136, 138
Harvey, Bernard 32
Henderson, Leading Aircraftman A 50
Henderson, B 118
Henderson, Flying Officer 57
HRH Queen Elizabeth 43-44, 46
Hesson, Captain Hugo 152
Hill, 2nd Lieutenant AN 89
HRH King George VI 32, 43-44, 46
Hollis, Sergeant 33
Holt, First Officer 127
Howden, GB 122
Hughes, Flying Officer FD 16
Hutchinson, Bert 109
Hyde, Pilot Officer 48
Ibbotson, Derek 158
Jackson, AJ 112
Jacobs Warrant Officer, Denzil 100

Johnson, Technical Sergeant JD 66
Jones, Flying Officer TJ 92, 94
Jones, Flying Officer ER 55
Kearney, Wing Commander WH 51
Kemp, Flight Sergeant T 58
Kennedy, Squadron Leader F 50
Kennedy, Jack 176
Kennedy, JR 128, 176
Kenny, Sam 126
Kent, Air Commodore the Duke of 32
Kersley, Thelma 50
Kidd, Wing Commander EC 17
Knott, HS 122
Knowles, Wing Commander EV 50
Lauder, Sergeant 16
Layton, Pilot Officer M 28, 33
Lees-Jones, Sub Lieutenant (A) D 99
Lenz, Warrant Officer LW 60
Leopold III ex King of Belgium 147
Lindgren, GS 123-24
Llewellyn, Flying Officer THA 27, 29-30
Logan, N 128
Londonderry, 7th Marquis of 122
Lord, Cyril 150
Ludlum, Lieutenant Commander T 78, 81
Lurkins, Sergeant EF 58
Lyons, George 145
Mackie, Flying Officer G 92-93
Mackie, Leslie 179
MacDonald, 'Mac' 94
Macreth, Captain AJB 179
Mann, Mr 139
Mathers, A 128
Matlack, Captain AE 81
MacAllister, Sub Lieutenant I 97
McAuley, Danny 128
McBratney, Wing Commander VHA 28
McCandless, Rex 182
McClelland, Robert 99
McClinton, Thomas 180
McCune, Robert 9
McDouall, Robin 164
McGonigal, Flight Lieutenant K 59
McKee, Mrs Margaret 168

McKenzie, Flight Officer LB 84
McMullan, Daniel 99
McNair, Wing Commander DIP 41
McReynolds, Colonel 21, 26
Medhurst, JA 152
Miles, Flying Officer R 92
Millar, Miss D 116
Milward, Anthony 159, 178
Mines, Sergeant H 39
Mock, Squadron Leader D 182
Monaghan, James 78
Moynihan, Captain DG 111
Murphy RH 116
Nash, Sub Lieutenant (A) WL 98
Neill, Sir William 123
Nicholson, Pilot Officer DF 42
Nugent, Sir Roland 123
Nutt, Elizabeth 181
Nutt, Martha 181
Nutt, Thomas 181
Nutt, William 181
O'Connell, 2nd Lieutenant W 66
O'Hanlon, Paddy 137
O'Neill, JRP 129
O'Shea, Sergeant T 41
Pakenham, 7th Earl of Longford 118
Panchak, Private First Class G 89
Paton, Pilot Officer AB 50
Patterson, Flight Sergeant 58
Petley, Sergeant 50
Phillips, Sub Lieutenant NE 97
Pickering, Sergeant JD 40
Pinkerton, Captain FW 126
Pollock, Mr 130
Pope, Wing Commander VA 54
Poore, Flight Lieutenant 92
Porteous, Fred 128
Price, Dr Alfred 32
Pritchett, Group Captain NAP 21, 26, 44, 131
Purvis, Leonard 117
Raff, Lieutenant Colonel E 51
Rebbeck, Sir Frederick 108
Richardson, Sergeant AA 58
Ritchie, WOp/AG M 22

Robinson, FA 116
Ross, Flight Lieutenant JS 92
Russell, Noel 170
Salt, Corporal 50
Schmidt, 2nd Lieutenant R 69
Selway, Wing Commander J 164, 168, 170
Shepherd, Sergeant 16
Siddall, Sub Lieutenant (A) T 99
Slattery, Rear Admiral Sir Matthew 159
Smith, Sergeant BF 40
Smith, Sergeant EA 48
Stagg, Aircraftman FJ 55
Stanley, Jean 177
Stapleton, Flight Sergeant 57
Stark, Admiral HR 76-77
Steele, Tommy 158
Stevenson, WHC 128
Stewart, Captain RM 152
Stokes, Captain R 117
Stroud, John 111
Swain, Commander JH 96
Swann, John 177-78
Taylor, Flight Lieutenant 48
Templeton, M 129
Tennyson, Pilot Officer T 50
Thomas, Flight Lieutenant 16
Thompson, Norman 128
Thompson, Tommy 94
Thurley, Ralph 168, 175-77
Tinsman, 2nd Lieutenant 65
Tomkins, First Officer WG 152
Tweed, Brian 139
Tweed, Mrs Greta 139
Tweed, Mr 139
Tweed, Lieutenant M 168
Wade, Sub Lieutenant (A) LP 98
Wait, Major GK 50
Waite, Sergeant JF 39
Wakefield, Flying Officer H 39
Wakehurst, 2nd Baron 147, 166
Walch, 2nd Lieutenant 73
Wallis, Sergeant MCC 48
Walton, Flying Officer R 25, 33-34, 40
Watkins, AC2 AJ 27

Watson, Lieutenant AW 97
Welford, Captain J 169
Welford, Sergeant P 39
Wheeler, Rosemary 179
Wightman, Pilot Officer 28-29
Wild, Sergeant C 48
Wilkinson, Squadron Leader AB 48
Williams, Corporal 50
Wilson, Sergeant Pilot H 23
Wilson, Bob 134, 145, 147, 149, 153, 161, 163-67, 171, 182
Wilson, Sergeant Pilot WJ 39
Wolby, Flight Lieutenant AL 52
Woosley, Flight Lieutenant EJ 73
Worner, Sub Lieutenant (A) GW 97
Wright, Wing Commander CFC 34
Yapp, Captain D 111

Organisations

Admiralty 33
Aer Lingus 115, 116, 118, 119, 150, 162, 166, 171
Aeronaves de Panama 173
Air Charter London 144
Air France 125-26
Air India 154
Air Kruise 144
Air Ministry 15, 78, 89
    Airfields Board 15
    Radiosonde Unit 89
Air Safaris 163, 164
Air Transport Charter 132
Air Ulster 161
Airwork Ltd 128, 150, 163
Alitalia 154
American Export Airlines 76
American International Airways 151
American Red Cross 86
    Club Belfast 86-87
    DO-Nutts Corner 86
Anglo-French Purchasing Commission 20
Aviation, Ministry of 170, 181
Avio Linee Italiane 126

BAL-AMi 147
Balfour Marine Engineering 146
BBC 142
Belfast Corporation 108, 114
    General Purposes Committee 108
Belfast Tradesmen's Social Club 151
Benfica FC 176
Bharat Airways 140
BKS Air Transport 144, 156, 158, 161, 165, 166, 169-71
    Air Survey Ltd 171
Boy Scouts 144-46
    1st Coleraine Troop 145-46
    3rd Coleraine Troop 145-46
British Army
    1st Battalion Royal Ulster Rifles 49
    5th Royal Inniskilling Dragoon Guards 147
    11th Special Air Service Battalion 47
    Glider Pilot Regiment 47
    Parachute Regiment 47, 49
    1st Air Landing Brigade 49
    72nd Infantry Brigade 44
    59th Infantry Division 44, 52
    61st Infantry Division 52
    Royal Armoured Corps 169
    2 Reconnaissance Flight 169
    Royal Army Service Corps 54
    Airborne Forces Depot and Battle School 47
    Battle School, Lisburn 55
British European Airways 109, 111-12, 114-17, 119, 122-23, 126, 128-33, 136-39, 141-44, 147, 150, 152, 154, 156, 158-59, 161-70, 174-79
    English Division 109
    Scottish Division 109, 178
    Training School 109
British Midland Airways 173
British Overseas Airways Corporation 109, 134, 140, 149, 164, 166-67
British South American Airways 109
British United Airways 165, 170-71
BU(CI) Airways 165
BU (Manx) Airways 165

Cambrian Airways 147, 161, 165, 171
Campbell College 21, 58
    24th General Hospital 58
Canadian Pacific Airlines 166
Capitol Airlines 165
Civil Aviation, Ministry of 108, 118, 119, 123, 125
Civil Repair Organisation 128
Commerce, Ministry of 123
Dan-Air 144
Derby Airways 164, 171
Distillery FC 176
Eason & Son 181
Eros Airlines 163
Falcon Airways 163
Flying Enterprise 168
Flying Tiger Line 150, 151, 166
Ford Motor Company 175
Fred Olsen Air Transport 150
Graham Construction 8, 16
Great Northern Railway 122, 130
H McGarry & Sons 79-80
Harland & Wolff 108, 149
Hunting-Clan Air Transport 142-44, 150
Imperial Airways 111, 175
Isle of Man Air Services 175
Killultagh Fox Hunt 180
KLM 113, 140, 150
Lancashire Aircraft Corporation 122, 144, 146
LIDL 183
Lisburn Museum 180
LMS (London, Midland & Scottish Railway) 116
Londonderry Air Charter 122
Luftwaffe 16, 18
Luxair 154
Manchester United 158
Mannin Airways 122
Maritime Central Airways 149
Martin's Air Charter 166, 168
Morton Air Services 150
MTCA 147, 148, 158
National Fire Service 115
North-West Airlines (IOM) 122

Northern Ireland Advisory Council 118, 123, 159
Olley Air Services 175
Orange Order 26, 152
Ordnance Survey 11, 180
Overseas Aviation 163, 164
Pan American Airways 76, 144, 149, 166
Passionist Province of St Patrick 73
Post Office 117
President Airlines 166
Railway Air Services 108, 109, 111, 113, 175
Riddle Airlines 166
Royal Air Force
    Army Co-operation Command 46, 48
    Bomber Command 34, 40, 41, 46, 57
    Coastal Command 15, 18, 20, 22, 28, 31, 34, 37, 40, 41, 46, 59, 108, 131
        Operational Research Section 31
    Ferry Command 22, 56, 61, 62
    Fighter Command 16, 46
    Transport Command 76, 82, 90, 92, 100, 107, 182
RAF Northern Ireland 46, 78
No 4 Group 100, 107
No 15 Group 15, 28, 42, 44, 77
No 18 Group 33
No 44 Group 56, 62, 92
No 67 Group 131
No 38 Wing 47, 50
No 24 Squadron 39
No 44 Squadron 41-44
No 47 Squadron 182
No 53 Squadron 39
No 59 Squadron 25
No 90 Squadron 34
No 120 Squadron 19-34, 36-41, 44, 46, 50
No 160 Squadron 41
No 202 Squadron 167-68
No 204 Squadron 21
No 206 Squadron 32, 35
No 220 Squadron 34-36, 39-41, 44
No 224 Squadron 26, 50-51
No 231 Squadron 52-56
No 233 Squadron 17

No 242 Squadron 93
No 264 Squadron 16
No 296 Squadron 47-50
No 296B Squadron 48-50
No 297 Squadron 47
No 413 Squadron 28
No 501 Squadron 55
No 502 Squadron 18, 22
No 504 Squadron 93
RAF Regiment
    No 2708 Squadron 52
    No 2775 Squadron 52
    No 2880 Squadron 52
    No 2883 Squadron 52
No 1 Armament Practice Camp 51, 77
No 11 Repair and Salvage Unit 32
No 104 Operational Training Unit 56-59, 67, 82
No 105 Operational Training Unit 57
No 108 Operational Training Unit 95
No 109 Operational Training Unit 95
No 1402 Met Flight 73
No 1680 (Transport) Flight 100-101
No 1332 Heavy Conversion Unit 92-95
No 1674 Heavy Conversion Unit 59-60
Air Training Corps 46
    Belfast Wing 46
Air Transport Training and Development Unit 75
Royal Canadian Air Force 21, 67, 149
Royal Canadian Navy 149
Royal Flying Corps 175
Royal Mail 154, 163
Royal Navy 18, 46
    Fleet Air Arm 76, 131
    803 NAS 98
    809 NAS 98-99
    879 NAS 165
    883 NAS 165
    891 NAS 97
    1837 NAS 96-97
Royal Ulster Constabulary 170
Saturn Airways 166
Scottish Airlines 113, 120
Scottish Airways 108, 109
Scottish Aviation 113, 131
Seaboard & Western AL 150, 151, 154
Short & Harland Ltd 43, 111, 128, 159
Silver City Airways 144, 154, 155, 156, 161, 163, 164
Skyways Ltd 117, 135, 144, 154, 163
Slick Airways 150, 151, 152
Standard Telephones 172
Starways 144, 154
Swedish Air Force 172
Toronto Film Festival 84
Trans-Canada Airlines 114, 164
Transocean Airlines 144
Transport Training Board NI 5, 183
Travellers' Club 164
Tyne-Tees Airways 166
Ulster Aeroplane Group 155
Ulster Aviation Ltd 119, 122
Ulster Television 150
Ulster Transport Authority 129, 156, 158
US Air Force 143, 144, 166, 173
    53rd Weather Squadron 149
US Army 44, 51
    1st Armored Division 51, 54
    34th Infantry Division 51
    503rd Parachute Infantry Regiment 51-53
US Army Air Corps 21
US Army Air Force 52, 62-64, 66-67, 76, 80, 82, 108
    Air Transport Command 64, 66-67, 75-76, 83, 89, 173
    8th Air Force 61, 65
    9th Air Force 61
    12th Air Force 51, 61, 62
    14th Air Force 66
    15th Air Force 61
    27th Air Transport Group 76, 79
    44th Bomb Group 64
    64th Troop Carrier Group 52
    91st Bomb Group 68
    24th Communications Squadron 66
    24th Weather Squadron 66, 88-89
    69th Ferry Squadron 62

132nd Army Airways Comms Squadron 90-91
311th Ferrying Squadron 64
312th Ferrying Squadron 64
321st Transport Squadron 64
325th Ferrying Squadron 64
1404th Army Air Force Base Unit 89
No 2 EWATC (Station 1009) 60, 75, 76, 78, 89
10th Station Hospital 66
RAWIN Station 88-89
US Navy 46, 77, 144, 151, 154
    Courier Service 68
    Communication Station 144
    Naval Air Transport Service 76, 78-79, 81-82
    97th Construction Battalion 78
Vauxhall Motors 165
Wheeler Airlines 152
Women's Auxiliary Air Force 26
Women's Missionary Association 133
World Air Freight Ltd 120

Aircraft

Airspeed Ambassador 141, 142, 147, 158, 161, 171
Airspeed Consul 122
Airspeed Horsa 47, 75
Armstrong Whitworth Argosy 182
Armstrong Whitworth Whitley 18, 47, 48, 49, 50
Avro 748 171
Avro Anson 113, 135, 171
Avro Lancaster 41-44, 47, 75
Avro Lancastrian 117
Avro Manchester 47
Avro Nineteen 109, 112, 113
Avro Shackleton 167
Avro Tudor 4B 144
Avro York 92, 135, 144, 150, 154, 182
Beech 18 172
Bensen Gyrocopter 182
Blackburn Beverley 153, 182
Boeing B-17 Flying Fortress 22, 34-36, 39, 44, 59, 61, 63, 67-75, 82, 84-85, 152, 182
Boeing Stratocruiser 149
Boeing WB-50 Superfortress 149
Boulton Paul Defiant 16
Bristol Blenheim 26
Bristol Brabazon 134
Bristol Britannia 166
Bristol Freighter 144, 150, 154, 155, 165, 169
Canadair C-4 North Star 149
Canadair C-5 North Star 149
Cessna JRC-1 Bobcat 68, 73
Consolidated B-24 Liberator 19-33, 35-41, 44, 46, 50-51, 59, 63-66, 75, 82, 92, 119, 120, 182
Consolidated PBY Catalina 25, 28, 29
Consolidated PB2Y Coronado 76-77, 79-81
Convair 240 168
Curtiss C-46 154
Curtiss Tomahawk 52, 54-55
DH Comet 4B 164
DH Dove 150, 168
DH86B Express 146
DH Heron 147, 154
DH89 Rapide 109, 112-14, 122, 125
DH Tiger Moth 148, 161
DH Vampire FB5 144
DHC-4 Caribou 172
Douglas A-26C 144
Douglas C-47/DC-3/R4D-4/Dakota/ Pinair 52, 63, 66, 68, 75, 82, 95, 100, 101, 112, 114, 116, 119, 126-29, 131, 132, 142, 144, 145, 147, 150, 154, 157, 161, 163-166, 168, 171-73
Douglas C-53 Skytrooper 63
Douglas DC-4/C-54 Skymaster 74, 75, 140, 144, 145, 149150, 152, 154, 163, 164, 168
Douglas DC-6B/R6D-1/C-118 Liftmaster 140, 151, 152,154, 166, 168
Douglas DC-7C/F 154, 166, 167
Douglas Globemaster 1 173
Druine D.31 Turbulent 168
Fairchild C-82 144
Fairchild C-119 143
Fiat G.212 126
Focke Wulf Condor 29-31

Fokker F.XXII 113
Fokker F.27 Friendship 162, 166, 171
General Aircraft Cygnet II 135
General Aircraft Hotspur 47-50
Gloster Gladiator 73
Grumman F6F Hellcat 96-97
Handley Page Halifax 47, 60, 75, 119, 120
Handley Page Hastings 167-68, 182
Handley Page Herald 165, 167, 171
Handley Page Hermes 163
Handley Page Marathon 146
Heinkel He 115 37
Junkers Ju52/3m 109, 111-12
Junkers Ju88 43
Lockheed Constellation 140
Lockheed Hudson 17, 22, 25-26, 34-36, 39, 41
Lockheed Model 12 68
Lockheed Super Constellation 151, 165, 166
Lockheed T-33a 144
Martin B-26 Marauder 82
Messerschmitt Bf 109 40
Miles Aerovan 122
Miles Falcon Six 122
Miles Gemini 122, 135
Miles Messenger 122, 135
North American Mustang 55
Percival Prince 147
Percival Proctor 135, 155
Piaggio P166 172
Piper Commanche 167
Saunders Roe Skeeter 169
Short Stirling 47, 92-94, 182
Short Sunderland 21, 25, 29, 81

Sikorsky S-55 150
Sopwith Camel 175
Sud Est Languedoc 125-26
Supermarine Seafire 96, 98-99, 165
Supermarine Spitfire 43, 55
Taylorcraft Plus D 135
Thruxton Jackaroo 161
Vickers Vanguard 162, 165, 166, 172, 177, 179
Vickers Viking 116, 131, 136-39, 142, 163
Vickers Viscount 141, 142, 150, 152, 153, 157, 159-61, 165, 166, 168, 171, 179
Vickers Wellington 47, 56-59, 131, 182
Vought F4U Corsair 96-97
Westland Lysander 54-55
WHE Airbuggy 182-83

Vessels

HMCS *Bonaventure* 149
HMS *Argus* 131
HMS *Audacity* 33
HMS *Bicester* 46
HMS *Furious* 131
HMS *Glorious* 131
HMS *Northern Pride* 33-34
HMS *Northern Spray* 33-34
HMS *Phoebe* 43
HMS *Powerful* 149
MSS *Elsa Essberger* 37-38
U-373 37-38
Convoy (ONS 102) 42
Convoy (HG 84) 42